Sussex

people and history

Sussex

people and history

Denys Skinner

The Crowood Press

First published in 2002 by
The Crowood Press Ltd
Ramsbury, Marlborough
Wiltshire SN8 2HR

www.crowood.com

British Library Cataloguing-in-Publication Data
A catalogue record for this book is available from the British Library.

ISBN 1 86126 519 0

Frontispiece and chapter opener pictures by Anthony Kersting. All other photographs by the author.

Frontispiece: Mermaid Street, Rye.

Map on page 8 by John Richards, reproduced from Ordnance Survey mapping on behalf of the Controller of Her Majesty's Stationary Office © Crown Copyright MC100038003

Typeset by Carreg Limited, Ross-on-Wye, Herefordshire

Printed and bound in Spain by Mateu Cromo, Madrid

CONTENTS

INTRODUCTION

Sussex, land of the South Saxons, controls most of the Channel coast between the Isle of Wight and the Dover Strait; a coastline of over 70 miles (113km), but with a breadth of only 20 miles (32km) makes for a relatively small county. It is divided into two administrations, East and West, which have their offices in Lewes and Chichester respectively. However, in the last decade a third, small unit was created, the unitary authority of Brighton and Hove.

The county is unable to decide its position in regard to the geographical regions of England. The eastern half tends to align itself with an eastern neighbour and accepts the bleaker continental climate. But as you travel to the west, the Kentish influence decreases and the balmier climes of Wessex become dominant. Everywhere Sussex merges largely unnoticed into its neighbours; scenically and culturally the borders are as one.

The population distribution in the county roughly follows the parallel geological lines, with the exception of the north–south A23 corridor. The coastal strip from Chichester Harbour in the west onward to Seaford is now largely urban; some areas are attractively residential but others are in dire need of improvement. Eastbourne is a town isolated by open countryside, downland and marsh-like levels. Bexhill and Hastings form another conurbation, then, finally, in the east, is lonely Rye. The north Sussex towns centred around Crawley and Gatwick are the industrial hub of the county, the airport and light industry offering employment for thousands. A ribbon of market towns along the central A272 constitute the third line of habitation.

Many writers have enthused over the visual beauty of Sussex. John Dennis, writing in his *Original Letters* of 1721, describes the view from the adjacent Leith Hill thus,

I saw a sight that would transport a stoic ... beneath us lay, open to our view, all the wilds of Surrey and Sussex together with a greater part of Kent, admirably diversified in every part, woods and fields of corn and pastures everywhere adorned with stately rows of trees.

Tennyson, who made his home under the county's highest hill, Blackdown, said,

You came and looked and loved the view
Long known and loved by me.
Green Sussex fading into blue
With a grey glimpse of sea.

Belloc, too, enthused over his 'Great Hills of the South Country ...'.

Continental invaders also have long enjoyed the living that this part of Britain offered, from the earliest appearance of man to the Norman, each brought with him aspects of his culture – combined they form the Sussex of today.

Few Roman place names exist in Sussex, for although the native Britons integrated well with their southern European masters, they appear not to have fully accepted the alien language, preferring to remain with their local tongue. In the fifth century a largely nameless county greeted the new invaders. This omission was soon rectified for each area took on the name of its conquering tribe: Suaseaxe – South Saxons – Sussex. The literate residents, who were mainly of Romano-British stock, were either quickly murdered or despatched westward, leaving behind them little evidence of the local names. Those that did survive related mainly to hills or rivers.

The Saxons also named much of the county where new settlements were established, mainly in the Downs or along the coast or river bank, where the tribe leader's name was used, often

Windmill at Chailey.

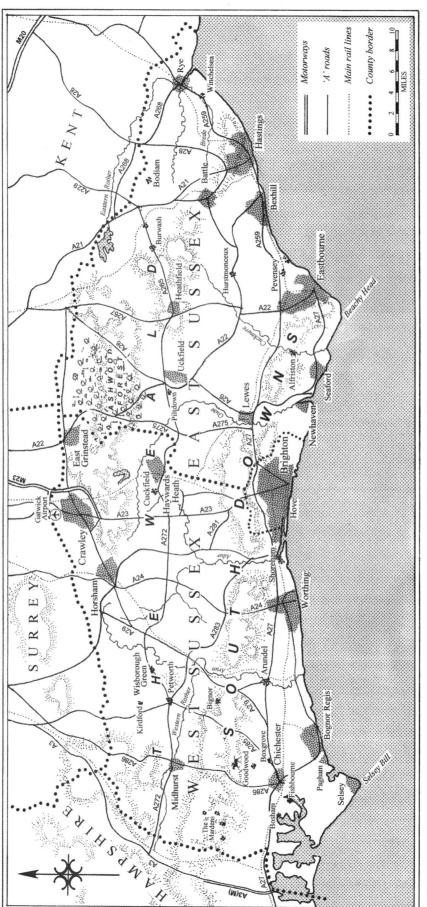

SUSSEX

combined with a further adjective or noun, for instance, Uckfield or Ucca's open land.

The Norman invasion had little impact on place names, the existing words being retained. Some alternatives temporarily emerged during the Domesday survey, but these were mainly caused by the inability of the French officials to come to terms with the local dialect. Upon the officials' return to Normandy, names reverted to their original spellings and pronunciation. In the Middle Ages many new communities were founded, with the majority following the Saxon tradition of taking up the name of the founder.

Over the centuries the old names have altered, paralleling the continuing progress to a more modern type of speech. No doubt these changes will continue and in a hundred years' time many could bear little resemblance to those now in use. The county dialect is now almost extinct; it never contained strong inflections and easily integrated with the Home Counties' speech that migrated south from London. Interestingly, the east of the county and Kent enjoy a similar dialect, but in the west the Hampshire tone made little progress across the border. Sussex words and expressions continue to be in regular use, often far removed from the Queen's English. Thus the Sussex native has a saying, 'We wont be druv' (= driven). This expression is interpreted by outsiders as pig-headedness or obstinacy. In reality, it translates to the fact that Sussex people cannot be pressed into making a hasty decision. All opinions and arguments must be heard; then, and only then, after much deliberation, will they agree on the appropriate action that has to be taken.

History is a living subject; Sussex realizes that, today, when reviewed tomorrow, is history. The student and the visitor, however enthusiastic they may be, can eventually tire of the past and seek something of our own time. Sussex is not lacking in what it has to offer. The countryside promotes itself, the Downs, the open forests and commons, along with the hidden villages of the Weald, ask to be explored.

With each land form having its own flora the beginner can enjoy this diversity on an equal with the dedicated naturalist, for much of the year the beauty can be viewed without too much effort.

From the roadside even a view of sullen winter heathland can be enlivened by the out-of-season flowering of a maverick gorse. As the year develops, undisturbed chalk slopes will be dotted with cowslips to be followed by nodding harebells. Who could pass a Wealden wood in May when bluebells carpet the ground with a blue heaven of colour? For the inquisitive, a network of reserves, managed by both local and national organizations, will provide the answer.

Wildlife species in the county have changed largely in parallel with agricultural practices. Of the larger, more visible mammals, the brown hare is the most notable evacuee. Not so the rabbit, who after the myxomatosis epidemic of the 1950s has thrived to become the Number 1 pest of the countryside. Foxes are more abundant, forsaking their rural habit to include the suburbs in their nightly scavenging. Various types of deer now roam free, no longer penned into private parks. Even the nocturnal badger can be found, although sadly the usual sighting of these noble creatures is that of a roadside corpse.

The status of many Sussex birds, too, has changed over the last half-century. The species that have suffered the most are those that rely on inefficient agriculture for their food and accommodation. Herbicidal sprays, mechanical harvesting and the reduction in verges, headlands and hedges have combined to make life difficult for many. It is not a complete picture of gloom for the local ornithologist, though, for in recent years the county has managed to attract new and returning species to its shores. The most notable example is that of the Little Egret, unrecorded prior to 1952 but now a common site at coastal inlets. The Chichester Harbour waters are an important overwintering ground for waders and wildfowl, and with the promontories of Selsey Bill and Beachy Head welcoming or bidding adieu to tens of thousands of passage migrants, the future remains bright for the local 'twitcher'.

The sportsman in Sussex is well provided for, be he a participant or merely a spectator. The

Alfriston Church. The cathedral of the eastern downs seen from the Cuckmere River on a foggy autumn morning.

coast, once only available as a trip round the bay, can now, with new marinas and the Chichester Harbour boatyards, offer the sailor facilities that are second to none.

Golf courses are plentiful, many with fairways that seem to blend easily into the natural beauty of their surroundings.

The English games of football and cricket are played in even the smallest village and there are many locations where a pleasant afternoon can be spent, pint in hand, watching the battle between leather and willow. County cricket is played at several grounds and at last the 'Seagulls', Brighton and Hove Albion, have made it to the dizzy heights of football's First Division. Tennis is not ignored: at international level the Eastbourne Tournament traditionally precedes Wimbledon. For horse lovers there is show-jumping at Hickstead, racing on the flat at the downland courses of Goodwood and Brighton, National Hunt meetings at Fontwell and Plumpton; and why not make a visit to Cowdray, the home of English polo.

Music and the theatre have always found a receptive ear in Sussex. Several of the earlier composers have visited, tarried, and no doubt received inspiration from the county. Young Benjamin Britten was a visitor to Bloomsbury Firle, Debussy completed *La Mer* whilst staying at Eastbourne and Elgar found Brinkwells, an isolated cottage set amongst daffodil woods above Fittleworth. Exponents of more modern music, too, have retreated to the county. The Forces' Sweetheart of the Second World War, Dame Vera Lynn, has found a home in mid-county and Sir Paul McCartney, of Beatles fame, has settled in East Sussex rather than his native Liverpool.

Throughout the year theatres in the area offer presentations of all forms of music, from classical recitals to the latest in pop gigs. The ultimate performance of opera takes place each summer at the open air theatre at Glynde. The world-renowned Glyndebourne Festival was founded in the 1930s and today retains the elegance associated with those earlier years.

The theatre, too, has always enjoyed a close affinity with the county. Numerous actors and artistes have made their homes within its boundaries, influenced in no small part by the relative ease of access to the entertainment of London. One of the most famous of the twentieth-century thespians was Sir Lawrence Olivier. When not performing he enjoyed the peace of his rural home below the Downs. Equally at home on stage or film set, he also became the first director, in 1962, of the Chichester Festival Theatre. When created a life peer in 1970 he took the title Baron Olivier of Brighton. At the other end of the entertainment spectrum, this premier resort was the home of that – for the age – controversial comedian, Max Miller, the 'Cheeky Chappie'.

Live theatre still thrives today and poor is the town that cannot offer its own arts centre where traditional touring companies mingle with variety and local production.

The fairly recent innovation of the arts festivals occur each summer. These range from two-week extravaganzas in the larger towns to local weekend events. All contrive to bring to the community a mixture of traditional and sometimes newer, thought-provoking, entertainment

Shopping can still be a pleasure in Sussex. Arundel and Petworth are meccas for the antique collector, while The Lanes at Brighton and the Old Town flea market at Hastings are places to browse without an obligation to purchase.

Do not confine yourself to the large towns where twentieth-century development turns each into a bland clone of its neighbour, move away to find the real Sussex. Here many small communities, seemingly bereft of county attention and assistance, are finding it difficult to survive. Fortunately, they are loath to expire for their people are proud and determined. It is in these hamlets and villages that much of the ancient history of Sussex may be found. Explore, learn and enjoy what the county offers, you will then start to understand this privileged part of England.

SUSSEX IN VERSE

If I ever become a rich man,
Or if ever I grow to be old,
I will build a house with deep thatch
To shelter me from the cold,
And there shall the Sussex songs be sung
And the story of Sussex told.

I will hold my house in the high wood
Within a walk of the sea,
And the men that were boys when I was a boy
Shall sit and drink with me.

                Belloc: 'The South Country' (1910)

God gives all men all earth to love,
But, since man's heart is small,
Ordains for each one spot shall prove
Belovèd over all.
Each to his choice, and I rejoice
The lot has fallen to me
In a fair ground – in a fair ground –
Yea, Sussex by the sea!

                Kipling: 'Sussex' (1902)

Higher and higher to the North aspire the green,
smooth-swelling, unending downs;
East and west, on the brave earth's breast, glow
girdle-jewels of gleaming towns;
Southward shining the lands declining subside
in peace that the sea light's crowns.

                A.C. Swinburne

1. Geology and the Sussex Landscape

One of the most difficult aspects of geology for the non-specialist is the immense timescale that is involved between the origin of the earth and the realization of the landscape that is recognizable today. This period has been likened to the face of a timepiece where the formation of our planet occurred at midday. Life as we know it arrived at a few minutes before midnight, and Man and recorded history just scrape home before the Cinderella hour by a few seconds.

During this period of four and a half billion years the earth was never in a tranquil mood. Since the formation of the oceans, land continually emerged from the waters, survived for a while, contributing sediments from its erosion, and then resubmerged. This process occurred countless times along with the folding and fracturing of the existing strata. Not all of these immersions were effected by the saline seas, vast freshwater lakes also imposed their presence on this developing earth. These seas and lakes, together with river systems, collected a variety of sediments, thus building up sequences of differing strata. Climate also went through great changes, fluctuations between extreme heat and ice age conditions. Arid desert-like periods and rainforest monsoons that make our current concern with global warming insignificant by comparison. These extreme conditions also produced characteristic desert and glacial sediments.

The rocks that make up the county of Sussex are young in comparison with those of other areas of the United Kingdom. The earliest rocks that are now exposed in the county were deposited in the late Jurassic period, around 145 million years ago, and are known as the Purbeck Beds. Many of the rock formations bear names that have no apparent connection with the county. They serve as a reminder that no area can be viewed in isolation and that similar strata occur in other localities. Local nomenclature does appear quite widely, largely for identifying subdivisions of the basic formations.

The whole of the county and the rest of southeast England were at one period enclosed under a dome of chalk. Today, the only remaining section of this in Sussex is the South Downs. Below the chalk covering, in the core of the dome, lay an upfold of older rocks now exposed at the surface known as the Wealden Anticline, the axis of which traverses north Sussex. Central and southern limbs of this upfold cross the county from west to east with the strata dipping regionally to the south.

The several soil and rock types that exist in the county will be examined chronologically, both their structure and place in the geological timescale, and later, their influence on the landscape.

In 1806 John Farey produced the first paper on the apparent geological divisions of Sussex. His observations were made from the windows of a stagecoach as he travelled throughout the county, but, in spite the primitive way they were collected, they proved to be surprisingly accurate. Other residents and the eminent geologists of the day, including Sir Charles Lyell, later amended and disputed some of his findings until in the 1860s definitive maps were produced by the Geological Survey at a scale of 1 inch to the mile (1:63,360). Investigation into our subsurface continues to the present day and the search for those valuable commodities oil and gas that takes place under the county's fields is a prime example.

The Jurassic Rocks

As mentioned previously, the earliest surface rocks of the Sussex system are three small outcrops of the Purbeck Beds of the Jurassic in the

The Devil's Dyke.

Harrison rocks. Adjacent to the Kent border, these are outcrops of one of the earliest Cretaceous rocks to be found in the county.

Heathfield, Brightling and Mountfield areas. These total less than 4sq miles (10.4sq km) in extent. The rocks comprise clays and shales, with thin layers of sandstone and limestone. It is thought that at the time these beds were laid down the climate was semi-arid and the area was covered by vast tidal mud flats. Continuing evaporation of the saline pools left brine which percolated into the main sediments, leading to the precipitation of gypsum. This mineral is now mined at Mountfield in the only 'safety light' gypsum mine in the United Kingdom. The excavated material is used mainly in the manufacture of wall plasters and plasterboard. The true limestone in the Purbeck Beds was at one time both mined and quarried but the sites are no longer in production.

The Cretaceous Rocks

The earliest rocks of the succeeding Cretaceous period belong to the Wealden Series (Hastings Beds) and have all been given local names. The Hastings Beds are subdivided into the Ashdown and Tunbridge Wells Sands plus the Wadhurst Clay. As may be expected from the names, all occur in the north-east of the county. The Ashdown Beds, named after the forest area, are the oldest division and are the most extensive, stretching from Ashdown forest to the coast. They consist of silts with subordinate clays and sands, with fine-grained sandstone occurring in places at the top of the formation.

The succeeding Wadhurst Clay outcrops in many areas in the north and the east of the county. Included in the formation are large pockets of ironstone and it was from here that the bulk of the ore was obtained for the local industry. The basic sequence is largely grey shales, topped in a few localities by red or purple clays.

The highest, youngest, and most complex division of the Hastings Beds is the Tunbridge Wells Sands. These extend into the west of the county, comprising mainly silty sandstones overlain by a medium-grained stone that is still commercially quarried, mainly for domestic decoration. A plethora of local names appear in this formation since each town or village wants recognition of its local outcrop, be it of clay or sand.

Opinions differ on the way these beds were formed. The original theory favoured a large freshwater lake with inflowing rivers, depositing sands and silts in deltas and silts and clays on to the lake floor. An amended belief is of a large plain criss-crossed by rivers which deposited the sandy beds, clays being formed from shifting mud banks, available only when the rivers were carrying little sand; periodic uplifting and subsequent immersion helped to stabilize the sediments and caused numerous repetitions within the sequence. Whichever theory is correct, this band of rocks still contains many mysteries that have yet to be explained.

Understandably, the most reviled soil of the county is derived from the Weald Clay. It rapidly becomes a glutinous mire when exposed to winter rains and readily bakes rock-hard when exposed to the summer sun. Despite these dubious qualities it is recognized as providing a strong fertile soil for crops and, once through

A weather-worn, free-standing example from the Harrison rocks site.

the difficult establishment period, regularly gives good returns. This clay covers the greater part of lowland Sussex, from the Surrey border south-eastwards almost to the Channel coast. Minor beds of sand, limestone and ironstones are found in the stratum, more especially adjacent to Horsham. Much of the clay was laid down on a vast, low-lying flood plain that was periodically immersed in brackish water. Those hillocks that survived above the water level for any length of time suffered erosion, and increased coloration of the clays occurred.

Towards the middle of the Cretaceous period, about 150 million years ago, the plains on which the Hastings Beds and the Weald Clays were deposited disappeared completely under the waves, not re-emerging for at least another 45 million years. Freshwater sediments were replaced by saltwater deposits. These mainly sandy deposits are referred to as greensands, the earlier designated as Lower Greensand followed by the upper greensand. Both include local vari-ations and greensand is a complete misnomer for one division (Bargate Beds), around Midhurst, which has a coloration similar to the red soils of Devon. These rocks or their subdivisions make only intermittent appearances in a narrow zone immediately north of and paralleling the South Downs escarpment and the total area they cover is substantially less than that of the clays. They are not present onshore east of Eastbourne.

During the formation of the Lower

Bedham sand pit. A working pit in the greensand hills north-east of Petworth.

Greensand the sea advanced, both to the west and the north; this in turn led to the waters deepening over the land that was to become Sussex. The rise in water levels meant reduced wave and current activity and a calmer environment, allowing finer muds to be deposited. This sediment developed as the Gault clays. Again only a narrow surface outcrop appears parallel to and north of the foot of the downland escarpment. As the seas retreated, the current activity increased, reintroducing sandier deposits. This Upper Greensand is also restricted to a narrow outcrop zone.

After the middle of the Cretaceous period, around 95 million years ago, there was another, more extensive marine advance. This did not occur in one continuous movement, but ebbed and flowed much in the manner that tides behave today. This pulsating inflow of water plus a general subsidence of the ocean floor gave rise to a deep marine environment. This great inundation of the land lasted for around 30 million years. Living in these seas were innumerable minute planktonic organisms, the shells of which, called coccoliths, were rich in calcium carbonate. As these organisms died or were devoured their remains drifted slowly down to the seabed as a thick, white, chalky ooze. This sediment, the basis of the chalk we all recognize, attained a thickness in excess of 1,000ft (300m). The purists have divided these chalk formations into three phases, the earliest, when the covering sea was relatively shallow and dry land not too distant, incorporated sand and clay material, resulting in a darker form of limestone. As the water depth increased, the sediments became purer with an end product of a whiter texture. Flints, which are common throughout the thin overlying soils, occur mainly in narrow, horizontal seams, at intervals of only a few feet, mainly in the upper part of the chalk. They formed from the silica contained in the skeletons of floor-based sponges. The silica was dissolved by the water and redeposited as small nodules of flint which were compacted at the same time as the surrounding chalk. It is thought that the nodules

were already in a hardened form when only a few feet below the seabed.

Towards the end of the Cretaceous period the land again began to rise, major earth movements took place and, as the sea grew shallower, the deposition of chalk ceased. The latest major upheaval of the earth's crust, the Alpine mountain building started in the mid Tertiary period. It is now that Britain as we know it began to take shape. A vast regional dome of chalk and underlying rocks was uplifted, stretching from the Pas de Calais in northern France through to Hampshire. The axis of this Wealden Anticline, which could be called a primitive mountain range, was centred over the Mayfield area. At the same time, much local buckling and folding of the strata took place. One large downfold allowed the sea to invade for the first time towards the gap that is now the English Channel, a process that was not completed until between 6,000 and 5,500 BC. Another downfold to the north resulted in the Thames Valley. The chalk, being the uppermost layer of the dome, was subject to the greatest stress. Being a fragile rock it readily fissured and began to disintegrate. Dissolution by rain and running water accelerated the erosion, a process that continues to the present. Man has also assisted in this erosion, a recent example is the run-off of silt from the prairie-like ploughed fields after a heavy downpour. Water, be it from fresh or from tidal streams, is a great scourer of the land and the river systems have had a significant effect on the landscape of the county. New areas of sands and clays formed on the surface of eroded chalk. These new rocks are placed in the Tertiary period and occur only in the south-western coastal plain. It is not surprising therefore that most bear names unrelated to the county such as the Bagshot Beds, London Clay and Reading Beds. The latest, and indeed the youngest of the rock formations underlying Sussex, does bear a local name: the Bracklesham Beds.

During the ice ages of the Pleistocene period glaciers did not reach Sussex but perennial snow and ice patches and permafrost were characteristic, giving rise to periglacial deposits. Only river alluvium and land reclaimed from the sea fall into the recent phase of the geological history.

The Topography of Sussex

The topography of Sussex is much less complex than its geology, with just five regions to consider. An imaginary line drawn from the centre of the Manhood peninsula, extending north-eastwards through Crowborough Beacon to the county boundary effectively bisects these areas. Departing from the shoreline, the Coastal Plain is the first to be crossed, then follows the South Downs and the Greensand ridges, ending with the Low and the High Weald.

The Coastal Plain is wedge-shaped, the widest in the west, along the border with Hampshire where it extends inland for up to 10 miles (16km). As one travels towards Brighton, the chalk ridge continuously nudges the lowland towards the waves, finally forcing its expiration at Black Rock just to the east of the town. Along the northern edge of the plain, to the west of the River Arun, there is evidence of several 'raised beaches'. These are considered to be the remnants of shorelines that evolved during the sea-level oscillations of the glacial Pleistocene. The main beach is 130ft (40m) above the present sea level and gives a good indication of the depth of the water inundation at that time. Many quarries have bitten into this shingle formation and it was in one, at Boxgrove, in 1993 that new archaeological evidence of one of our forebears was discovered dating from the interglacial warm period, half a million years ago.

The Seven Sisters, where the chalk meets the sea, to the east of Cuckmere Haven.

The surface soils of Sussex tend to follow west to east patterns, largely corresponding to the underlying rocks. Those of the plain are mainly poorly-drained alluvium overlying Tertiary rocks. The water table even in summer lies only a few feet below the surface, and, to achieve any agricultural return, effective drainage is needed. Where this has been undertaken a fertile soil results. Behind the coastal development of the Selsey or Manhood peninsula the land is meshed by the drainage ditches; the local name is 'rife', after the Old English word for a rivulet. The early efforts at land drainage must have been successful since, by the time of the Iron Age, the area and that of the Downs were the population centre of what was to become Sussex. Many of today's place names bearing the suffix 'ham', a homestead, offer fur-

ther evidence relating to the position of these early settlements.

Throughout the ages these soils were found to be highly suitable for the cultivation of cereal crops, and one named variety of wheat was developed at Chidham and bore the village name. The plain enjoys a protected microclimate, the Downs shelter it from the northerly winds, the adjoining sea provides the warmth and the maritime air, even if boisterous, is largely free from pollution and gives a intensity of light far superior to that of the land beyond the hills.

In recent years the area has moved more into the horticultural market with the Dutch influence becoming apparent. Acres of glass have been erected and now exotic flowers grow alongside the more tender salad crops. Vast

Firle Beacon, looking across the Cuckmere levels; Alfriston is in the middle distance.

The Western Downs above Harting.

fields are devoted to the production of lettuce, their automated harvesters appearing alien in the landscape. As the plain tapers towards oblivion, residential housing buries much of the soil. The A27 trunk road forms a rough boundary to the plain and, on approach to Worthing from the west, the road comes up to the dip slope of the Downs, seaward cultivation ceases and from here to Black Rock it is all seaside suburbia.

The chalk downs leave their confrontation with the English Channel between Seaford and Beachy Head to aim slightly north of west and eventually leave the county at the original end of the South Downs Way at Buriton. The Downs may be likened to an unequal sided horseshoe, our 80-mile stretch (129km), the South Downs, being the shorter side. Once over the border the chalk expands into the apex plateau of Hampshire and Wiltshire before narrowing and returning eastwards as the North Downs. This longer leg stays clear of the county, traversing both Surrey and Kent.

The cliff face at Beachy Head has an uninterrupted drop of over 500ft (153m), confirming it to be the highest sheer chalk precipice in England. As the Downs make westward progress they enlarge both in the vertical and the horizontal plane. Firle Beacon tops 700ft (214m), Ditchling is 100ft (30m) higher, further to the west Graffham Down climbs another 20ft (6m). Butser Hill in Hampshire is the highest top at 888ft (270m).

Chalk is a relatively soft form of limestone, but surprisingly resilient to local erosion. This resistance is largely due to its permeability which restricts the availability of surface water run-off. Continuous running streams are to be found only in the deepest escarpment valleys, usually at the base of the chalk a few feet above the water table. A few winterbournes exist, these tending to flow in the late winter period when the chalk aquifers reach saturation point. When not flowing, the beds of the streams appear little more than small depressions coursing through the landscape. When in spate their power can be frightening as the residents of Chichester found in 2001.

One of the more common features of these chalk hills is the abundance of dry valley systems. These may vary from shallow depressions through wide-bottomed, winding troughs to deep-cut ravines. The most famous of this last type is the Devil's Dyke, a few miles to the north of Brighton. Opinions differ as to the formation of these features, one being that in the distant past, when the water table was higher springs and streams once flowed from their heads, cutting into the chalk. Their present dryness is explained by a lowering of the water table to its present level, down cutting of the main river systems or a climate change. A second view is that their formation occurred during one of the many cold periods of the Pleistocene. Water held in the chalk then became frozen, rendering the ground impermeable. When the temperature rose, streams and meltwater combined with chalk debris to scour out the valley sides. When viewed from the Weald the downland escarpment appears as an equable horizon broken only by four river gaps and several lesser 'wind gaps'. These larger dry gaps are believed to have been cut by early rivers that failed as the water table in the chalk fell.

To the west of Brighton and continuing across the Hampshire border there is a secondary line of hills lying along the main dip slope. These are not a continuous feature but form a well-defined, lower, minor escarpment, again with the steeper slope facing north. The surface capping of this range differs from that of the higher tops and, as before, opinions differ as to the reason why.

Much of the downland is surfaced with a thin layer of clay with flints, considered to be a relic from the former Reading Beds' clay which has been much modified by the extreme climatic changes that occurred during the Pleistocene. This covering is very moisture-retentive, proving difficult to cultivate and leading, especially on the western section, to large areas of coppiced woodland. Some of these woods could well date from a time before the arrival of man, with a virgin soil never having been disturbed by plough or hoe. To the east, the clay capping has combined with a loess thought to have arrived from the bed of a dry North Sea during the early part of the last glacial period. Where a deeper deposit of this soil exists the surface tends to decalcify, and this has allowed lime-hating plants to colonize. The Lullington Heath nature reserve is a good example; here several varieties of what are loosely termed heathers exist, such as *Calluna vulgaris* and *Erica cinerea*.

The natural vegetation of the downs was a mixture of scrub and trees, the short-grazed turf so beloved by writers and tourist authorities is a totally man-made feature. Our earliest inhabitants, nomadic hunters, favoured the lower lands where food and shelter were more plentiful. When the first primitive farmers arrived from Europe they found that their Stone Age implements were able to strip only the lighter chalk downs. Small parcels of land were cleared to provide areas where their crops could be planted. The harvests were mainly fodder for the animals, with any excess for human consumption. The transition from hunter to farmer was a gradual and sporadic process and it was not until the semi-nomadic neolithic man was established that the face of the Downs began to change. As the fertility of the small patches of cleared land diminished, larger areas came under the axe, both for pasturing and food production. The ancestors of our present-day sheep and oxen were found to thrive on the uplands. The sheep, with their close-grazing habit, created through the centuries the sward that so typifies the downland scene. Sadly, much of that landscape has disappeared in the last century, because where sheep no longer graze scrub soon returns. The final indignity imposed upon these hills occurred in the 1940s when misguided politicians decreed that much should be ploughed up in the name of food production. Tons of artificial fertilizer were, and are still, being poured on to the ground; the soils have been forced back into a condition that, if abandoned, would be similar to that which greeted our forebears: centuries of evolution destroyed in only a few years.

The Greensand ridges and Gault Clay strike parallel to the chalk escarpment, widening in the west of the county and looping around the Western Rother valley to return eastwards, at the same time encompassing the highest hill of Sussex – Blackdown – which tops at 918ft (280m). To the east of the A24 road these formations occur only irregularly and have little

CHALK FIGURES

The Long Man of Wilmington. Cut into the northern slopes of the Downs this mysterious figure inspects the East Sussex Weald.

Throughout England, wherever a chalk scarp provides a suitable, short-cropped grass face, there you will find examples of open-air artistry. East Sussex has two of these chalk figures, both on the Downs adjacent to Alfriston.

The Long Man of Wilmington appears on the north face of the Downs above the village that bears his name. He is a tall figure, 226ft (69m) in height, and in each hand he holds a staff or spear, their lengths surpassing him by a few feet. The complete figure has been designed so that, when viewed from the lower ground, he does not appear to adopt an unduly squat pose. His origin is a mystery; is he a relative of the Cerne Abbas Giant?

This is doubtful, for the first report of his existence was in the eighteenth century, when a drawing showed his hands holding agricultural implements, a hoe and a rake. The existence of these tools cannot be verified for there is no disturbance to the chalk where the heads would have been positioned. The outline was originally cut direct through the turf into the chalk, but in 1874 white bricks, thought to be longer lasting, were inserted into the outline. The Man lies only a few feet below the route of the South Downs Way but he is not visible from the trail, so that many of the walkers remain ignorant of his presence.

continued opposite

CHALK FIGURES *continued*

The White Horse of High and Over keeps a watchful eye on the Cuckmere River.

The second feature is of a white horse carved into a hillside above the river Cuckmere. Again, his origin is uncertain, tradition relates it to a drinking club from an Alfriston hostelry. In the early 1920s a group of local lads, probably after a wager, left the inn after closing time, completed the animal during the hours of darkness and returned to the village before daybreak. The story is hardly plausible – could these locals, who were agricultural workers, create a design that is so correct in proportion and posture in just a few hours of darkness? There is a further questionable story relating to the animal. During the Second World War he took refuge under a temporary covering for it was thought that his shape would provide enemy pilots with a definite marker. On both tales the jury is still out.

impact on the landscape. Further to the west the raised beds of the greensand are relatively infertile and contain pockets of fast disappearing, low-level heathland. Mesolithic man favoured this terrain, as his discovered artefacts confirm. It is conceivable that it was he who started the denudation of these lands. He was not a farmer, as was his successor on the Downs, but integration of both peoples and ideas obviously occurred. Close to the Surrey border lie pockets of a sand that was used in local industry, that of glass-making. Examples of this long-departed

Ambersham Common, an outcrop of the Bargate Beds.

enterprise may be found in the war memorial at Kirdford.

The overlying clays on the gault combine to form an almost impenetrable mass. These soils are largely given over to grass production, but where the greensand does not intervene between the chalk and the clay, the lime-rich debris has interacted with the clay to create a more friable medium.

The Weald, or the Sussex Vale, covers much of the county, extending from the greensand hills northwards and eastwards through to the coast. It is divided into the Low and the High Weald, roughly corresponding to the underlying strata of clay and sandstones. The High Weald now also encompasses the coastal levels between Hastings and Rye. The word 'weald' is a derivative of the Saxon word for woodland, 'wald', and is an apt description of the area, for, from the arrival of vegetative cover, it was a forest,

largely inhibiting colonization by early man until the Saxons began small, regularized clearances. Mesolithic man did find that the greensand hills and the sandier ridges of the High Weald were able to offer him a reasonable living, for here the tree cover was a little less dense.

The underlying rocks of the Low Weald are almost totally clay-based, although in the west, around Horsham, small pockets of limestone and sandstone occur. These are more resistant to erosion and form minor ridges erupting from the flatter plain. The covering topsoils of the region are again of clays, and combine to form a heavy, sticky land that easily defeated early man's attempt at clearance. The tree cover that spread northwards from Europe after the last ice age, when the land bridge over the area of the present Channel was still in existence, comprised mainly types of birch, pine and hazel. As the temperature rose, other species arrived, notably oak, elm and beech. The oak, with a deeper root system, became the dominant tree of these clay lands, so much so that it has been referred to as 'the weed of the woodlands'. Beech, with a shallower root, decided not to compete and made its home on the thinner soils that overlay the chalk downs.

Local Building Materials

Many of the old buildings and farmsteads were built with locally quarried sandstones, the varying hues of their walls reflecting the quarries from which they were obtained. Most of the stone came from the Ardingly Beds of the High Weald, where several hundred old workings have been identified. On excavation, the stone being relatively soft, it was sawn *in situ* then left to harden with exposure. Different ridges produced varying qualities of stone; the higher grades were used for domestic or church building, while those of inferior texture were relegated to use in farm buildings, paving or even road construction.

The principal stone obtained from beds in the Weald Clays are the Paludina Limestones and a locally named Horsham stone. The 'Winklestone' represents the former and is recognized by the massed fossilized shells of a freshwater snail; it is not usually used for domestic building. The generic name for the limestones is Sussex or Petworth marble. Horsham Stone is

Winklestone: a solitary lump of this limestone embedded in a church wall.

a calcareous sandstone that is easily split into a ripple-surfaced slab. This feature ensured that it was almost entirely used for roofing or paving, where the shallow ridges gave a non-slip surface. This is a dense material requiring a roof to be low pitched and constructed with a substantial timber frame, the size and corresponding weight of the slabs decreasing as they approached the ridge. Many of the buildings that used this material are characterized by their sagging ridges. The stone is rarely found outside a 20-mile (32km) radius of the town and, since the quarries have been closed for many years, there exists a thriving market for second-hand tiles.

The chalk country provided other building materials, a hard, chalk stone, 'clunch', being used as an infill for timber-framed buildings. Flints were occasionally mined but usually just collected from the shore, then knapped to form a smooth profile. These were then incorporated into other materials; several buildings in the Shoreham area still show evidence of this type of construction. A later development was the bonding of flint cobbles into the facings of buildings or walls. This style of building was widespread throughout the Downs and the coastal plain, and in places also extended a few miles into the Weald.

Brick-making was, when the bricks were handmade, a thriving, localized industry. The individual clays, plus the fuels used and the varying firing methods, provided village housing with a diversity of colours ranging from a rich red to yellowish brown. The standardization of today's housing is, scenically, no match for these earlier buildings.

Because of the impervious nature of the clays, rainwater run-off is a major feature: there are over a third more permanent streams per square mile (2.6sq km) in the Weald Clay than in the sandier areas of the High Weald. In times of flooding large quantities of sediment are washed downstream leading, over geological ages, to a rapid denudation of the clay. To the north of Lewes several small ridges occur, each capped by flinty gravels; these are the remains of a material that spread across the lowlands from the Downs during the penultimate ice age. Since then general erosion and the fact that the rivers have cut their way to a lower level mean that today's flows are 100ft (30m) below the tops.

The High Weald, which is the last section of the imaginary line that was drawn through Sussex, has recently received more government and local attention than its sibling. It is now designated an Area of Outstanding Natural Beauty (AONB), which merits a long-distance trail, and the highest area, Ashdown Forest, is rated as a Site of Special Scientific Interest (SSSI). To the west, which is the smaller part, the underlying rocks are predominantly sandstone, while to the south-east clays and sandstone intermix. The surface soils over the whole area are clay-based, which helps to explain the winter waterlogging

that can occur even on some of the higher summits.

The AONB of the High Weald has been subdivided into nine smaller units, several of which relate mainly to the adjoining county of Kent and only two of which are really entitled to an upland description. These comprise a series of lifts subordinate to the main ridges and cut through by rivers and streams, the local name being 'ghyll', in places creating impressive sandstone cliff scenery. The western ridge which extends almost from the Surrey border into Ashdown Forest is not conducive to successful large-scale agriculture and large areas remain covered by ancient woodland. Some areas have been cleared only to be replaced by uniform parcels of commercial conifers. Bands of ironstone lurk a few feet below soil level and the dis-

Ashdown Forest. Typical flora of these sandy soils.

A hammer pond. Hawkins pond in St Leonards Forest.

covery of this ore, together with the wealth of timber for fuel, enabled the area to develop into one of the main centres of the Sussex iron industry.

The Iron Industry

As you walk through the Sussex countryside, in certain areas of the Weald many stream beds are adorned by a rust-coloured sediment. This is an indication that the surrounding soils, or those upstream, contain traces of ironstone. Most of this ore has been obtained from opencast workings from the Ashdown Beds or ridges in the Weald Clay, although some had to be excavated from pits up to 30ft (9m) in depth. Little evidence remains of these workings, for the mines

were backfilled after the ore had been extracted. The original ore was thought to have been discovered in early marl pits; this marl was spread on to cultivated land and acted as a primitive fertilizer and soil conditioner.

The industry existed before the Roman occupation but it was developed and extended during their stay. After their departure, the industry went into decline and was not revived until early Tudor times. At first, iron was extracted by the bloomery process which used primitive open hearths. This method led to an abundance of residue slag, cinders and unburnt clay, a material much favoured by the Romans to surface their expanding road system. The introduction of hammer forges and the arrival from the continent of blast furnaces were the incentives needed to further revitalize the industry. Sussex now became the industrial heartland of England, a position that it held, largely unchallenged, until early into the eighteenth century.

The new processes were dependent on both water power and fuel. The county had an abundance of both. Small streams, normally in narrow valleys, were dammed to provide a head of water, the reservoir of power that the forge mills and furnaces needed in order to exist. The ponds that were formed were unsurprisingly called 'hammer ponds', a name that is still common in the High Weald today. Many infant flows were, in their upper reaches, diverted to enhance the main flow, then followed down the valley through a series of ponds, each servicing its own mill. The Wealden woodlands were originally able to produce a plentiful supply of local fuel and large areas were stripped of any timber that could be converted into charcoal. Later, as the supply became more distant, and with only primitive transport available, a managed system of replacement planting was introduced.

A further boost to the prosperity of the county occurred in 1543 with the first successful casting of a cannon. From then on ordnance manufacture ran in parallel with the basic iron works. A further and closely related industry was created in the east of the county, that of gunpowder manufacture. The powder produced quickly gained a reputation for quality, indeed, Lord Nelson insisted on it for all his ships. The last Sussex ironworks finally closed in 1826, although two abortive attempts at resurrection took place later in the century.

Ashdown Forest, which lies on the stratum of the same name, is the largest area of lowland heath in the south-east of England. It covers much of the most northerly sandstone ridge of the AONB and is home to the highest point, Crowborough Beacon. In the thirteenth century the area was decreed a royal deer park for hunting, but with the commoners' rights for grazing and fuel being maintained. This was the origin of the scenery that we enjoy today, for heathland requires the constant control of the vegetation,

be it by natural or mechanical means. Should this cropping cease, then, as has occurred on the Downs, scrub, followed by woodland, soon invades. The beauty of Ashdown was lost on the nineteenth-century traveller William Cobbett, who, when on his rural rides in 1822 wrote, 'Verily the most villainous ugly spot I ever saw in England.' Although renowned for its open landscape, one-third of the forest remains tree-covered, the woods being predominantly of oak and birch.

The remaining portions of the High Weald are a glorious mixture of sandstones and clays. Most of the sands enclose wide river valleys, and the southern ridge, which, in effect, forms the boundary of the area, drops its drainage streams into the rivers Rother and Brede. When these were dammed they provided the energy for the iron furnaces and forges, the Wadhurst Clays supplying the raw materials. The ridge continues to the south-east before terminating at the cliffs at Fairlight. Again commercial forestry is commonplace, more especially on the northern slopes that have been cleared of scrub and rubbish timber.

The High Weald, as it approaches the coast, merges with river floodplains and land that has been reclaimed from the sea. Although technically still in the AONB, it is best described in conjunction with the Sussex river systems.

The Sussex Rivers

The Sussex rivers, with one exception, steer towards, and discharge their waters into the English Channel. The exception is the Western Rother which originates in Hampshire and uniquely parallels the structural features before joining the Arun above Pulborough. In the north-east of the county, small streams flow northwards off the sandstone ridges to enhance either the Medway or its tributaries, but before crossing the county line have not combined into any resemblance of a river flow.

Five rivers, plus an overgrown stream – the Brede – are responsible for the county's drainage. Three winterbournes also exist, these

The River Cuckmere. The final few yards of a sluggish, meandering river, viewed from the Haven.

have seasonal flows, appearing only when the chalk aquifers become full and, having small surface catchment areas, they take their water direct from the downs. Four of the main rivers, Arun, Adur, Ouse and Cuckmere, cut through the east to west chalk barrier, while the Eastern Rother finds a leisurely course through the High Weald. This last river drains off the sandstone around Mayfield and Rotherfield and then continues in an ever widening valley to form the county boundary, finally swinging coastwards to collect the Brede and reach its end at Rye. In their infancy many of the river-feeding ghylls are cut so steeply that they have defied any attempt at clearance and cultivation and the trees that line their slopes today are probably direct descendants of the ancient Wealden forest. In the lower levels the influence of man becomes evident; the

flat water meadows are networked by drainage ditches. These rifes are relatively recent additions, for, over recorded history, the area has seen several inundations from the sea, salt marsh and mud flats alternating with pasture land. During the Roman occupation the Isle of Oxney was indeed an island. After each retreat of the sea man has renewed his 'improvement' of the re-emergent lands; the river bends have been straightened, new cuts dug and ditches inserted. All of these measures tend to create an austere landscape. The last large-scale drainage occurred sixty years ago during the Second World War. Little has changed since then apart from the continuing eradication of the hedgerows and the construction of sterile flood banks.

The 'half' river Brede wanders among sandstone cliffs which were, in Roman times, the coastline around Winchelsea and Icklesham. It may be likened to a tributary of the Rother for they share the same outflow and their levels are similarly hatched with ditches and dykes. Their history too is comparable, although the small river has a more marine feel to its reaches, for upstream from Rye the inland cliffs are a constant reminder that in the none too distant past this land was under the waves. Natural and man-made reclamations have united to form the profile of today's land. These levels tend to be more intensely farmed than those of the Rother lowlands, but outside the main towns there is little evidence of habitation and the area remains a

haven of peace and solitude. It is uncertain when Rye developed into the port for the region; it thrived for centuries, but by the end of the reign of Elizabeth I, as the sea continued to retreat, the decline had started. One hundred years later Rye Harbour was declared 'to be choked with sand'.

Of the rivers that break the chalk barrier, the Cuckmere is both the shortest and has the smallest catchment area. With its headwaters around Horam, it manages to flow over an almost complete sequence of the Cretaceous deposits, finally breaching the Downs only a couple of miles from its mouth. The whole length of the river is defined as sluggish. This characteristic is well in

TWO TOWNS – ONE PROBLEM

Both of the county's administrative centres share the same problem, that of flooding. The causes of these disasters are, however, completely different. Lewes suffers from the overflow of a permanent river while Chichester is the victim of an intermittent winterbourne. Flooding has occurred throughout the centuries but recent media involvement has increased the public awareness of the problem.

Lewes was founded by the Saxons, it then gained a Norman castle and developed on the west bank of the Ouse akin to a hill town with narrow streets and alleys winding steeply away from the river. A complementary area of development on the flatter lands below the eastern ridge of chalk is the main sufferer when the river floods. A small winterbourne occasionally spews from the chalk but its sporadic flow has not allowed a stream channel to develop, and when there is flooding from this source then an area to the south of the town suffers.

The Ouse and its main tributary the Uck flow off the permeable sand ridges of the Weald. Normal rain falling on these sandstone rocks tends to be absorbed; it is when saturation is reached that problems arise. Then immediate run-off occurs, raising the river levels and posing a threat to the towns and villages in the upper reaches. The peak level slowly rolls down the valley and, as it closes on the sea, the tidal influence increases, continually raising and lowering the discharge through the

town. The danger peaks can now be accurately calculated, but nature will still retain the upper hand as the suburb of Cliffe and the riverside properties can testify. In the final days of the last century large areas became submerged, both residential and industrial units suffering extensive damage.

Chichester has the same problem but from a differing source. The river Lavant is another winterbourne, that rises in the Downs inland from the city. It starts to flow in a valley that, for the greater part of the year, remains dry and becomes culvertized in its journey through the town before fragmenting into the coastal plain. Chichester must thank one of its earlier settlers, the Romans, for the danger: it was they who originally diverted the stream away from the uninhabited lands on to its present course. The culverts should in normal years provide adequate passage for the waters, but twice in the last decade of the millennium they failed. The birth of a winterbourne usually occurs in late winter after the rains have saturated the aquifers, but in 1994, and again six years later, the river was born before Christmas. The earlier flood did considerable damage to the eastern parts of the city, a flood plan was inaugurated, yet the same problem occurred. This time continual pumping of water from the stream into 13 miles (20km) of pipeline saved the city. Road and rail communications were interrupted for days but at least Chichester remained dry.

The River Lavant at Singleton. A weed-choked winterbourne in mid summer.

The Ouse at Lewes. Harvey's Brewery was one company to suffer in the 2000 floods.

evidence just inland from its outflow at Cuckmere Haven; here the course has been straightened and shortened, the original flow remaining as isolated oxbow lakes. An excellent view of these features, known locally as 'The Meanders', may be obtained from the hills on either side of the Haven. Any interference with the river does not extend inland from the chalk cut at Alfriston. Upstream from here the flood plain survives largely intact, the only intrusion being the construction of a right-bank reservoir at Arlington.

The Cuckmere is the only river of Sussex that does not have its entry into the Channel disfigured by industrial or residential development. The remoteness of the Haven made the river popular with smugglers and Alfriston, being only a short distance inland, was energetically used as a distribution centre.

The Ouse has the second largest catchment area of the Sussex rivers, 70 per cent of which is above the tidal limits. It is regarded as an eastern river although its main headwater is in the west of the county just off the main Brighton road. It first circles to the north of Haywards Heath before collecting several run-offs from the Tunbridge Wells sands and the Ashdown beds, the permeability of these beds having a marked impact on the flow of the river. The Ouse becomes tidal at Barcombe and, as with its two siblings to the west, all have a tidal limit several miles above the Downs breakthrough. The tides usually stop at an abandoned lock or weir but the influence of the sea extends further through the drainage system, this being more especially notable in times of flood.

The Ouse needs two bites to conquer the chalk. The inland break is narrowly cut below Mount Caburn, where the town of Lewes, the river and the main rail and road systems all squeeze through the tiny gap. The river then continues through a flood plain where a misfit tributary joins. Opinions differ as to the origin of this small Glynde Reach, one theory is that from its early life the flow was in reverse to that of today and the Cuckmere benefited from its waters. Once a wider breach of the chalk has

been effected the river soon discharges at the port of Newhaven.

Much of the river no longer adheres to its original course. In the lower levels straightened waters flow between artificial banks and above Lewes discarded oxbows remain as evidence of its earlier wanderings. Man's tinkering with this river extends far upstream of the tidal limit thanks to the eighteenth-century Upper Ouse Navigation. This enterprise needed eighteen locks, numerous cuts and twenty years of construction to reach the terminus. Small pockets of riverside industry were created along the banks in the form of water and paper mills, but barge traffic was always sparse, final closure taking place in 1840. Relevant artefacts may still be found along the banks and two countryside hostelries, 'The Sloop' and 'The Anchor', are reminders of its previous existence.

Both of the West Sussex rivers flow for the greater part of their length over the clay lands of the Weald. The smaller, the Adur, is dual-headed, the branches of which are not differentiated by name, and join forces to the west of Henfield. At one time it was thought that some of the tributaries of the Upper Arun were the original headstreams of the Adur; this theory has now been rejected and replaced by the view that the Horsham stone outcrop has always formed the barrier between the two river systems. Below the fusion of its two branches the river winds through a wide flood plain. When in flood, if viewed from the Downs, it appears that the whole of the Sussex Weald is under water. These floods do not, however, extend into the coastal plain, for the bridge and causeway at Bramber form an effective barrier.

Steyning is today 6 miles (10km) inland from the sea, but as late as the Norman period it was a thriving estuary port. Natural silting plus opposition by the local landowner led to its demise. A new port was then established on the coastline at Shoreham; this, however, had only a short life since in the middle of the fourteenth century the sea devastated the facilities and the adjoining town. Four hundred years passed before a new cut was made through the shingle bank; this reach was then canalized and the present port established.

As at Lewes, road, river and an abandoned railway squeeze between the chalk hills; however, here all three modes of transportation abut one face, forsaking a mid valley route. The final flow of the river is through the apex of the coastal plain. Land to the east is residential, while to the west the remaining patch that is not covered by housing is occupied by Shoreham Airport.

The largest river of the county, the Arun, along with its tributary the Western Rother, controls the drainage for the west and the north of Sussex. Stream capture is almost entirely on the right bank of the main flow, but to the northeast of Horsham the river is unable to collect all of the sandstone run-offs, a few dropping into the basin of the Surrey Mole. After an initial westerly run, the river swings left to continue over the clays virtually due south to Littlehampton. The Rother tributary flows over more permeable rocks collecting, en route, water from the sandstones on either side.

Immediately below the junction of the two rivers lies a large flood plain known as the Wild Brooks. This was previously used as summer grazing, the land converting back to bog and marsh with the advent of the winter rains. To increase the productivity of these meadows the water table was lowered by means of increased and improved drainage. Recently, new conservation management and the introduction of a bird sanctuary are steering the Wild Brooks back towards their former state. Here the chalk hills have begun their retreat from the coast and the river has created a reasonably wide break before continuing in contained banks across the coastal plain to the sea.

This river has received less 'improvement' to its course in comparison with others, thanks to the Wey Arun Canal, which was constructed in the early nineteenth century to provide a through route from the Thames to the south coast. In the upper reaches of the river it was built adjacent to, but separated from, the main stream, only one straight cut being made to the

north of Arundel. Originally the river flowed to the east of the town but it was diverted to provide a trading link to the sea. The early line is now only traceable by a hesitant ditch. The Rother was also canalized in parts, but by being a smaller stream it had less impact on the surrounding lands.

Sussex finally secured its complete coastline between 6,000 and 5,500 BC when the sea broke through the land bridge. Before this inundation, the east of the county was an extension of the continental plateau and formed a barrier to the Atlantic waters; however, it was a further 2,000 years before the depth of the sea stabilized and a profile resembling that of today was formed. In Roman times the tidal inlets were deeper and the promontories extended further into the Channel. The port for Chichester was developed at the head of an inlet that is just 2 miles (3km) from the present city. This complex tidal inlet is today protected by a fragile sandbar that extends across the mouth of the harbour. At one time this spit projected into the open sea; tides and winds then forced it to reverse direction before it finally settled on to its present bearing. Should this low-lying barrier ever be breached, then a large area will be at risk from flooding and the outline of the harbour will change substantially. On the eastern side of the Selsey peninsula the entrance to Pagham Harbour has also had a troubled life. Collected shingle increased the eastward movement of the spit and man also intervened, draining the inland salt marsh for cattle pasture. The dry period of this land lasted for only a few years, for in 1910 the sea broke through the shingle at a point west of the previous entrance and reformed the lagoon.

The greatest erosion from the coast has taken place close to Selsey, with the site of a Saxon cathedral now being below the waves, half a mile (800m) beyond the present shoreline. This land continues to retreat at a speed of up to 10ft (3m) a year. Sea defences are helping to slow this erosion, but certain areas can be maintained only by the continual replacement of the shingle beach. Further to the east, between Bognor and

---

SUSSEX AND THE SEA

Without the neighbouring sea Sussex would be but half a unit. So involved is the county with the Channel that it has adopted a stirring march as its unofficial anthem. There are few outdoor summer events where the strains of 'Sussex by the Sea' are not heard. The adjoining waters have been, and in certain circumstances remain, protector, provider and adversary. Several times in recent history this stretch of water has formed an effective barrier against potential invaders, the last successful invasion being almost 1,000 years distant. Since that day our waters, in collaboration with those to the east and west, have prevented landings by continental aggressors: the French, the Spaniards, and more recently the Germans have been unsuccessful. Over the last few centuries our small ports provided bases for England's explorers. Their position faced both the Continent and the south where the majority of the voyages were destined. London was reasonably close and departure from a Sussex port obviated the need for a passage through the tricky Dover Straits.

The sea has also provided a rich resource of marine food, with the small harbours housing accumulations of inshore fishing boats. The black net houses on the beach of Hastings Old Town are a reminder of this once thriving industry. The sea forms the trade link, both legal and illegal, with our outside markets. The waters between our ports and the Continent offered the early entrepreneurs a smoother journey than the Kentish Straits and it was through them that the continental influence became established before extending into the rest of the country. Shipbuilding was also an important local industry and in the last two centuries tourism linked to the sea has created employment for thousands of workers.

Besides being a friend, at times the sea is an enemy, continually encroaching and attempting to engulf large areas of the county, only to return, at a later date, the unwanted remains of its earlier meal. The prevailing coastal drift is from west to east, this ensures that the remnants are returned to the land on a different section of coastline.

Littlehampton, two further villages have succumbed to the sea.

The mouth of every Sussex river has at one time suffered from the effects of encroaching shingle that forced its outflow eastward. Protective barriers were needed to stabilize any new cuts that were made. Long stretches of sea protection arrived with the urbanization of the coastline on either side of Brighton; groynes and sea walls feature most often. The groynes capture the drifting shingle while the walls were built to provide a permanent barrier against the waves. These concrete barriers are not a perfect solution since an undercurrent is formed at the base of the structure and, over time, the shingle is dragged seawards, leaving the wall vulnerable.

The east of the county has a more undulating coastline, cliff faces alternating with sections of reclaimed alluvial lowlands. The stretch between Brighton and Eastbourne belongs almost entirely to the chalk. Here too erosion continues but less speedily than to the west. Falls from the cliff

face tend to be more spectacular and are certainly more newsworthy.

A large shingle foreland known as the Crumbles lies to the leeward side of Eastbourne. This feature is the third constructed by the sea at or near to its present position. From the eleventh century this beach developed rapidly, attaining a width of 2 miles (3.2km). This protective presence greatly assisted the reclamation of the inland levels. From around 1600, redistribution of the shingle commenced with the shoreline retreating quite spectacularly. Later, 200ft (60m) of land on which were built three Martello Towers, disappeared in a little over thirty years. Today a defensive line of groynes has slowed the migration of material from the bank, but the threat of flooding to the levels remains.

Another set of cliffs, this time of sandstone, lies to the east of Hastings. As with the chalk, they continue to lose their battle with the sea. These cliffs are variable in form with sections underlain by clays, and when the clay becomes

Hastings net houses. These tall, black buildings, on the beach at the entrance to the Old Town, are the remnants of a once thriving inshore fishing industry.

saturated mud slides and land slipping occurs. Where there is some protection from the waves the cliffs have a stepped profile; those that are more exposed tend to have a vertical facing. As the land retreats, so the erosion at the adjacent, south-western end of the Winchelsea Beach occurs. This has necessitated the provision of a long sea wall to protect the Pett Levels. The Winchelsea Beach, again consisting of onshore-drift shingle, is a recent formation, hardly existing before the sixteenth century. Before then the sea was again in its invasive mood, the original settlement of Winchelsea being submerged in 1287.

The largest open sand beach of Sussex lies to the east of Rye and extends beyond the county boundary. This is a wide, gently shelving beach backed by a series of dunes. Two other small stretches of sand occur, East Head, which is the bar to Chichester Harbour, and another to the immediate west of the Arun mouth at Climping. Many of the county's shingle beaches are underlain by sand but this more pleasant underfoot surface is exposed only between the tidal limits.

2. The Arrival and Development of Early Man in Sussex

Sussex has never provided an abundance of fossils for the collector, unlike the coastlines of Dorset and the Isle of Wight where the action of the sea upon the soft cliffs is continually exposing new treasures. The most prolific area for fossil hunting in the county occurs where the sandstones, clays and shales drop into the sea to the east of Hastings. This 4 mile (6.5km) stretch of coastline has also revealed the imprinted footprints of dinosaurs, but the first major find of these creatures' remains occurred almost 200 years ago in a pit on a sandstone ridge in the centre of the county near Cuckfield. In 1822 the wife of a Lewes doctor unearthed teeth from an unknown reptile. Detective work was carried out on the find and the creature was named *Iguanadon*, for it was felt that the teeth resembled those of a present-day lizard, the iguana; however, later research proved them to be from a large, herbivorous dinosaur. This discovery was a great boost for local archaeologists for they were the first remains of a dinosaur to be discovered anywhere in the world. The teeth were found in a quarry and later similar finds were made in the area. The original site was believed to be to the south of the present town but details were not recorded and, as all traces of these pits have been eradicated, the exact position cannot now be determined.

Man is believed to have originated in Africa before slowly spreading north through the Old World to our shores. The complex story of his evolution is gradually being unravelled as new fossil finds are made. Perhaps they do not now cause as much excitement as was once the case, and such is the extent of our knowledge of our ancestors that hoaxers are unlikely to go long before they are unmasked. But this was not always the case.

The discoverer of the Sussex Iguanodon.

The Piltdown Hoax

In the latter years of the nineteenth century archaeologists embarked on a world-wide journey to discover a 'missing link', a creature that would provide the connection between apes and modern man. As early as 1865 a possible candidate was unearthed in what was then Prussia when parts of a skeleton were discovered in a limestone cave. Was this the original Neanderthal? Thankfully the remains were not claimed as such for detailed examination proved them to be of recent deposition. Other discoveries followed from France, Belgium, Gibraltar, and, from further afield, the former Dutch East Indies. All were exposed as hoaxes, or remained not proven, but these findings provided the impetus needed for many expeditions searching for our ancestor.

The neighbouring county of Kent offered another Neanderthal but this too was rejected, for the skeleton was revealed to be that of a recently deceased female. British palaeontology was in despair and desperate for any discovery that would enhance its standing in the science.

Iron Age village.

GIDEON ALGERNON MANTELL

Gideon Mantell was born in Lewes in 1790, the son of a shoemaker. At the age of fifteen he was apprenticed to a local surgeon and six years later he gained a diploma from the MRCS. From an early age he was interested in geology and palaeontology, with his first venture into print, in 1813, being an article in the *Sussex Advertiser*, 'Geology of the Environs of Lewes'. The following year saw the publication of his first full geological paper. In 1816 he was appointed military surgeon at the local artillery hospital, bought his first practice and married Mary Ann Woodhouse.

Over the next two decades he continued his literary output. This was mainly of a localized geological theme interspersed with an occasional medical paper. In 1825, a year after his wife found the Iguanodon, he was elected to The Royal Society. In 1833, the family moved to Brighton where he opened his house as a fossil museum, the first in Britain. Five years later he was 'much broken in health and spirit'. He sold his fossil collection to the Natural History Museum for £4,000 and moved to London.

In 1841 a carriage accident left him in persistent pain; this changed his whole attitude to life, and he became morose and dispirited. Although he was now taking opium in an effort to relieve the pain, his literary output continued unabated. Concentrating as before on his favourite subjects of geology and palaeontology, he now extended his area of research outside of his native county.

Mantell committed suicide in 1852 by swallowing thirty-two times the maximum dose of opium. The remains of his extensive collection was bought by the Natural History Museum, which now held over 25,000 of his specimens. This Sussex worthy is not only honoured by the plaque on his Lewes residence, but also part of his diseased spine remains pickled in a jar, on a shelf, at The Royal College of Surgeons.

One local exhibitionist believed he had the answer. Any find, no matter what, was pronounced to be 'new'. New forms of prehistoric mammals or reptiles, new types of flint rubbish, in fact anything that could be inflated through his own published papers was so. When his period of self-promotion finally waned the country was ripe for further exploitation; it had not long to wait.

Piltdown is a cluster of houses in mid Sussex, 7 miles (11km) north of Lewes, and lies on a gravel plateau raised slightly above the River Ouse. The settlement first came to national prominence in 1912 when the journal *Nature* announced, 'Remains of a human skull and mandible, considered to be from the early Pleistocene period has been discovered by Mr Charles Dawson in a gravel pit ...'.

Volumes have been written on Piltdown Man, but none has been able to identify conclusively the chief arranger of this fraud, and, with all the suspects being long gone, it is unlikely that he will ever be named. Suspicion falls on three men: Dawson was the prime suspect, but in league with him was his life-long friend Arthur Smith Woodward, who by 1912 had progressed to become a keeper at the British Museum. The third member of the trio, who was probably less involved, was a French Jesuit priest studying in Sussex, Pierre de Chardin. Dawson was a solicitor practising in nearby Uckfield. With a passion for archaeology and geology, he had already written several papers on the subjects and had been made an honorary collector for the British Museum, presenting them with several small fossils. He was also a steward for Barkham Manor, and it was in a small gravel pit in the grounds that the first finds were made. It is not clear when the first discoveries were unearthed but it was in February 1912 that Woodward received a letter from his friend cataloguing them, pieces of a skull and several animal teeth. Although he was at first sceptical, a site visit was arranged for June when the pit had dried out. Excavations continued throughout the summer and further fragments of skull, more animal teeth, flint implements and half of a lower jaw emerged. It was now decided that there was enough evidence to make an announcement; but before the official disclosure in December someone leaked the details to Fleet Street. This early publicity was certainly advantageous to the hoaxer.

The meeting held at the Geological Society in London was described as 'interesting'. Dawson partially outlined the sequence of his discoveries and incorrectly dated the gravel in which they were found. Whether this was in ignorance or deliberate, who knows? Woodward produced a plaster-based mock-up of the head of Piltdown Man (known as *Eoanthropus dawsoni*, 'man of the dawn'), compiled from the available skull fragments and half jaw bone. The revelations were well received, any doubts that some archaeologists may have had were swiftly overridden, for the missing link had been found in Britain.

Over the next two summers excavations and related publicity continued. In 1913 de Chardin unearthed a tooth that was missing from the jaw bone. A year later further animal bones were uncovered, culminating in the discovery of a fossilized elephant's thigh bone. When the recovered tooth was analysed more queries were raised, but again these doubts were suppressed.

Dawson died in 1916 leaving Woodward to battle on alone; this he did enthusiastically for, in the following year, he revealed that, before his death, his friend and the Frenchman had made yet another find. Two miles (3.2km) from the original site further skull fragments, a rhinoceros tooth and a molar identical to that of the man had been discovered. Piltdown II surely confirmed the authenticity of the two specimens. Professor Haldicka, a renowned hoax demolisher from the United States, commented that the two teeth were so similar that they must be from the same jaw.

In the 1920s more examples of primitive man emerged, several teeth from China (Peking Man) and Neanderthals from Israel. These last, Mount Carmel fossilized men, had human jaws and ape-like brows, unlike Piltdown where the reverse was true.

It was not until after the Second World War that Piltdown began to be exposed as a fake. An earlier geological survey had corrected Dawson's

views on the associated gravel beds, and, when further tests were made on the relics, each was pushed back into a later period of evolution. In 1953 the whole scheme began finally began to unravel. Woodward was not around to witness the truth for he died in 1944. The British Museum at last gave permission for further tests on all the remains. A fluorine-based test was used; this test was subject to error but it brought into prominence Kenneth Oakley.

A chance remark made to Oakley led him to pose several questions. Why was the site of Piltdown II not given the same scrutiny as the original? Indeed, where was it? The British Museum had throughout appeared to accept without question or research the facts that were handed to it. Only now was it willing to authorize the comprehensive testing of all materials. The results from the teeth were startling. There was evidence of artificial abrasion of the molars; this was in reverse of that encountered through normal wear, and, when a modern chimpanzee's tooth was stained, it became identical to that of Piltdown. The staining of the majority of the bones was, according to Dawson, due to the presence of ironstone in the gravel. In fact, it had been either artificially induced or a paint-like substance had been applied. More chemical tests on the animal teeth proved that their owners had never walked the lands of Sussex. Piltdown Man was dissected fragment by fragment. The press had another field day ridiculing finds that just forty years before were being hailed as the greatest discovery of the twentieth century.

As we have seen the leading perpetrator has never been exposed. Dawson was the chief suspect but did he work alone or was it a group conspiracy? In 1996 a fourth name was added, that of Martin A. C. Hinton who in the thirties became keeper of zoology at the British Museum. A trunk bearing the initials MACH and containing stained bones had been found in the museum. When these were analyzed by two British palaeontologists, Gardiner and Currant, it was found that they had been stained in the exact same way as the Piltdown fossils.

In 1912 Hinton was working as a volunteer at the museum and was known to have an abrasive relationship with Woodward, his superior. It has been suggested that it was he who planted the Piltdown bones to ensnare and embarrass Woodward, the bones in the trunk being used for practice before treating those in the actual hoax.

This is a plausible explanation but poses more questions. Did Hinton collude with any or all of the suspects? If Woodward was to be the victim, how was it that a man in his position acted in such a naive manner and accepted the planted material without question? Plus, from where did these bones originate? These questions can never be answered; the gravel pit has disappeared and Barkham Manor has a thriving vineyard. Indeed, the only visible signs remaining of the earlier dramas are a memorial erected in 1936 to 'Mr Charles Dawson, solicitor and antiquarian' and a sign now hanging outside the local hostelry.

Piltdown Man. The only visible sign of the county's greatest hoax.

The First Residents

The earliest inhabitants of Sussex belonged to the Lower, or Early, Palaeolithic age. This period encompassed over half a million years, so the date they arrived from the Continent can only be guessed at. It is thought that it coincided with the warm spell before the last ice age. Britain was at that time still connected to Europe by a wide land bridge so it was relatively easy for this Early Stone Age man to migrate northwards. He led a nomadic lifestyle and had an omnivorous diet. The only evidence of his existence was, until recently, the remains of his tools, flint knives and hand axes together with the accompanying waste materials.

Sussex is not a treasure house of Palaeolithic finds. This is mainly due to the lack of any large-scale gravel extraction, for it in in these beds that the tools would be most likely to survive. The greatest number of recognized sites occurs on the 'raised beaches' at the northern edge of the coastal plain. The Goodwood–Slindon beach is over 100ft (30m) above the present sea level and dates back about 500,000 years. It was adjacent to this beach at Boxgrove that the earliest fossilized remains of Early Stone Age man were discovered, and nearby substantial finds of his axe heads have been made. There have also been discoveries of tools on the Downs, more especially between Brighton and Eastbourne, adjacent to or very near river courses. Few sites have been confirmed from the Weald, surely confirming that this forest was once seen as an intimidating area.

The ice ages did not entail an uninterrupted lowering of temperatures over the county, warm periods fluctuated with increasingly arctic conditions. It was during the cold centuries, when the landscape resembled the tundra and the food supply had migrated southward, that our Palaeolithic residents vacated the area, only to return again as the climate improved. The final exodus took place as the ice sheets approached the Thames Valley. There now follows a gap in our history of over 30,000 years, for it was relatively recently, 8,000BC, when the climate had improved enough for man again to colonize Sussex.

Neanderthal Man

The popular image of our early ancestors is that of the Neanderthal, a humanoid with a thick skull, brow ridges, and a sloping forehead, all signs of a primitive creature. In fact, their brain volume was equal to or even exceeded that of modern man. In the early part of the last ice age, about 50,000 years ago, the Neanderthals ranged over much of Europe but did not appear to favour our lands, for no trace of their culture has been discovered here. Theirs was a short life since by 30,000BC they had vanished, superseded by a type that is generally recognized to be our first, true parent. No one is certain for the reason behind the demise of these early creatures, an ice age genocide by the Upper Palaeolithic invaders has been suggested as the cause, or perhaps it was continual interbreeding between the

two species that ended the life of 'Ape Man'. The Early Stone Age people were also thought not to have taken up residence in our county, France being their most popular home. Boxgrove has proved that theory wrong.

Mesolithic Man

The missing years in Sussex archaeology come to an end with the final retreat of the glaciers. The flora and fauna again expanded northwards over the still existent land bridge, pulling with them another age of man. These Mesolithic, or Middle Stone Age, people were the first of our ancestors to populate Sussex comprehensively, remaining in charge for about 4,000 years. They were still nomadic hunters but had embodied the culture of both family and territorial groups. From evidence recovered from known camp sites, it has been calculated that each of their territories covered upwards of 400 sq miles (1,000 sq km).

BOXGROVE MAN

Boxgrove is a small village about 3 miles (5km) north-east of Chichester and is usually associated with the ruins of its Benedictine Abbey. However, it was here in 1993 in a commercial gravel pit that animal remains and flint tools dating from the Palaeolithic Age were uncovered. The tools were mainly hand axes, plus debris from their manufacture, while the animal bones were from large carcasses such as rhinoceros, horse and giant deer. A study combining the archaeology and the geology of the area suggested that the site could well have been in continual use for thousands of years. The excavations have been to the seaward side of the raised beach or cliff, suggesting that this was either a grass or mud, flat area that was used for the procurement and subsequent processing of the carcasses. The absence of claw or teeth marks on the bones shows that they had not been stolen from other predators, but that these early humanoids were able to undertake hunting themselves. The rhinoceros has no known predators and, as the recovered bones were from both young and fully-grown animals, the fact again

gives weight to the view that this early resident could successfully hunt should the need arise.

The most significant find on the site has been that of a shin bone, the oldest semi-human remains yet to be found in Britain. In western Europe only one other piece of humanoid fossil that is of comparable age has been discovered. In 1907 a jaw bone, thought to be about 400,000 years old, was unearthed in a sand pit near Heidelberg, in Germany. This bone was found in isolation, but in the same stratum remains were found that were almost identical to those of Boxgrove. The shin bone has been calculated to be that of a male, almost 6ft (2m) in stature and of powerful build. Marks appearing on the bone correspond to those made by the teeth of wolves. This poses the question, was he a victim of these animals or were the marks made after his death when the pack were enjoying a meal?

Two years after the Sussex shin bone find, further excavations on the site revealed a tooth that appears to predate that of the tibia. No doubt more finds will emerge from future digs.

The early Mesolithic campsites are mainly on the Lower Greensand ridges, to the lee of the Downs. Their tools are now more varied, arrow- and spear-heads and the first true axe heads appear, but imported, primitive implements continued to be used in tandem with the newer products. A cluster of sites on the sands above the Western Rother all bore evidence of fire-eroded flints, suggesting that these were camps with small cooking fires. An isolated pit near Selmeston church in East Sussex also yielded over 6,400 worked flints.

In the period from 7,000 to 6,000BC there was expansion into the western Weald, although most of the recorded Sussex sites are of a later date, the Late Mesolithic Period, that is up to 4,300BC. Again the sandy soils were preferred for the main centres of habitation. In the high Weald rock shelters were used as temporary camps; one hearth discovered at High Hurstwood was formed of sandstone blocks and the surrounding area gave up over 4,000 items of recognizable usage.

Their is little evidence of occupation of the low Weald, the extensive tree cover being more than a match for the primitive tools that were available then. It is thought that the Downs did see quite extensive Mesolithic activity, but much evidence from this early period has been lost by erosion. The finds that have been made on the hills from the later age consist mainly of flint tools and associated debris; usually these have been uncovered by the modern plough. This Stone Age man still remained a hunter gatherer, and, like his predecessor, his diet was controlled by his ability to kill or collect. From the riverside and shoreline sites that have been examined it appears that fish also featured on his menu.

His home was only a temporary shelter, for he was still a nomad at heart. It consisted of a shallow pit dug into the sandy soil and roofed with branches that were interwoven with other vegetation. Cooking was done on an open fire and water was heated by dropping hot stones into skin containers since pottery was still in the future. From the analyses of ashes from these Stone Age fires it appears that hazel was the pre-

dominant woodland tree, oak not taking over until after the climate had warmed further.

The Mesolithic population of Britain was thought to consist of no more than about 10,000. Given that the northern uplands were not conducive to colonization, Sussex was probably home to only a few hundred. It was during this period that the continental land bridge was finally breached, Britain was alone and our Sussex families were able to continue unmolested from European infiltrators or their influence for many centuries.

Neolithic Man

The next culture to invade our county was the Neolithic, or New Stone Age. This period was used by earlier archaeologists as a dumping ground for any discoveries whose age they were unable to identify. Any new artefact that was difficult to recognize was deemed to be Neolithic. Because of this uncertainty, it was originally thought that the age extended over several millennia, but today's thinking has reduced the period to less than 1,000 years.

In spite of its relatively short duration, this was the period when the southern counties started to develop. Farming and general husbandry began to appear; no longer was man just a scavenger and hunter. The cultivation of wild grains that could be converted into animal fodder originated in the Middle East, extending in turn through the Balkans and mainland Europe before coming to a temporary halt at the Channel. This farming innovation was introduced to Sussex by southern European peoples who first colonized Ireland and south-western England before extending along upland ridges and the chalk plateaux into our county.

This was no invasion since the newcomers were few in number and acted more as traders, bringing a measure of civilization. These Neolithic peoples again favoured living on the higher ground, where tree and scrub clearance was easier. The climate enjoyed by these uplands was also balmier than that of today, for the temperature was a few degrees above our present-day values. The domestication of animals, notably of cattle and pigs, took place and operated in parallel with the earlier economy of hunting, fishing and gathering. These new activities obviously brought their practitioners into contact with the indigenous tribes who were ripe to assimilate the new practices. Arable farming is thought to have arrived at a slightly later date. The extra land needed for these crops came largely from woodland clearance, the system originated in the Mesolithic, but, with new tools becoming available, the cleared areas greatly increased.

The term New Stone Age refers to a period when an improved form of tool appeared: the axe head now featured a longer-lasting, polished surface. No longer were likely flints just collected from the land or sea shore surface, but active mining for them took place. An experiment carried out in Denmark proved that one individual using one of the new axes could clear an acre (about half a hectare) of woodland each week. Not that the labourers worked alone, for these peoples lived in communities rather than in family groups as was the earlier system. Although a community culture was adopted, they were still semi-nomadic, moving on when the surrounding area was exhausted and could no longer provide.

The latest arrivals brought with them basic items of pottery, but no complete examples of their utensils have yet been discovered in the county. From the shards recovered, two differing types have emerged, characterized both by design and age. Each was crudely made, round-bottomed and fashioned without the aid of a wheel; the later type does however bear traces of ornamentation.

Neolithic Remains in the Landscape

The New Stone Age was the first period of history that left any evidence of existence on the landscape. Three types of disturbance remain visible today: flint mines, causewayed camps or enclosures and long barrows. Flint mining has left its mark on the downland surface by a series of grass-covered depressions, all that remain of the mine shafts. The nucleus of the industry was centred on the Downs a few miles inland from Worthing, with other sites in the west of the county and a solitary one east of the Cuckmere river. These miners certainly worked for their rewards for, after the clearance of the surface material, shafts were dug into the chalk to a depth of 50ft (15m). When a seam of suitable flints was encountered galleries were tunnelled from the core into the lode-bearing levels. This was a massive operation considering that the only tools available were picks shaped from discarded animal bones. At the Cissbury site up to 200 pits have been identified within a radius of a few hundred yards. This makes it the second most densely worked area for flints in Britain. Several of the Sussex flint sites along with the causewayed camps were incorporated by the later Iron Age people into their fortified settlements.

There are eight known causewayed camps in Sussex, but only five show the characteristics from which they are named. These camps consist of a roughly circular central area enclosed by a series of concentric ditches and banks, the earthworks being broken at intervals by the unworked causeways. Several opinions have been put forward to explain their working but no definitive answer has yet been agreed. The size of these enclosures meant that a communal effort was needed for their construction; this gave rise to the suggestion that they may have been a semi-permanent home for a collection of tribes, or were they only a ceremonial site, the significance of which we are still not able to comprehend? Any excavations that have been made at the camps have yielded only general debris characteristic of the period, but nothing conclusive.

The third intrusion on the landscape is the long barrow, or its smaller relative the oval barrow. Only two areas of downland contain these relics and, since the county total is fewer than a dozen, they are a rare item when Sussex is compared with the counties to the west. These earth mounds are always situated on the upper slopes of the hills, but below the crest, and do not conform to a standard size, some reaching over 200ft (60m) in length. The mounds are usually surrounded by a ditch which could be causewayed at one end. They are generally agreed to be burial tombs for tribal chieftains or elders, each mound being used for successive internments from the same tribe. Further excavation of these barrows is needed before a truer picture of their purpose will emerge.

The Bronze Ages

The transition from stone to the metallic ages was never as sudden nor dramatic as the names may imply, both cultures coexisting for many centuries. As with most novelties, the possession of bronze implements, the shapes of which were largely based on those of the flint era, was a status symbol and available only to a few select members of the tribe.

It was generally believed that the introduction of bronze technology into Sussex corresponded with the invasions from the Netherlands of the so-called Beaker People. The human remains of these new peoples are easily distinguished from those of the Neolithics for they were of larger stature and possessed a significantly rounder skull. The name Beaker relates to the type of pottery they used for drinking vessels. These cups were thin-rimmed, often elaborately decorated, and uniquely had a flat base. Remains of this type of pottery have been recovered from both known domestic sites and round barrows.

The Beaker–Bronze connection now looks a little suspect, since in Ireland, where Bronze Age relics occur, there is no trace of Beaker pottery. So, was the metallic connection made through Ireland, by an invasion or through trading routes from the Continent where metalworking was already well established?

Bevis Thumb. An unobtrusive long barrow on the downs near Compton.

The earliest recorded finds of flat bronze axes in the county are from isolated sites and no general pattern of distribution has been determined. Early Bronze Age settlements are recorded mainly on the Downs and the Lower Greensand ridges, with a concentration in the area to the north of Brighton and near to Beachy Head. Lone sites have been found on the Pett Levels and on the coastal plain. It could well be that the intensive agricultural disturbance of this latter land has destroyed any evidence that may have been there.

Round Barrows

The round barrows (tumuli) pepper the landscape of the Downs and, to a much lesser extent, the northern sandstones. Almost a thousand have been listed locally, and of this number 90 per cent are of a standard design: an upturned bowl encircled by a ditch that may vary in depth between a few inches and several feet. A slightly more complex shape is found in the west of the area; here the bowl rests on a ledge of level ground inside the circling depression. These monuments are known as 'bell barrows' since their form appears to resemble an inverted church bell. The distribution of this type suggests that they are not endemic to the county but are outliers of the common Wessex mound.

The round barrows can usually be dated accurately and are all placed in the Early or the Middle Bronze Age period. The early examples are of a solitary internment with the body in a contracted position; weapons or ornaments were also included in the tomb for the occupant's use in the next world. The weapons or tools were almost exclusively of flint – bronze or copper artefacts are rarely in evidence. Copper was an metal used early on the Continent but it made little inroad in Britain since it is relatively soft and was probably suitable only for personal ornamentation. Occasionally beakers or bowls were included in the burial chamber alongside the body, this pottery containing sustenance for the journey ahead. The later barrows are characterized by evidence of cremations, the ashes

Round Barrow. A well-camouflaged example on Iping Common.

being contained in an urn totally unlike those used for food preparation. Personal weapons were normally absent, any that were found were of metal, not stone. Some of the later barrows contained evidence of multiple cremations along with bones from an earlier interment; this supports the view that these earthworks were established family monuments.

The abundance and accessibility of the barrows has meant that the vast majority have, in the none too distant past, suffered from investigation and subsequent plundering. Those who undertook these excavations unfortunately kept only sparse records of their finds.

The Iron Age

The Mid to Late Bronze Age eased easily into the Iron Age. It was during this period that the way of life first began to change for the residents of Sussex. Before then the area was sparsely populated; now, with growing tribal unrest on the Continent, an increasing number of immigrants flowed across the Channel. These newcomers brought with them new ideas and improved implements. In the Early Bronze Age man was still semi-nomadic; now, with increased farming commitments and the growing pressure on available land, Iron Age man began to realize the need to establish a stable base. Each family, clan or tribe was forced to curb any desire to roam

BUTSER, AN IRON AGE VILLAGE

The transition from bronze to iron had little impact on agricultural methods, apart from the availability of improved tools. Accommodation and ancillary buildings underwent little change. A replica Iron Age village has been reconstructed at a site which is a couple of miles over the Hampshire border. The first project undertaken at the Little Butser Experimental Farm was the building of a typical 'ideal home', the construction being based on evidence taken from Maiden Castle hill fort. The resulting building is circular with wattle walls which were coated with a daub of clay, straw and chalk; this design proved strong enough to support a free-standing, conical, thatched roof. The completed building was highly weather-resistant.

A common feature of the farm sites that have been investigated is a series of four post holes; these are believed to be the basis for above-ground granaries. But this may be too simple an explanation since Butser has found that grain stored in underground sealed pits will survive uncontaminated for several years. The pits could also be used for the storage of other essentials such as silage, clay or water, while the post holes could well be the foundations for byres, barns, or even chicken houses since poultry arrived in Britain in the first millennium BC.

Improved strains of wheat and barley were imported, and recent analysis of these seeds has found that they contained more than twice the protein of more modern varieties. Further experiments at Butser with the improved plough found that, when fitted with an iron shoe and hauled by a pair of oxen, it would be quite capable of turning over the heavier loams found at the foot of the Downs. The cattle and sheep farmed during this period were tough specimens and able to survive on poor or thin pasture. Recovered bone samples from both animals, apart from those of a few young bulls, were from old or diseased creatures, implying that they had died when their meat was beyond its best and that they were reared mainly for the production of milk and wool.

and to establish a territory that would support both them and their animals. Solitary standings did occur, but the trend was for units to combine and create a defensible enclosure.

Arable farming was now developing with the Downs providing most of the suitable land. The design and strength of early ploughs confined their use to the lighter lands of chalk and sand; the ploughshare had not yet arrived and cultivation was confined to the scratching of surface drills. An improved plough was introduced by the invaders known as the Belgae or the Celts. Their cultivation technique was to cross-plough areas into a square field plan. These fields were normally on the higher ground with the lower slopes being retained for animal pasturage. The continual ploughing of the same area combined with rainwash led to the creation of banks or lynchets along the lower edge of cultivation. Evidence of this form of working is still visible today at several locations along the Downs.

Another feature of the Downs which has yet to be fully explained is the cross-ridge dykes. These are linear dykes of single or multiple earth banks. Over sixty examples have been found, many of which were sited near to known settlements. Approximately half of these earthworks extend over ridges at the tops of the scarp slopes of hills. The general view is that these ridges were constructed as territorial tribal boundaries, while the minority opinion is that they are just scattered remains of early drove roads.

The use of round barrows for ceremonial internment was discontinued in this period. Cremation was still practised but the ashes, still contained in distinctive pottery, were now buried in unidentifiable, level graves. As the bronze period gave way to another metal age it is a sobering thought that the vast majority of these peoples probably never owned nor even handled a metal implement during the whole of their lifetime.

The technology of iron manufacture, as with many of the early civilized crafts, originated in the Middle East centuries before its arrival in Sussex. This coincided with an infiltration of

The Trundle. Earthworks of an Iron Age hill fort.

refugees from south-east Europe. Each succeeding wave of arrivals brought with it more advanced manufacturing techniques, both for metals and also for pottery. The increasing demand for material goods was largely satisfied by the emergence of craftsmen. Metal workers, potters and, from the agricultural economy, weavers, established their trades in the larger communities. A barter system of trading operated at first, but as the Roman occupation drew near this was supplemented with a form of locally-produced coinage.

Unlike the transition from stone to metal, when both materials continued in use, once iron work arrived on our shores bronze was relegated almost immediately to the manufacture of less important articles, jewellery becoming a typical outlet for it.

It was during the Iron Age that settlements finally began to spread away from the main downland conurbations. The earliest iron workings appeared to the north of Hastings, spreading further inland as the demand for the metal increased. Soon the iron workings in the High Weald needed protection from predators from the north who had no iron of their own and felt that their needs could best be satisfied by violence rather than trade. In order to counteract this threat, a series of hill forts was constructed along the higher ridges that today overlook the northern boundary of the county.

The coastal plain below Chichester was another area favoured for colonization. Several different types of pottery have been recovered from sites in the area and, as these remains differ substantially from those discovered at other local excavations, they could well be imports. The principal settlement for the area was believed to have been situated near to Selsey, on land that has now disappeared under the waves.

As was noted earlier, the agricultural systems of the Bronze Age continued into the next period of history largely unchanged, with, perhaps, minimal fortifications being added to the enclosures. By 400BC changes began to take place; inter-tribal squabbling introduced the need for a secure area that could be readily defended. The establishment of the hill forts not only provided the outlying settlements with havens to which they could retreat in times of trouble, but also created centres for administration, craft workings and trade. The larger centres, which all occur to the west of the River Arun, were all constructed through a co-operative effort of several clans and had the effect of regionalizing the downland.

As the Iron Age drew to a close, Sussex received a further inflow of would-be residents from across the Channel. The Roman Empire had extended through France and in both 55 and 54BC Caesar made forays into Kent. Both proved ineffective and the occupation of Britain was delayed for a further ninety years. The influence of Rome spread throughout the south-east of England decades before the first successful invasion. Trade with the Empire increased markedly, probably creating the first trade imbalance in our country's history. Any goods with a Roman connection were welcomed by the more affluent, who also felt that it was to the south that they should look for future protection, should their northern neighbours prove troublesome.

It is in this pre-Roman period that the personal names of local leaders were first recorded. One, Commius, was the first chief to have a coinage struck that bore his name; previous earlier tokens were either borrowed or traded from continental sources. Verica, one of the sons of Commius, formed a close alliance with the Roman imperial household, this culminating in AD40 in a visit to the Emperor Claudius. The reasons for this cross-channel journey will be outlined in the following chapter.

CISSBURY HILL FORT

During the Late Bronze–Early Iron Age (1,000–400BC) a large number of hill forts or enclosed units were constructed on the Downs, the majority being sited from the centre of the county westwards, with Caburn above Lewes being the main eastern outlier. By the time of the Middle Iron Age the majority of these forts had been abandoned; of those remaining Cissbury was by far the largest example. In size it is the second largest camp in Britain, being surpassed only by that of Maiden Castle in Dorset.

The enclosed central area of Cissbury, parts of which contain evidence of ploughing, exceeds 60 acres (24ha), but, when the surrounding ramparts are added a total nearer to 80 acres (32ha) results. The ramparts are not of a uniform height; to the north and the west of the fort the natural steepness of the hill is used as part of the fortification. On the southern dip slope higher artificial earthworks were needed to provide the same protection. In places these banks rise over 40ft (12m) above the associated ditch.

The wooden retaining wall at this site was of a design unique to Cissbury. Vertical timbers were set side by side in a trench, then anchored back into the rubbish of the ramparts. It needed a mammoth feat of engineering to protect this hill-top site, at least 10,000 tree trunks each 15ft (4.5m) in length were needed for the retaining wall and incalculable tons of chalk had to be raised from the ditch to form the ramparts. Timber has only a limited lifespan; decay, plus the action of rain and frost on the exposed chalk, combined to cause the partial collapse of the embankments into the ditches. Repairing this system of defence would be difficult and the temporary abandonment of the site took place before the arrival of the Romans. Agricultural activity, however, continued spasmodically through to medieval times.

The earlier flint-mining pits are still visible in the south-western corner of the enclosure as grass-filled depressions. Opposite to them there are remnants of Romano-British field lynchets. The hill is now in the care of the National Trust, ensuring that it will remain as an interesting visitor attraction.

THE CHICHESTER DYKES

To the north of the city and lying in the shadow of the Downs, is another of the county's unsolved mysteries. Three blocks of bank and ditch earthworks extend from the Bosham stream in the west almost to the River Arun. The date for the construction of these works is subject to speculation, a period between the first century BC and early in the first century of the Christian era is now thought to have been the most likely date, although some historians have now extended this to include the twelfth century. The current consensus believes them to be either tribal boundaries defining the land blocks held by neighbouring chiefs or a defensive system against northern raiders. Their design would have had little impact on warriors on foot but would certainly have blocked any infiltration by charioteers. Interestingly, the majority of the Roman villas that have been discovered in the vicinity are outside the earthworks.

With the discoveries at nearby Fishbourne and Bignor, plus the arrival of Boxgrove man, the dykes have received only scant attention from archaeologists, but both Iron Age and Roman pottery have been found near to the entrenchments. Several quite detailed maps of Sussex were published during the eighteenth and the nineteenth century; none indicated the existence of the feature until the publication of the Ordnance Survey map of 1875. It is regrettable that they were missed from the earlier maps for in the last 200 years many roads, farm tracks, buildings and even a disused railway have all combined to blur the evidence of their existence.

Desecration. A twenty-first century telecommunication mast erected in the centre of the Trundle hill fort.

3. THE ROMAN OCCUPATION

The Roman occupation of Britain brought the country out of prehistory and into the age of recorded history. Each previous influx of continental peoples introduced to the residents not only improved material goods, but new cultures which were adopted and readily assimilated into their own customs and daily life. British society had been developing for several thousand years and at the end of the Late Iron Age had attained a standard equal to that which was enjoyed in mainland Europe. This similarity of life style owes much to the latest of our invaders. This race of peoples, loosely named Celts, was a troublesome crowd who expanded from their base in Germany to the west and the north.

All of these early residents and invaders were deficient of one basic aspect of life, that of literacy; they were unable to leave any written evidence as to how they spent their days. All that has been discovered of these early lives is due to archaeology and supposition. Combined, they have provided what is believed to be a reasonably accurate picture of the times in which they lived. However, any future large-scale discovery could well rewrite the history books. From the arrival of the Romans, or a few decades before, the written word became the chief information provider of what is known as recorded history. Apart from a short period in Anglo-Saxon England when literacy was temporarily lost, this medium, along with that of art, remains the primary source for referral. It was not until late in the nineteenth century that photography, followed by voice recording, began to challenge it for supremacy.

It must be acknowledged that these early works cannot be completely accurate, for there may well be bias in recording any event, as there is still, of course. These reports were written in a foreign tongue which, sometime in the future, would require translating into the native language. Names of tribes, kings or chieftains begin to appear in the documentation, but as these are 'Latinized' the Roman translations must be accepted and one can only ponder on their Celtic dialect form. Repeated copying of the texts again gave the opportunity for unintentional errors to arise. Other examples of writing support the literary texts and provide further information on this period. Examples are inscripted stonework, marks on manufactured goods and early examples of graffiti. Coinage also greatly assists in the dating of events; a coin which bears the name and image of the local ruler served a dual purpose: besides being a monetary unit, it was also a form of propaganda, continually imposing his presence on his subjects.

One further introduction as prehistory lost its prefix was the introduction of the rule of law. This ran in parallel with the advancement of the literate community and began to regulate the life of the individual, both by the state and his fellow man. The first laws were probably inefficient in many respects and were open to corruption, but they were there. Once the Empire expanded into Britain the residents soon found that they were subject to new decrees, taxes and regulations.

In the years leading up to the first forays into Britain by Caesar, in 55 and 54BC, the Celtic tribes were relatively small and self-contained, each individual unit ruled by a 'king'. This system of land control was slowly reformed and, by the time of the first colonization of the country by the Emperor Claudius, almost a century later, Sussex was home to one large clan, the Atrebates. Their authority at one time extended from the Channel coast to the Cotswolds, but lately they had lost territory to several bellicose neighbours.

Caesar's two short expeditions landed in Kent and had little impact on Sussex. Before his second departure he did extract from many of the

Fishbourne.

local leaders pledges of support for Rome. This allegiance also included the imposition of an annual tax, and, although not physically occupied, the southern counties of England became a virtual province of the Empire.

Celtic Trade

Sussex was between two cross-channel trading routes with the Empire: to the east was the short sea route serving northern Gaul and the Low Countries, and traffic from Brittany and the Mediterranean was routed through Hegistbury in Dorset. A year before Caesar's first raid on Britain his navy destroyed the maverick fleet that controlled the western route. This event led to the development of smaller independent cargo traders who were quickly made welcome by the Sussex ports.

As the years passed, the imbalance of trade between the Continent and Britain was reversed. Many of the goods exported were essential for the well-being of the Roman army: grain, cattle, hides and iron were typical commodities that left the county's shores. British agriculture was now producing grain in excess of local needs, the exporting of the surplus proved to be of great benefit to both parties. Imports into Britain were mainly of luxury or non-essential items.

Pre-Invasion Politics

The Atrebate tribe of Sussex received a further migration of Gallic relatives around 50BC, accompanied by a new leader Commius. This man was once a strong ally of Caesar, but then supported the wrong side of a continental anti-Roman revolt and was forced to flee for his life. Commius was succeeded by his son Tincommius, who, like his father, had coinage struck which bore his Latin name. Then followed a series of family disputes. Tincommius was ousted by his brother Eppilus, who, in turn, was deposed by another brother or half brother Verica. This chief continued with the tradition of personal coinage, calling himself *Rex* or king. Eppilus, when rejected, travelled only a few miles to the east and became leader of one of the Kentish tribes. Verica stayed to rule the Atrebates for over three decades and at all times maintained friendly relations with Rome.

The tribal lands to the north of the Thames now began to influence the south coast. Two tribes, the Trinovantes and the Catuvellauni, were among those who had originally agreed to Caesar's arrangements regarding taxes and cooperation; but as their leaders were succeeded by younger men, who felt less inclined to honour the treaty, tensions increased. The Romans appear to have largely ignored the signs of dissent that were issuing from the southern counties; this was probably due to the local troubles that they were experiencing from Gaul and Germany. Invasion plans needed months of preparation and to invade Britain would require a larger navy. Increasing the size of the Empire appealed to the military leaders who saw it as an opportunity to boost their reputation, but the foot soldier was less enthusiastic, for them the land over the sea constituted an unknown hazard and they would rather face a foe they knew than an unfamiliar enemy.

The Catuvellauni finally became the premier tribe of southern Britain and the Atrebates lost to them the northern part of their territory; Verica now ruled only Sussex and parts of Hampshire. These two tribes controlled all of the southern counties and surprisingly formed an uneasy alliance. Verica remained true to Rome while the Catuvellauni's leader, who had two expansionist-minded sons, tended to distance himself from the Empire. Trade between Britain and Gaul remained at a high level and the boys were of the opinion, probably correctly, that Rome's need of Britain was greater than the reverse. A third son was pressed to invade his northern neighbours; when he refused he was forced to flee to Gaul where he sought the assistance of the Emperor Gaius ('Caligula'). The Catuvellauni were now considered a threat to the security of the Empire. An invasion was planned, the army was assembled at Boulogne, but, at the eleventh hour and for no apparent reason, the undertaking was cancelled.

Gaius was murdered in AD41 and succeeded by his uncle Claudius, who continued to monitor the events that were taking place across the Channel. A Catuvellauni empire, now anti-Roman, was not acceptable and, although the earlier invasion was cancelled, the army remained prepared. When Verica was exiled a year later and sought assistance from Claudius, the Emperor decided to act. The first documented invasion of Britain was about to begin.

Invasion

It was in the early months of 43AD, probably May, that the invasion began. An army of around 40,000 assembled at Boulogne under the command of a sixty-year-old veteran Aulus Plautius. The main landing took place in eastern Kent and was largely unopposed. However,

when Plautius moved inland he met strong opposition from the part-time warriors of the Celtic tribes. These defenders were mainly enlisted agricultural workers who were hardly in favour of an extended campaign, for, if their conscription developed into a prolonged absence from their lands, then food production would be put at serious risk. After several hard-fought battles the Roman forces reached the Thames where they rested, regrouped and awaited the arrival of Emperor Claudius.

While the main landings were taking place in Kent, a subsidiary force sailed westwards with the aim of making contact with the pro-Roman Atrebates who had their base somewhere in the south-west of the county. Chichester was the most probable location for this Celtic centre, but it could have been nearer to the sea at Selsey, at a spot that has long since been eroded away. No

Sidlesham, an ancient port on the Manhood peninsula. Was it the site of the first Roman landing in the area?

confirming documentation exists for these invaders nor where they made landfall. Opinion favours Fishbourne, which is at the head of the Chichester Channel. There are two other feasible options: at the time of the invasion the inlet now known as Pagham Harbour extended further towards the present city and a quay on this inlet remained operational until well into the sixteenth century. The other alternative site is on the western, Chichester Harbour, side of the Selsey peninsula. Just inside the harbour mouth, on the eastern shore, and at the present protected by the East Head spit, is an area known as Roman Landing. Was this the place where the landing was made? It is certainly nearer to the lost settlement of Selsey, if this was the immediate destination of the invading army. Whichever part of shoreline first encountered the Romans the occupiers were well received by the local tribe and soon began to develop a base camp and port at Dell Quay which is only 2 miles (3.2km) from the present city centre.

The main section of the army remained adjacent to the Thames, probably controlling both banks, and awaited the arrival of Claudius who wished to take command of the prestigious final assault on the Celtic capital Camulodunum (present-day Colchester). It is almost certain that Plautius had already negotiated with the local defenders, for the city was easily captured. The Emperor, according to one inaccurate report, remained in Britain for only sixteen days, but a more likely period would be two months; in any event, his was a short stay for he was eager to return to Rome to receive the expected accolade for the conquering of 'that island over the sea'. Before Claudius left, he, or Plautius, it is not clear who, charged Vespasian, who was an emperor-in-waiting and leader of the 2nd Legion, to bring bring into the Empire 'all lands in the south and south-west of the island'. It is documented that during his campaign he 'fought thirty battles, subjugated two war-like tribes, occupied more than thirty towns, plus the Isle of Wight.' It is unlikely that any of these skirmishes took place in Sussex, for, in the absence of their previous leader Verica, the Atrebates

remained true to Rome. Vespasian established his base at Fishbourne from where he continued his conquest of the adjoining areas to the west. By AD47 the southern coastal lands from Kent to Dorset had, in effect, become a Roman province.

The name of Verica now ceases to appear in the written records; possibly he died or returned to his homeland for it was Cogidubnus who was installed as the local king. This new ruler's background is also unclear, he may have been recruited from a local tribe or brought over from Gaul. Whatever his origins, his appointment was a success, for, throughout his reign, the kingdom developed and prospered. Chichester became the *civitas* capital for the area; this roughly translates as a local government unit or, in today's term, the county town.

It was general practice for the Roman authorities, once an occupied area had become stable and was no longer threatened by exterior forces, to establish a local governing authority. This assembly consisted mainly of local leaders who were made to follow strict Roman directives. The administration of an area was, like all Roman law, extremely complex. The public faces of local government were tribal leaders who were overseen and controlled by officials of the occupying power. This system ensured that any resentment from the lower ranks of society was directed against their fellow tribesmen, leaving the Romans free from criticism. This policy of enforced delegation was found to be less successful when applied to Britain than to other parts of the Empire. After the Boudiccan revolts, this kingship idea of control slowly began to be reformed. Those who were not Roman citizens, the vast majority, were then allowed to follow their Celtic codes, provided that they were not in direct conflict with the overriding Roman law. Even a successful leader was not immune from change and it is believed that it was in about AD80 that Cogidubnus was eased into the palace at Fishbourne. Although the *civitas* remained in place, greater emphasis was now placed on the education of the populace into the advantages that the Roman lifestyle would give them.

Chichester, Noviomagus Regnensium

The full Latinized name for Chichester suggests that it was not built on the site of an earlier settlement, but was a new foundation for the Regnenses. This supports the theory of an alternative Selsey settlement, but no doubt arguments will continue as to whether this early Selsey site ever did exist.

Chichester is acknowledged to be one of the premier Roman towns of Britain, but has yielded little of its early life, any secrets that have been revealed have come from excavations for new building developments. The whole area of the Roman settlement is now almost completely blanketed by housing and industry, this leaves little opportunity for future discoveries.

As previously noted, the town first began life as a military base for the 2nd Legion's advance to the west. The port was only a short distance away and, although the base was recorded as being at Fishbourne, the main garrison was probably housed in the town. Fragmentary evidence of timber buildings which served as barracks has been discovered in the central area. The military occupation was only fleeting, for by AD47 the process of expansion and conversion into civilian use had begun. A Romanized street plan was introduced which, by the end of the first century, was complete with a typical grid system of roads. By this time a forum, amphitheatre and public baths were all well established. The forum was thought to have been sited where the two main thoroughfares intersected, a position later dominated by the market cross. The amphitheatre, or entertainment centre, lay to the south-east of the main centre, well outside the defensive ramparts.

One of the most important finds relating to the period was made in 1723, when a tablet was unearthed dedicating a temple to the gods Neptune and Minerva. This inscription was authorized by Cogidubnus who was described as 'great king of the Emperor in Britain'. It was after the death of this pro-Roman leader that the town was afforded the title of *civitas* capital. It is thought that, besides holding the legislative

Market Cross, Chichester. A medieval edifice erected on the main intersection of the Roman grid system of roads.

authority, the town must also have become the commercial centre for the region, but little evidence has emerged regarding the trades and services that were on offer.

The first protective earthworks were constructed towards the end of the second century; they consisted of a rampart with two ditches. Four gates opened through the ramparts with the London road, Stane Street, leaving from the eastern one. Over the next two centuries further improvements were made to the defences, first a masonry wall was added, followed by the addition of external bastions and recut ditches. The earthworks remain visible and are now enhanced by medieval flint walls.

Chichester prospered during the third and the fourth century, but after the departure of the Roman armies life in the town began to deteriorate. Many from the Romano-British aristocracy

City Walls, Chichester, built on early earthworks.

decided to emigrate at the same time as the army, for they needed the protection that Rome afforded. Alone they would be easy prey to the North Sea raiders. Throughout the southern counties villas and farmsteads were abandoned, leading to a general reduction in commercial activity; when coupled with the departure of law and government it is little wonder that the town began to suffer.

Urbanization of the country was promoted, but not in Sussex, where only the one town was developed. Here, it was believed that building luxury homesteads for the wealthy was the main incentive that was needed to inspire the workers, who were by far the largest section of the community, into a higher standard of living. In spite

FISHBOURNE PALACE

Fishbourne is inescapably linked to Chichester, not only is it almost adjoining the city but King Cogidubnus is believed to be the reason for its existence. Like its neighbour, it began life as a military outpost, but by AD50 a timber house, with a separate building which was possibly used as servants' quarters, had been constructed. A decade later the first masonry building arrived. This was subdivided into living accommodation and a bath house for the owner, plus staff rooms; all were elaborately decorated and provided with mosaic or marbled floors. It is generally accepted that the palace was given to the retiring king, by the Empire, for services rendered to Rome over the preceding thirty years. Work commenced on this new building sometime after 75. This complex covered an area of approximately 10 acres (4ha) and, although other villas of a comparable size have been found elsewhere in Britain, they are all of a much later date; for a first-century building this was unique.

This enlarged building consisted of four wings arranged around a formal garden. Each wing served a different purpose. The owner's accommodation was in the south, overlooking gardens that stretched down to the shoreline. The official wing was to the west, visitors' rooms and an ornate entrance hall filled the remainder. The whole was adorned with elaborate paintings, stucco and mosaics, with all the decorative materials and the

workmanship showing their Italian origins. Changes were soon made to the building for, by 100, two bath houses had been installed plus further mosaics added to the north wing. These alterations suggest that the complex was then in the process of being converted into self-contained units. At the same time the standard of accommodation was downgraded but was still superior to that of the average villa.

Towards the end of the third century a fire brought the life of the palace to an abrupt end. It is not known whether the fire was accidental or whether it was a deliberate act by piratical raiders. Whatever the cause, the outcome was the abandonment of the site with no attempt at rebuilding. As with many of these early establishments, much pilfering of the fabric took place, the materials then emerging in later constructions.

Fishbourne was not discovered until 1961 and, as parts of the building are hidden by the modern A27 road, it is unlikely that they will ever be examined. Large sections have been excavated and are now preserved with covered protection. Limited opening of the site first took place in 1968, now it is a year-round attraction and provides the visitor with an extraordinary insight into the lifestyle and luxurious living that were available to the elite members of the Romano-British community during the first part of the Roman occupation.

of this propaganda, the agricultural workers in a Roman province very much the underprivileged. It was the town dwellers that benefited from this new Romanized Britain. However, from the last quarter of the first century until well into the third, Sussex, as a region, enjoyed a peaceful and undisturbed period of advancement.

Roman Villas

Any map of Sussex that records the sites of known Romano-British villas will confirm that the majority were built on the western Downs where the land was most actively farmed. Many of the villa complexes developed from a collection of timber farm cottages that had, in turn, succeeded earlier round houses. Over the decades, the wood was replaced by more permanent stone buildings that provided increased comfort for residents. From one basic structure the villa expanded, often intermittently, but always in a geometric design. Corridors were constructed from the original base; these, in turn, spawned further rooms; when an optimal length was reached the building continued at right angles. In many of the larger complexes the

process was repeated until a rectangle was formed, the enclosed space being then entered by a gate in one wall. One wing of these larger villas usually provided luxury accommodation for the owner; the other sides served as the home farm for the estate, providing stabling for the animals and storage facilities for the arable crops. On occasions separate buildings, as at Bignor, appeared outside the main rectangle.

As Chichester was becoming the commercial centre for the area, it was obvious that the majority of the downland villas would be sited within a day's journey of the market town and with easy access to the main road system. The advantages were twofold: transportation of goods to market was a simple and quick operation, and, as many of the landowners were also leading members of the legislature, they needed their country retreat to be not too distant from their place of work.

Although most of the villas are found in the western Downs, one lone farmstead has been discovered east of the River Ouse. It was sited on Ranscombe Hill overlooking the river and near the Mount Caburn hill fort. Excavations revealed it to be from the second or third centu-

---

BIGNOR VILLA

Bignor villa was discovered in 1811 when a large stone was upturned by a local farmer when ploughing. Over the next few years the total plan of the villa was revealed, but it was not until the 1950s and the 1960s, when more excavations took place, that the significant finds were made.

The villa site, on what is believed to be the foundations of an earlier farmstead, sits on a south-facing sandstone ridge in the lee of the Downs. The progress to a complete villa was slow, the original stone building was built about 220 and superseded earlier, timber houses. A corridor and small wings were added later, but it was not until the fourth century that final expansion enclosed the courtyard.

Bignor is renowned for its series of mosaics, all of which date from the middle of the fourth century; one, discovered only in 1975, is of geometric design and is over 80ft (24m) in length. The interior furnishings were considered to be of luxury standard, with the bath suite subdivided into rooms, all heated by a hypocaust capable of producing a different temperature in each. The collection of outbuildings, which included stables, barns and accommodation for servants, was enclosed by a wall and situated away from the main complex. By the end of the century the fabric of the villa had already begun to decay and it was finally abandoned a few years later. The villa was less than half a mile from Stane Street but access to this main road was by a trackway that climbed the Downs parallel to the main route and closed with it only on the crest of the hill. As with Fishbourne, many of the exhibits at Bignor are under cover; there is public access throughout the summer months.

ry; the only significant find from the dig was portions of an early corn dryer.

Few of the county's villa sites have been thoroughly researched, several adjacent to the coast are covered by development and are unable to offer any new revelations. The building at Southwick was a courtyard villa of the early second century, but, from the evidence gathered, it was in existence for only a short time, probably less than fifty years. Angmering was one of the first to be built in Britain, work starting about AD70. In spite of later additions, the construction of a bath house and with the main rooms adorned with imported Italian tiles, it again had only a short life span. A third coastal villa discovered on the outskirts of Brighton was found to be of a standard farmhouse design.

A villa-cum-farmstead was sited adjacent to a Roman road in the Downs at Chilgrove, a few miles to the north of Chichester. Further to the west, close to the Hampshire border, runs a minor road, the B2146. One mile south of the village of West Marden there appears on the map the name Busto Copse. The adjoining house is not named but does bear this unusual title. An unmarked farmstead and burial ground that were excavated nearby showed that the settlement belonged to a man with the name of Busto Mephar. This is hardly a Latinized name and it suggests a Middle Eastern connection; if this is correct, then this citizen of the Empire took up residence far from the land of his birth.

Many of the changes affecting Sussex, both physical and in the lifestyle of its residents, that occurred under the Romans took place within the first few decades of their arrival. The capital was established and under the new legislation the lives of the people were for the first time under a form of control, ostensibly by their own leaders. The tax system introduced was not popular, but it did provide for a security that previously was often absent. The local industries were revitalized, the improved road system now gave a year-round availability to communicate and the increased trading opportunities all combined to make the county one of the most prosperous regions of the province.

Agriculture

When the Romans arrived in Sussex the agricultural lands were concentrated on the southern Downs and the adjacent lower levels, with the former Iron Age farmsteads spread haphazardly across the landscape The new masters did not change the basic system, but concentrated on collective distribution and improved marketing of the products; with a large occupying army to feed, the Romans drew the individual units into an industry that would make Britain self-sufficient and provide an excess for export. New crops were introduced, notably a hardier cereal crop, oats. New vegetables and fruit arrived, and one product that is always remembered: vines, and the science of viticulture.

Other local industries were expanded and improved. For centuries salt had been produced on the coast by evaporation; this process requires much effort for little end product and, when the salt springs of the Midlands were in full production, the coastal pans were largely abandoned. The main area of the region to receive attention was the eastern High Weald; here many of the iron ore sites were revitalized and enlarged.

The Iron Industry

There was an increased demand for iron from both the civil and the military authorities. Other areas of Britain produced the ore but Sussex was in a favoured position, being only a short distance from the provincial capital Londinium and the Channel ports where there was a great export potential. The ore pits and bloomeries which processed ore into workable metal seemed to have been worked independently with no overall central control. A few sites where fragments of tiles bearing the stamp of the British fleet were discovered suggest, however, that the navy may have had exclusive use of several sites.

The industry was well established by the end of the first century. This boom period lasted for well over 150 years before over-production and deforestation around the sites caused them to be uneconomic. The largest of the known sites was at Beauport Park, east of Battle. This was one of the naval units, and archaeologists who made a study of its large slag heap (much of which had disappeared into Victorian road-making schemes) calculated that in its lifetime the total production of the finished metal from this one site must have exceeded 50,000 tons (50,800 tonnes). Excavations made near to the heap revealed the existence of a small but well-constructed bath house. Similar digs made at other East Sussex sites have also revealed evidence of attached village communities.

Other natural materials were quarried in the county. Sandstone was used for buildings and road construction used the debris from the quarries, slag from the iron workings and gravel that was dredged from the river courses. However, none of these activities had any long-lasting effect on the landscape. Strangely, chalk used for conversion into agricultural lime or as a poor substitute building material appears to have been imported from the Kentish North Downs. The Sussex hills remained unscarred by intrusive quarrying.

The Road System

The tracks of our early residents usually linked the settlements or the essential sites of one tribe. A few interconnecting long-distance trails had been established, usually on the higher ground where the main food-producing areas were situated. Here, on the lighter soils, the going was easier and the way did not suffer from winter flooding. The Romans did not invent the road, but they were responsible for the construction of a network of maintained roads throughout Britain.

The perception of a Roman road is commonly of an unremitting straight line that tends to ignore any intervening physical feature. The truth is somewhat different, for the surveyed line was followed by the road builders as closely as possible, but where a small deviation would make for easier construction then this was done. River crossings or sharp inclines were the most common causes for these bends.

Which way to Londinium? Signpost on Bignor Hill.

It was common practice to build small settlements, known as posting stations, on arterial roads, at intervals of between 10 and 15 miles (16 and 24km), for 15 miles was considered a good day's march. These units were designed to provide rest areas for the military, but also featured stabling where horses could be changed. Later, as a type of courier service was established, they acted as a point where goods could be collected and despatched.

There were four main roads from Sussex converging on Londinium. These were some of the first to be built in Britain, with construction of all four beginning within a decade or two of the occupation. Only Stane Street, which connected Chichester and London, could be called a provincial route, the others were of a commercial nature, linking the iron- and corn-producing areas to the capital. The eastern road from Pevensey, or the port of Anderida, did not take a direct line to the capital. The first few miles followed the coastline westwards, then a right-hand turn was made towards the Lewes area, where it made an end-on connection with the London road. An unusual feature occurs on this last road: when it prepares to leave the county, a stretch of several miles here was surfaced with iron slag. This material was widely used as a base material, but this is the only known instance of its being used in this manner.

STANE STREET

Stane Street was the name given to the 57-mile (92km) length of Roman road that was built to connect the capital of the province to the regional capital of Chichester. There are several instances of the name appearing in today's address books and on cottages and farms, and on stretches of the modern A29 road to keep faith with the title bestowed on its predecessor. This was the second trunk road to be built in Britain, with building starting not long after the invasion. Chichester was originally developed as a military base and, although it had its own port, there was a need for a secure and usable direct line of communication between the two centres.

Stane Street has been well researched since long stretches now form part of the county's network of primary routes. In a few isolated locations traces of the original embankment, or agger, may be recognized without departing from the tarmacadam. The road is usually referred to as running from its southern terminal northwards, but it is almost certain that it was surveyed and built in the reverse direction.

A direct alignment between the two towns would have meant the road taking a climb over the summit of Leith Hill, plus a difficult double ridge crossing of the South Downs. A compromise to the route was forthcoming and a three-alignment route was decided on. The original line was followed to Ewell in Surrey, then a slight deviation to the east took it to Pulborough, where the third leg found a coomb through the main escarpment of the Downs and a gentle descent direct to Chichester.

Two stations have been discovered on the Sussex stretch of Stane Street, both on or near to the Arun. The southern site at Hardham, at the junction of two roads, had a lifespan of less than a hundred years before the facilities were moved 2 miles (3km) to the north. The precise location of the new station has yet to be discovered but there is a cluster of villa sites a little to the east of the main road and one of these could have provided the necessary accommodation and stabling. The second smaller station was at Alfoldean, a little to the east of the modern road, at a point known locally as Roman Gate. In the mid 1930s, when the river was especially low, wooden piles that supported the piers of a bridge were revealed; these were still hard and in good condition. Here, remains of the enclosing earthworks are still visible, unlike at Hardham where the railway and commercial developments have combined to erase all traces of the ramparts.

Another road left Chichester on a north-westerly heading for Silchester. Before it left the county a posting station was established on the greensand ridge at Iping. Local opinion is that there is a lost town adjacent to the station. A modern road now bisects what is thought to be the site of this town, so any future excavations would prove difficult. Coins bearing the date 70 were found on the line of the road, the early dating of these helped to confirm that the Sussex roads were among the first to be constructed in the country.

There are two cross-county roads; one leaves the Lewes road north of the town and follows an underdown route to join Stane Street at Hardham, while the other departs from Brighton, passes westward by Chichester en route to Southampton Water on a line that is not too dissimilar to that of today's trunk road. Other minor roads connected to the main arterial roads served villas, other farming communities and centres of industry. These lesser road were built to a lower standard and consequently little evidence of their existence remains. In a land charter of 930 mention is made of a road called Stanstrete which extended from Chichester southwards into the Selsey peninsula. This road was probably built to serve the lost settlement that is thought to have existed in the area.

The larger of the Sussex rivers, all of which gave access to the Channel, were used for the conveyance of goods soon after the occupation was complete. Unfortunately, there is little documentary evidence to be found on their use. The Arun did, however, have the distinction of receiving a Latin name, Trisanto.

Modern Stane Street. The A29 at Pulborough.

Ancient Stane Street. The distinctive agger is well preserved on this section of the old road as it climbs Bignor Hill.

Religion

The Romans worshipped several gods, but they were few in number when compared to the Celts. Some gods had only a local appeal while others were revered over a much wider area. Rome was generally tolerant of the religions practised by the peoples that it administered, and over the passage of time the fusion of creeds often took place, leading to temples being built to serve differing beliefs. There were several Romano-Celtic temples erected on the Downs, often on sites of earlier Iron Age sanctuaries; two examples in close proximity were at Chanctonbury and Lancing. Christianity was one of only two religions, Druidism being the second, that were not tolerated by the early Roman leaders. By the fourth century Christianity had spread throughout the Empire and in 314 Constantine issued an edict which gave Christians full freedom of worship. The order was shortly followed by the acceptance of Christianity as the official religion of the Empire. Sussex, however, had to await a further three centuries and for a new occupier before it was converted to the new faith.

During the third century the Empire came under attack from several directions. On the Continent internal rebellions when combined with outside tribal forays forced a large part of the British garrison to be redeployed to Gaul. This depletion of the resident army allowed the Picts, whose homeland was Caledonia, or Scotland, the opportunity to make invasion threats against the northern border of the province. Sussex remained largely unaffected by these troubles and suffered only from sporadic raids along the coast by raiders from northern Europe. These pirates were a continuing nuisance to the cross-channel trade routes and so a series of forts was built along the coastline of south-east and eastern England, several doubling as bases for the Roman navy. The last of the chain, which were known as the Saxon Shore forts, was built at Pevensey.

Inland, the peaceful lifestyle continued in the same pattern, the early farmstead villas were

---

PEVENSEY FORT

The fort at Pevensey was the largest of the chain and construction is thought to have begun about 335 on the site of earlier harbour buildings. It could not be built to a standard Roman design, either a square or rectangle with evenly spaced bastions, for the only suitable land was on a narrow peninsular bounded by the sea on three sides. To accommodate the maximum area of land, almost 9 acres (4ha), the fortifications were built in an irregular oval with the bastions also irregularly spaced.

The original walls were 11ft (3.4m) thick and over 20ft (6m) in height and were raised on a bed of imported chalk and flint. There were three gates to the fort, the two main entrances were in the eastern and the western extremities with a small postern gate in the north wall. Exploration of the central area revealed traces of timber buildings, similar to those found in other military depots. Coins of the late third and the early fourth century have also surfaced, plus two brick stamps. These were discovered by Charles Dawson (of Piltdown fame), and, like his later forgeries, were probably 'planted' during his excavations. The fort was at one time home to a detachment of the Roman fleet, but over the centuries the sea has retreated and today the peninsula is a low inland ridge, a mile from the shore line, leaving the remains of the fort to oversee marshland to the rear of the coastal development.

The *Anglo-Saxon Chronicle* reported that in 491 there was a vain defence of the site which culminated 'in a terrible massacre'. Of whom and by whom is uncertain. After this battle the fort was abandoned and remained a ruin until the Normans used the walls as a basis for their castle. Further improvements were made to the fabric during the medieval period and piecemeal restoration continued up to the Second World War when a gun turret was added, completely obscuring the north gate.

either enlarged or abandoned. If the second was decided upon, the majority of the houses re-emerged on what was considered to be a more convenient site. Life was certainly good for the elite in this period of the occupation.

The Final Years

As the third century rolled into the fourth, there was a period of great unrest in the Empire. New leaders emerged, survived for a few years and then were either deposed or murdered. Britain remained largely unaffected by the continental maelstrom but did suffer from more attacks on its northern borders by tribes eager to take advantage of the fragmentation of the controlling army. Complete peace was returned to Britain thanks to a new emperor, Constantine. Backed by a reformed and reinforced army he was able to secure the boundaries once more and make dialogue with the invaders. Both sides honoured the treaties that were negotiated and the country remained trouble-free for a further half century. With the threat of war lifted, Constantine embarked on a programme of regeneration and restoration for the urban communities; as each town was rebuilt the opportunity was taken to enhance its defences. The Continent was not enjoying the same peaceful interlude as the northern province and problems resurfaced again in Britain in 367 when the invading peoples combined to attack simultaneously. This time large sections of the Roman army were less than enthusiastic in defending the country and consequently it suffered several defeats. For a year there was no effective control of Britain until a new commander, Theodosius, supported by troops from Gaul, restored Roman authority. He then reactivated the work that was started by Constantine several decades earlier, and it was during this later programme of improvements that Chichester received its enhanced protection.

Around the turn of the century renewed attacks were made on all the provinces of the Empire and for the first time the heartland of Italy was no longer immune. In 407 a decision was made to withdraw the army from Britain in order to concentrate on the defence of the mainland provinces. Three years later the country was officially instructed to arrange its own protection. There had been Saxon raids on the southern shores for many years, but now, with no organized opposition to them, the process of colonization gained momentum. There was no immediate destruction of the Romano-British settlements by these invaders since Chichester was known to have continued, albeit as a declining commercial centre, until the middle of the fifth century. Local government ceased almost immediately for, as the Romans withdrew, the majority of the British officials left with them, no doubt hoping to continue with their affluent lifestyle abroad with continuing protection.

The light was now extinguished on Sussex. For the following two centuries few events are recorded in literature or as evidence left in the fields. Conjecture and supposition return as the basis for the early years of the next period of the county's history.

Pevensey Fort. A Middle Age bastion built on Roman earthworks.

4. The Lost Years and the Saxons

After the abandonment of Britain by Rome the country slowly descended into what have been labelled 'the lost years of English history'. The next two centuries are years of mystery for there are no accurate written records of the events that occurred nor of the lifestyles of the residents in this period. The scanty information that is available again comes from archaeology and accounts that were written years later.

With the departure of the Roman army and the widespread exodus of the British aristocracy, literacy in England became virtually non-existent. The remaining population, consisting largely of agricultural workers, had never received any form of education. For decades they had lived under a protectionist system that always offered a ready market for their produce. Almost instantaneously their market and the protection that the army provided had disappeared.

The Germanic invaders who soon began to fill the vacuum created by the departure of the Romans were also illiterate. Evidence of their lifestyle before their arrival on British shores has come either from Roman texts or from much later Anglo-Saxon writings. Information taken from either could easily be less than accurate. The Romans regarded the Saxons as enemies, any writings were probably biased and were used as local propaganda. The later English accounts were drafted from recollections that had been passed verbally through several generations. A span of 200 years allows ample time for individual memories to fail or the facts to be altered to suit the teller's beliefs.

There are but three 'publications' that refer to the events that took place in this unidentified age. The first was compiled in the sixth century by a north-country cleric by the name of Gildas. The main purpose of his *De Excida Britanniae* seemed to be to denounce the evils of the day in the strongest language. The second was begun in

731 by the Venerable Bede, another monk, residing in Northumbria. It gave a good account of events that took place in the seventh and the eighth centuries but lacked detail about the invasions and the early years of occupation. The most authentic recording of events that affected Sussex comes from the *Anglo-Saxon Chronicle*. This journal is devoted to the southern counties, but, once again, as its composition did not start until the reign of Alfred, about 892, information concerning the dating of early events could well be suspect.

The Invading Tribes

The post-Roman invasion of England was made by three Germanic tribes, each concentrating on a specific area of the country. The Angles originated in Schleswig Holstein; the Saxons who became the new residents of Sussex, arrived, as the name suggests from Saxony; and the Jutes may possibly have lived in Jutland, but recent thinking believes them to be from east of the lower Rhine. These tribes were closely integrated and marriages between their leaders were common. The Romans also had trouble differentiating between the three and in their literature the were collectively referred to as 'Saxons' or 'barbarians'.

Piratical raids were made on the southern counties by these tribes long before the Romans departed. Some reports even hint that there was often a tacit agreement between the raiders and the defenders for a proportion of the eventual spoils. Archaeological remains from other parts of the country confirm that the Roman army frequently used Saxon mercenaries in defence of England against attacks by both the Picts from the north and the Celts from the west. Known Roman cemeteries in the lower Thames valley have revealed belt fittings corresponding to

Sompting Church. The tower from the south-west.

those worn by Saxon warriors. Although no confirmation of such activities exists for Sussex, it is quite probable that paid-off members of the Roman army dispersed to find relatives who had arrived and settled in the county generations earlier. From about 430 there was a marked increase in the number of people of Germanic origin arriving in the country, but it was several decades later before a concerted invasion took place.

The Saxon invasions were concentrated on the coast of south-east England from Essex, through Sussex and into Wessex. The continuity of the occupation was broken on either side of Sussex, as Bede revealed, from an unknown source: 'The people of Kent, the Isle of Wight, and that part of Hampshire that lies in the shadow of the island are of Jutish origin.' This racial distribution is probably oversimplified, for, by the time that the account was written, many of the tribal boundaries were less than definite.

The first battle of the invasion took place in Kent in about 455, but it was another twenty years before the Saxon king Aelle, supported by two of his sons, made landfall on the Sussex coast. Surprisingly, the landing appears to have taken place in the west of the county near Selsey, on the part of the peninsula that is now lost to the sea. The advance through the county was made in a leisurely but uncompromising manner, the invaders being victorious in any confrontation that occurred. The British defenders were systematically eased eastwards and inland. The absence of Celtic place names from the modern map of the county tends to confirm the thoroughness of the Saxons in eradicating the previous culture. Any of the residents who attempted resistance were either driven out, enslaved or destroyed. The final battle for control of Sussex took place in 491 at the Roman fort at Pevensey. The Saxon army was under the command of Aelle or his son Cissa, or possibly it was under dual command, no matter, for reports state that the British garrison was totally destroyed. The losers may have been survivors from previous skirmishes who gathered

Pevensey Castle. The East Gate bastion, showing varying periods of construction; note the herringbone feature on the upper levels.

for a final stand or local men enlisted to fight for their homeland; the answer will never be known.

Saxon Place Names

Many of the Sussex towns and villages bear names that originated from Old English words or phrases. The passing centuries have obviously effected changes both in spelling and pronunciation, but the essential formation of the words is still evident.

As mentioned earlier, the Romans referred to all the Germanic tribes as Saxons; the remaining

Britons continued with the tradition in spite of a large proportion of the invading force having originated from the Angles. In time, the descendants of the settlers of both Sussex and Wessex began to favour the name of Angle. It is not known what brought about this change but by the reign of Alfred the language was known as English and by the eleventh century all the territories under Germanic rule had become *Engla land*.

One of the first acts undertaken by King Aelle after completing his conquest of the county was to rename the Roman provincial capital. In honour of his principle son Cissa, Noviomagus Regnensium became Cissa's Castra, or fort. In time this Old English form became the modern Chichester. Two other sites in the western sector of the county also relate to his offspring; Cissa again features in the name of the Iron Age fort in the downs behind Worthing – Cissbury – and the name of his brother Wlensing is preserved in Lancing.

The most common settlement names of the county contain the letters –ing, from the Old English –*ingas*. These three letters usually form the suffix of the word but may appear in a different position, as in Rustington. Both forms are patronymic and relate to the abode of an earlier relative. This collection of names is mostly found near to the downland ridge and may be sited on either side of the main axis. There is one exception to the rule in an area colonized by the maverick Haetingas tribe. The group remained semi-independent for nearly 200 years, but did conform to the standard form of nomenclature. Their capital became Hastings and a forest outlier gained the name of Brightling. The –*ing* was the first phase of place-naming but was not adopted until late in the sixth century; then, as development spread into other areas of the county, new forms of naming arrived.

The lowly farm was the basis for several suffixes; –*ham* or –*hamm* was one of the earliest. It was first used for a semi-isolated pasture but later came to be adopted as a word for a hamlet or estate. Many farms that developed into larger

settlements carry the ending –*tun* or its modern rendering –*ton*. This was first attributed to a hedged or fenced enclosure, in effect, a field. The –*ton* names fall into three linguistic categories: some combine it with the physical properties of the site, while others are formed with the addition of a personal name; the third, and less frequently found type, includes the category of the involved person, Kingston being a prime example. There is one further, small subcategory which combines two word endings into –*ington*; this example almost always uses a personal name as the first element of the word.

As the Wealden forest was slowly infiltrated by expansionist farmers new word endings appeared: *hurst* is the name applied to a general area of woodland, while –*den* or –*dene* refers to a more localized feature, a wooded valley. A further name for pasture is *ley*, this time an area reclaimed from the forest and remaining encircled by trees. With the later development of organized settlements in the east of the county it is here that more modern place names appear; the collection of –*fields* that occurs around the lower slopes of the Weald is one example.

Saxon Sussex Agriculture and Land Use

It is one of English history's unsolved mysteries as to how and why bellicose piratical tribes managed to transform themselves into an industrious agricultural community. Possibly the members felt that their new-found home was, indeed, greatly to be preferred and they were willing to adapt to a peaceful rural lifestyle, taking up arms only much later when the Vikings threatened. The Saxons were not town dwellers so Sussex, with only one developed centre, suited their way of life; Chichester after receiving its new name was left to decay. The Romano-British villas were distrusted and ignored and the roads were treated with suspicion since many were paved, a type of construction that was not known in their homeland.

The majority of the early settlements were family units which collected enough of the surrounding land for their immediate needs. Most of the farms were at first centred on the coastal plain in the shelter of the Downs. Group communities soon developed in areas where the soil was found to be most fertile, and one such was centred between Worthing and Littlehampton. As the population increased, new settlements were established in the river valleys and on the loams that parallel the northern scarp slope of the Downs. The Saxons were generally not happy with the thinner soils of the chalk hills, but there is evidence of a cluster of farmsteads on the eastern Downs between the Ouse and Eastbourne. This was an area devoid of villas and it has been suggested that the occupants of these sites were there at the invitation of the British landowner. In return for the land, they were to provide manpower for a local army should danger threaten.

With the closure of the Roman iron industry the Wealden forest was allowed to regenerate. By the time of the early English settlements the woods had largely returned to their pre-Iron Age condition. Small open areas did exist where the iron working sites remained inhabited, but these were few in number and remained totally isolated from the events that were taking place only a few miles to the south. With one exception, the peoples of early Saxon Sussex did not feel inclined to investigate the Wealden forest. The exception was the breakaway tribe, the Haestingas, who centred themselves on the dry land between the Romney and Pevensey marshes. As noted earlier, this clan isolated themselves from the remainder of the kingdom and were unique in attempting to recolonize the edges of the forest block.

As generation followed generation, individual family units combined to form larger manors. To regulate the expansion of these estates, a system of land control, or charters was established. These charters gave each group a section of land suitable for each of their farming needs, a cattle or swine area on the heavier clay soils, a parcel of arable loam, which was usually adjacent to the settlement, and a strip of downland for the grazing of sheep. This system of land division led in south Sussex to a series of narrow strip parishes running in parallel on a south–north axis. Most of the unsettled areas of the forest were allocated to the manors in separate parcels located as directly as possible north of the parent centre. This form of distribution led at times to multiple estates having several outlying areas. When this occurred, a right of passage was granted for the driving of herds over the intervening land.

The earliest recorded charter for Sussex dates from around 675 and relates to Stanmer, an area on the Downs to the north-east of Brighton. This document confirmed outlying swine pastures in the present parishes of Lindfield, Ardingly and West Hoathly, the last area being almost 20 miles (32km) from the home farm. Distances of this magnitude between the main centre and its pastures seem to have been common.

The most conspicuous evidence remaining on the ground of these outstations are the lines of old trackways that joined them to the main centre. The majority of these short drove roads followed the lines of the parishes and ran parallel on a south–north axis. Those that originated near to the coast crossed the Downs through a convenient gap or, where this was not possible, they negotiated the steep scarp slopes by well-graded terraces. There are good examples of this latter feature on the hills above Steyning. It is probable that some of these drove roads used routes that were in existence before the arrival of the Romans. Roman roads were again not in favour, although in the Billingshurst area, which is bisected by Stane Street, there are several examples that closely accompany the road and match its straightness. Most of these drove roads still function in the present-day road system, but a few have been downgraded and exist only as a green lane or right of way. These old drove roads may easily be recognized if encountered away from the tarmac for they had a minimum width of 30 to 40ft (9 to 12m) and were usually bounded by a high hedge bank.

The last four centuries of Saxon rule saw

great changes to Sussex, both in commerce and agriculture. In the seventh century still the only recognizable town was what was left of Chichester and there were few settlements larger than a hamlet, but by the time of the Norman invasion a network of towns and commercial or administrative centres had been created. The countryside no longer consisted of small individual units; these had been amalgamated into large estates, each having its own centre to which the tenant farmers paid their dues. These estates were continually combining or dividing and new centres developing, so it is almost impossible to identify the areas that belonged to any individual.

The main administrative unit of late Saxon Sussex was known as a rape, a name that was continued by the Normans. Each rape was divided into hundreds which consisted of a hundred taxable land areas known as 'hides'. For an unknown reason, the size of a Sussex hide was deemed to be smaller than those in the rest of England. Justice was administered and tax collected at a hundred court which all freemen of the district were obliged to attend. The courts were held at a convenient and permanent location within the hundred and their regularity gave the opportunity for the attendees to indulge in local trading. It was not long before permanent markets were established at these meeting places. The estates soon benefited from these trading centres, especially if the court could be persuaded to settle near to the centre.

Early Sussex Towns

As we have seen, the Saxons were a rural people who shunned urban living, so before the eighth century there were few settlements in the county that could be referred to as a town or village; with the increase in population many of the residents were forced to accept living in close proximity to their neighbours. The old capital of Chichester, when it began to be reoccupied, was considered to be subordinate to nearby Selsey. There is no physical evidence of the rebirth of

Saxon Cottage, Steyning. Possibly built on an earlier site, this unusual dwelling has at the further end an accentuated 'cat slide' roof.

the city since the early Saxon buildings were structured in wood and it was late in the period before stone or masonry was adopted as the common building material. Early stone buildings were rather crudely constructed since the masons apparently had difficulty in converting from the comparatively soft medium of wood into the harder stone. These substandard efforts were none too durable and became easy targets for subsequent redevelopment. By the end of the ninth century the city had regained much of its former importance, because the *Chronicle* reports that in 892 'the townsmen put the Danes to flight and slew many hundreds of them.' It is unlikely that Chichester could call on enough of its residents to defeat the Danish army and so in all probability it served as a defensive depot for the surrounding countryside.

The other settlements that were enlarged into towns or commercial centres were situated adjacent to either rivers or the coast. The River Adur claimed two such sites close to each other. At the time, the river was a large, tidal inlet, and Botolphs and Steyning coexistied as neighbourly ports on its western bank. Steyning, once known as the Port of St Cuthman, developed into a thriving unit and soon became the capital of the central region. Botolphs never became more

SILLY SUSSEX

The derogatory remark of 'silly Sussex' is usually applied to the county in general, although on occasions it has been amended slightly and applied to individual residents. The origin of the expression is unknown, but it could easily refer to the less than erudite saint, St Cuthman, and his involvement with the mid-Sussex town of Steyning.

Cuthman was a West Country peasant who received a calling from God to leave his home and seek his destiny elsewhere. He decided to travel eastwards and, as he was unwilling to abandon his aged mother, he constructed a hand cart that was large enough to convey her and all his worldly possessions. Together they roamed the southern counties, ever drifting towards the morning sun. Cuthman's woodworking ability was on par with his intelligence and, as they approached Steyning, the cart disintegrated. He took this as a further divine sign to stay in the town. This he did and built a wooden church on a site now occupied by the Norman building.

When people referred to Cuthman's escapades as 'silly' then they were paying him a compliment, since our modern word derives from the Anglo-Saxon *selig*, which means blessed. If this explanation is the true source of the saying then both he and Sussex deserve to be treated with some reverence.

St Cuthman. A millennium statue of the wandering saint.

than a village, existing for only a short period before it expired early in the sixth century, only to re-emerge several centuries later.

The River Ouse had a similar collection of hamlets; Beddingham was a Roman villa which appears to have been usurped by Saxon squatters early in the occupation, Bishopstone was sited on a hilltop overlooking the estuary and adjacent to a fifth-century cemetery. Neither increased in size or stature, and it was left to Lewes, which started life as another inland port, to start its journey to becoming the county town of East Sussex. The importance of the town to the surrounding countryside was confirmed with its establishment as a fortified burgh by Alfred in his campaign against the Danes.

Coastal towns developed around the ports of Hastings, Pevensey and Eastbourne; these were not only centres for craftsmen but, with their direct access to the Channel, they proved to be suitable locations for merchants and traders. The original port of Winchelsea may also have reached town status, but this is only speculation for any direct evidence is missing.

In the tenth century, because of the increased commercial activity taking place in Sussex, a number of mints were established to issue the needed coinage. These were located in the larger commercial centres of Hastings, Lewes, Steyning and Chichester. An emergency mint was temporarily set up inside the Iron Age fort at Cissbury. The reason for this is unknown or why

Lewes Castle. The keep built on Saxon foundations.

The medieval gatehouse to Lewes Castle.

this particular site was chosen, since there appear to have been several more suitable alternatives.

Again, the majority of the emerging towns and commercial centres were to be found in the catchment area of the Downs. The Weald and the eastern part of the county retained their sparse populations for a few more centuries; indeed, as late as the thirteenth century East Sussex could muster few towns that were large enough to contribute to the economy of the county.

The Decline of the Population

The early Saxon period is also known as the Dark Ages, with 'dark' describing two differing aspects of the time: the absence of recorded data which would have shed light on current events has already been noted; the second could well refer to the general recession into which the county slowly descended. Sussex did not remain immune to the decline, but the Wealden forest provided a protective barrier against the intertribal aggression elsewhere in the country.

When a country enters a lengthy period of recession then the population level tends to stagnate or to follow a similar downward trend; this certainly happened in the fifth and the sixth century.

It is thought that the population of Britain towards the end of the Roman occupation could well have totalled almost six million. When Domesday was commissioned in 1086 England supported less than three million. Given that the population of the southern counties grew steadily in the years before the end of the first millennium, it is difficult to determine what caused the earlier drastic decline in the population and in the number that the county could support. It is known that there was the large exodus of Britons before or shortly after the main Germanic invasions, but no explanation has been forthcoming as to why a populace of millions was unable, or unwilling, to repulse a force whose numbers were in only the tens of thousands.

Two theories have been offered to explain the dramatic loss of population. The first concerns the agricultural system; during the boom years of the Roman occupation the land was intensively cultivated with little thought being given to any sustainable fertility. Many areas were now worked out and could deliver only a much reduced yield that would provide a living for fewer people. There is some evidence to support the second theory; the *Anglo-Saxon Chronicle* states that, 'in 664 a great pestilence ravaged the island of Britain ...'. The death of four kings within a decade was also noted, but not specifically linked to the pestilence. Bede also mentioned a pestilence that swept Britain in the seventh century. Early historians argued that this visitation could not have been the Black Death since the rat carrying it had not yet arrived here. This argument looks increasingly suspect since the bones of the black rat have been discovered in several Roman wells; if the disease did occur then it could well have decimated the residents, for the outbreak in 1348 reduced the population of medieval England by over a third.

The Return of the Light

Little is known of the political history of Sussex after the decisive battle at Pevensey and the death of Aelle in 491 until the baptism of a new king Aethlewahl shortly before 675. During these two centuries the county, although a relatively small county and ruled by kings whose names have gone unrecorded, retained its independence from the aspirations of its more powerful neighbours.

After Aethlewahl, Sussex endured a succession of local rulers; many are listed in a series of charters which are connected to the cathedral at Selsey. Apart from showing that several kings appear to have ruled simultaneously, they reveal little else of historical importance. Late in the seventh century Wessex, under the leadership of Caedwalla, annexed Kent, Surrey and Sussex. This acquisition gave the western kingdom total control of the coast of southern England. This period of Wessex rule was not long-lasting since by the middle of the next century the Mercian king Offa had imposed his authority on at least the western section of the county, granting two royal titles to local individuals. The Hastings area remained outside his control until 771 when 'he did subdue the men of Hastings in war', entitling him, in the following year, to be referred to as *Rex Anglorum*, 'king of England'.

There is now another short break in the history of the southern counties until 825, when Egbert of Wessex defeated the Mercian king and re-established the West Saxons as the dominant power in the south; Sussex was only too happy to realign itself to its near neighbour. This period of history is complex and poorly documented. During the five centuries of Saxon occupation the number of 'kings' that received recognition is in excess of 200 and the number that ruled unsung during the unrecorded years will never be confirmed.

The Return of Christianity

The greatest social change to the peoples of Sussex came with their conversion to

Christianity. The Romans had at first tolerated the religion, then endorsed it, but it was only the army and the educated section of Romano-British society that accepted the faith. The peasants were never introduced to the Christian God and remained with their local idols. When the Romans and the aristocracy abandoned Sussex they took their faith with them, leaving behind a pagan country. The new overlords brought with them more gods – Thor, Woden, Frig and Tiw are names that have survived through mythology to the present day.

It was Pope Gregory who reintroduced Christianity to England. He knew that the king of Kent had a Christian wife and it was to the county that he despatched in 597 a Roman monk with the mission to convert the island. The monk had immediate success but the conversion had only a fragile base and several areas soon lapsed. In the same period large areas of northern England were converted by Celtic monks from Ireland. Rome became concerned with the success of the Irish preachers and it was from the friction that arose between the two sections of the one faith that the saviour of Sussex emerged.

Wilfrid (or Wilfrith) was a troublesome character who, when Bishop of York, fell out of favour with both the king of Northumbria and the papal archbishops. Two expulsions from the country and a prison sentence persuaded him that his duties would more likely be appreciated in heathen Sussex. His first visit to the county was in 665, when, after one of his expulsions to France, he and his crew were shipwrecked. The local pagans, following the tradition of purloining everything the sea delivered, fell upon the survivors. In a manner not recognized by their faith the sailors fought back and were able to make good their escape.

In 681 Wilfrid returned to the county. Nearly 100 years had elapsed since the first Roman missionaries landed in Kent to begin their campaign, and isolated Sussex was the only area that throughout had remained pagan. The return visit was a success, for he had the support of King Ethelwalch who was a practising Christian.

Mythology now combines with reality during the five years that it took Wilfrid to complete his mission. Bede tells of several miracles that were effected by the Bishop during the campaign, including a local version of the five loaves and twelve small fishes. Wilfrid so impressed the king with his teaching that a large section of land on the Selsey peninsula was given to him; here he established his see and built a cathedral. This building remained the principal place of worship in the county until after the Norman conquest when it was displaced by Chichester.

Saxon Churches

These churches are the oldest buildings in the county to display, above ground level, fragments of their original fabric. Constructed over 1,000 years ago, it is little wonder that in the intervening centuries they have had to endure much restoration and rebuilding. Wilfrid, after the conversion of the Sussex people, must have built churches where they could worship, but since these were erected from the standard building material of the age, wood, they have left no evidence of their existence. Many of the stone buildings, or parts of them, date from the late Saxon period and were built over the sites of the previous timber buildings. These stone churches may have been constructed either before or after the Conquest since the local masons continued with their traditional designs well after the Norman arrival.

For a sparsely populated county Sussex was well endowed with churches. It is thought that there may have been in excess of 150. Domesday listed only 111, but as this was a purely economic census and if the church had no land value it was omitted from the count. Early charters list at least nine churches in the borough of Lewes, none appears in Domesday; similarly the cathedral at Selsey receives no mention either.

The distribution of the churches followed the general pattern of the population, with the concentration increasing markedly from east to west and from north to south. The majority of the sites were adjacent to either the Downs or the coast, or on the sandier regions in the west of the county. Apart from one isolated instance close to the Surrey border and a corridor to the north of Brighton, the Wealden forest is devoid of recorded sites.

It is in the small villages and hamlets that have remained free from residential dormitory development or commercial activities that are to be found the best preserved elements of the Saxon mason's work. The churches in these settlements have retained more of their original features than those in the more populous areas where restoration has been more widespread.

In East Sussex Bishopstone and Jevington are typical examples of the period, not only for their architecture but also their position on the Downs. In mid Sussex two churches served the adjoining parishes on the western bank of the Adur: Coombes may now be reached only through a farmyard, while Botolphs is a remnant of a larger building in use when the hamlet was a thriving port. In West Sussex there are fine examples to be found at Selham, which is one of the churches built on the sandstone ridge that parallels the northern slopes of the Downs, and a downland variety at Up Marden. Selham is featured in Domesday, but no church is mentioned and so this tiny building could well be a post-Conquest construction to a pre-Conquest design. Up Marden is an ancient settlement first mentioned in a grant of about 920. The church is believed to be partly thirteenth century, but

Selham. Basically Saxon, it is one of the smaller Sussex churches.

Worth. A non-traditional church design inherited from Surrey.

St Mary's Sompting. The only building in Britain that has retained its Rhenish roofed tower.

These are two of the larger and most significant Saxon churches in Sussex, one lying close to a northern boundary of the county and one to a southern. The church at Worth – not to be confused with the nearby buildings of Worth Abbey – is an enigma. Although at one time the parish was the largest in England, no one has ever explained as to why a church of this size came to be built in what was only a clearing in a forest. When the church was built in the early part of the tenth century the area was under the control of Surrey, with Worth being part of the king's estate, and it is thought that the construction was authorized either by him or by a member of his immediate family. The church is quite different from others in the county, and the large chancel is unique in an English church of this period. As it is more substantially built and better finished than the majority, the theory persists that possibly Worth had attached to it a college of secular or monastic clergy. These facts and its isolated position suggest that it was built by masons either from Surrey or from further to the north. A roof fire in 1986 gave the opportunity for a thorough restoration of the building to be carried out.

The church of St Mary's at Sompting lies just inland from the Channel and at the foot of the Downs. It is a complex building, with the tower and part of the nave being pre-Conquest, the remainder being added between the twelfth and the fourteenth century. The tower is the most striking feature with remnants of Roman brickwork existing in two of the walls, but it is the tower roof that makes the church instantly recognizable. The roof is of a Rhenish type; there are later examples of it in both Koblenz and Cologne, but this church in Sussex is the only Saxon tower that has retained its original roof form.

the thickness of the nave wall suggests that the present building is a rebuilding of the Saxon original. Close to the site of today's building lies a Saxon cemetery where graves dating from between the late fifth and the early eighth century have been discovered. As some of the later interments were obviously Christian it strengthens the belief that today's church rests on earlier wooden structures; the first was probably a pagan temple, then, as Sussex was converted, a Christian church was erected on the site.

King Alfred

After three centuries of non-interference from the Continent, Britain was again subjected to piratical raids. These new attackers came from both Norway and Denmark and planned their raids roughly to match the geography of their homelands; so it was the Danes who created problems for the southern counties. Both sets of raiders were referred to by the Anglo-Saxons as 'Vikings', or pirates.

The first raids were made into the north of Britain in 795; four decades later Kent became the target. Sporadic forays continued for a further thirty years then an organized invasion took place. Over the next ten years large swaths of the country fell to the invaders, but surprisingly Sussex was spared. In 871 Alfred was crowned King of Wessex. His early encounters with the Danes resulted in a series of defeats and he was forced into a period of hiding in the Somerset marshes. Emerging from the levels, he was able to reform his army and rout the invaders. Following a treaty between the two leaders, England was divided. The Danes retained control of the eastern counties, the Danelaw, and Wessex was granted the remainder of England.

Alfred remained King of Wessex until his death in 899 and it was during these years that his influence was felt in Sussex. In this period peace treaties between warring factions were always fragile affairs, and with this in mind Alfred decided to establish a chain of fortified enclosures, known as burghs, along the Channel

---

BOSHAM

King Cnut or to give him his English title, Canute, held lands in the west of the county mainly around the port of Bosham which lies on one of the western arms of Chichester Harbour. Tradition says that Canute built a palace there, but even if the story is not true the village became the premier maritime community in Sussex. Another tale refers to his attempt to make the sea obey his command. This story may have arisen from the series of groynes that were being built along the coast, since these obstructions do reduce the action of the incoming waves.

A further story connects the Canute family to the church of Holy Trinity. The date of the church is unrecorded, but it was in existence when Edward was on the throne for he granted the

lands to his 'kinsman Osbern'. He later became the second Bishop of Exeter. The connection to Canute is through a small grave in the nave of the church; throughout the centuries this was said to be that of his daughter who died when still a child. The grave was opened in 1865 and was found to contain the skeleton of a young girl, but there was nothing from which to date or identify the remains.

Earl Godwin based his fleet at Bosham and it was from here that he departed for his short period of exile. This west Sussex port then offered the shortest and most convenient route to Normandy and was used again by King Harold on his visit to Duke William. This last journey is graphically illustrated on the Bayeux Tapestry.

Holy Trinity, Bosham. According to tradition, the resting place of Canute's daughter.

coast. These stretched from Portchester in the west to Dover in the east. Sussex received five of them, four were in developed towns and one was at Burpham. This overlooked the River Arun, 2 miles (3km) inland from the future town of Arundel and to where the defences were soon relocated.

Alfred had other links with Sussex. He owned several large estates in the county and his father is believed to be buried at Steyning. The King was also a literate man, he learnt Latin and was the author of three works. His literary achievements did not go unrecorded since his future biographer, Bishop Asser, held an exploratory meeting with him in the county at Dean. Several villages lay claim to this meeting place, but the most likely spot was at West Dean which is an unspoiled hamlet close to the banks of the River Cuckmere.

After Alfred's death Wessex continued to prosper and expand; the increase in territory came mainly from the Danelaw and was achieved through a series of local wars. The retention of these lands was aided by the sympathetic and even-handed rule offered by the conqueror. As the first millennium drew to a close, a new Norse threat disturbed the tranquillity of Sussex. The raids increased in ferocity as reported in the *Chronicle*: in 994 'They advanced and brought the greatest evil that any army could, burning, plundering and manslaughter – but in Sussex and Hampshire.' Again in 1000: 'and everywhere in Sussex they plundered and burnt as is their custom.' The fortunes of Wessex now fluctuated, battles were won and lost, territories regained then lost once more. This confused period was finally stabilized in 1016 when the Dane Cnut was proclaimed King of England. In 1017 Cnut divided England into four earldoms, Wessex being placed under the control of Godwin. His credentials are unclear, but he became overlord of the richest province of the country. He and his family were largely responsible for the power politics of the last three decades of Anglo-Saxon England after the death of the King in 1035.

Two of Cnut's sons briefly followed their father as king, but when the second son, Hardecnut, died in 1042 the Wessexonian Edward (The Confessor) was elected as ruler. Edward, who had spent twenty years in exile in Normandy, was very much subordinate to the all-powerful Earl Godwin. There was a period of improved relationship between the two when the King married Godwin's daughter. No heir came of this union and Edward gave the impression that he was in favour of a Norman duke being named as his successor. These thoughts were believed to have been converted into action when he increased the Norman presence at his court and invited William, the Duke of Normandy, for a state visit. William assumed that this was to be the occasion when he would be named as the future king of England; when the proclamation was not made the Norman realized that his control of England could never be made through diplomacy, war was his only option.

A further dispute between the two English leaders almost led to a local war, but, as support for Godwin appeared to be temporarily on the wane, he accepted from the King an order expelling him from the country. Godwin remained in exile for only a few months then returned and assembled a fleet which at first concentrated on regaining the support of the south-eastern ports. Pevensey and Hastings were two Sussex ports that pledged their allegiance both with ships and men. Godwin's son Harold now joined his father; with this assistance and that of his new-found friends from Kent and Sussex, plus some local residents, Godwin faced the King on the banks of the Thames at London. The King, realizing that his forces were inferior, agreed to a treaty of 'full friendship' between the two. Godwin was reinstated into his former position and also managed to obtain the banishment of all of the court's Norman guests.

When Godwin died in 1053 his son Harold became the new Earl of Wessex. He was successful in quelling and defeating attacks on the northern borders of his territory and quickly became the outstanding figure in the country and was recognized as the obvious successor to King Edward. The King despatched Harold to Normandy as his ambassador in 1063 or 1064; although the departure from Bosham is recorded on the Bayeux Tapestry, the actual date remains vague, as is the reason for the visit. Again, little is known of the discussions that took place, but the outcome did not find favour with the King.

Edward died in January 1066 and, since there were continuing problems with the borders of northern England, the prime consideration for the ruling council was the urgent appointment of a military leader. Harold was the obvious choice; he was elected king and immediately took his army northwards. By mid September he had regained control of the last remaining obstacle, Northumbria, and looked forward to a leisurely return to his capital. Events did not agree to his plan, for, while the English army was involved with the Norsemen, William had been preparing for an invasion; on 28 September 1066, the most momentous day in the history of Sussex, William landed at Pevensey and began the last successful invasion of Britain.

Bosham. The port of King Harold.

5. NORMAN SUSSEX AND THE EARLY MIDDLE AGES

Origin and Development of the Duchy of Normandy

In the eighth century the Duchy was part of the Charlemagne empire, which stretched from Germany through France and into Spain and Italy, but after the death of this Holy Roman Emperor in 814 the empire began to disintegrate. The development of Normandy now ran roughly in parallel to that of Britain. Both countries received visitations from the northern Vikings, and it was these peoples that developed the tandem cultures of the two territories. The Vikings used the rivers of northern France to reach the interior of the country; Paris and the Seine valley were overrun and in 911, after a locally signed treaty had been arrived at, a large area adjacent to the Seine became Scandinavian property. Further territories were obtained by conquest and negotiation and by the middle of the century Normandy was fully established.

The name Normandy derived from Northmannia, or land of the Norse (north) men. This name was not universally accepted for a later report in the *Anglo-Saxon Chronicle* stated that Harold defeated the Norsemen at Stamford Bridge then was killed by the 'Freneyscan', or French, at Hastings. Similarly the Bayeux Tapestry describes them as 'Franki'. The first Norman kings of England carried on with this tradition, dividing their subjects into French or English.

Despite being under Scandinavian control, the Duchy of Normandy retained many characteristics of a French province, apart from the abolition of the monarchy. Rollo, the first Viking ruler, made the decision to terminate the royal authority and establish a line of hereditary counts, later referred to as dukes. Large numbers of new Scandinavian settlers arrived in the province in the tenth century, but these were quickly and easily assimilated into the French culture and, by the time of the conquest, the Scandinavian language was little used.

With their ancestors evolving from the same or neighbouring tribes, it is understandable that there was a close affinity between the cross-channel neighbours. Marriage between members of the two courts was a common occurrence and one of Duke William's claim to the English throne was the fact that his great aunt Emma was the mother of Edward the Confessor. When he was seven Edward was despatched, along with his French mother, into the care of the Norman court. Here he remained until 1042 when he returned to be crowned King of England. It is obvious that his exile in France influenced his early promotion of Norman acquaintances into the English court and probably gave rise to the suggestion that, should he have no natural successor, then the throne of England should pass over the Channel to the then Duke of Normandy.

Mention was made in the previous chapter of the visit of Harold to Normandy. This had an unfortunate beginning for the Englishman. Shortly after leaving Bosham his ship encountered a storm and he was forced to make an emergency landfall on a shoreline that was controlled by a count who had recently been subjugated by William. Harold and his men were arrested and released and allowed to continue their journey only after intervention by the Duke. While in Normandy he accompanied and assisted William in two minor victories. He also signed some form of allegiance to the Duke. It is unclear what was included in this for the two parties issued differing versions of its contents.

Battle Abbey.

When Harold was proclaimed King of England, William concluded that the Englishman had reneged on the pact and it was time for him to act and fight for the crown that he believed was rightfully his.

In the years leading up to 1066 William had stamped his authority over the greater part of northern France and had gained the support of his near neighbours. He was now in an expansionist mood, for many of his new-found allies were seeking rewards for their continuing support, indicating that the gift of new lands would be most acceptable. The establishment of two local religious houses had gained the Duke the blessing of the Church on his forthcoming venture, and his marriage to the daughter of the Count of Flanders, who was his nearest rival, stilled any possible trouble from that direction.

The Year of 1066

This was the year that changed dramatically the history of both England and Sussex. It started with the crowning of Harold early in the year, for Edward had died over the Christmas period. For a few months a cross-channel 'cold war' of propaganda existed, this being easily won by the French. A papal blessing for the forthcoming crusade was given; this, in effect, prevented any other foreign state from assisting Harold, for this would be seen as a fight against the Church. In fact, the Pope had no option but to agree to William's demands since his palace was situated in an area of Italy that was controlled by Normandy. William also sponsored a Norwegian, Tostig, who was Harold's brother, into a series of raids on the south-eastern coast of England. These were probably made in order to test the English defences.

Harold spent the first half of the year building his army and hoping that his barons in the north would be strong enough to quell any local disturbances that might arise. He considered that the immediate threat to his crown would come from across the Channel and it was in the southern counties that he based the majority of his forces. A large army reserve was concentrated in

inland Sussex and his navy was centred on the Isle of Wight, from where it made periodic patrols along the coast. It was during one of the navy's absences from its home base that Tostig first attacked, forcing the island residents to resupply and refinance his ships. He then continued with a cat-and-mouse game with the English defenders, ransacking many of the local ports before returning to his homeland.

Throughout the summer William continued to build his invasion force. With coercion, or at times the plain bullying of his barons, he amassed a fleet of perhaps 2,000 ships and 14,000 men. Many of this army were mercenaries bought from other European states. He assembled this armada at Dives where it was kept in an advanced state of readiness for over a month. This strategy ensured that Harold was unable to stand down any of his defenders. Given that many of these men were only on a two-month enlistment and that harvest time was approaching when their prescence would be needed in the fields, it is not surprising that the morale of the defenders became suspect.

In late August a large Norwegian fleet crossed the North Sea to Shetland then drifted south along the Scottish and Northumberland coasts, plundering and slaughtering as it went. At the mouth of the Humber it met Tostig's invasion force and combined to attack York. Harold had to make an agonizing decision: should he keep his forces in the south or force march them to defend his northern borders? He and his army went north, leaving the southern counties unprotected against any invasion. As the English army moved, so did William, redeploying his forces to St Valery-sur-Somme.

The decisive battle of the northern campaign took place at Stamford Bridge, 8 miles (13km) to the north-east of York. The city had surrendered to the Norsemen on 24 September and it was arranged that 150 children of prominent Yorkshire families were to be handed over the following day as surety for the continuing supply of provisions. It appears that the Norse intelligence was less than adequate on this occasion, for a large proportion of the army were allowed

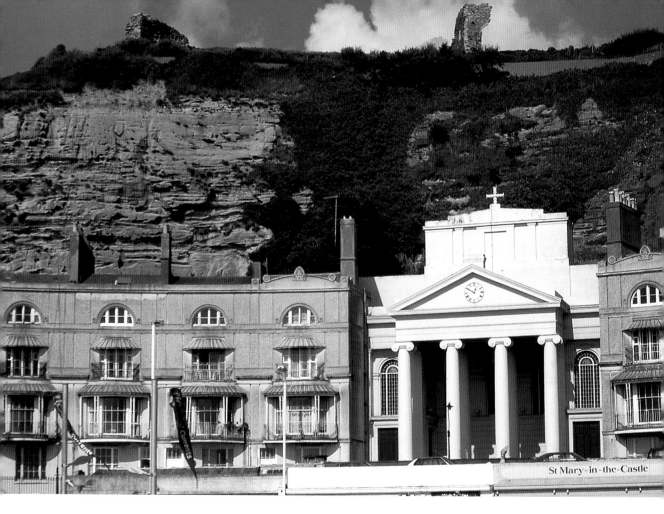

Hastings Castle. The ruins of the castle now overlook the town's sea front.

to return to the ships, replete with bounty. Those remaining in the city overnight left the following morning for the hostage rendezvous poorly armed.

Harold and his English army proved victorious in a series of hand-to-hand encounters that lasted all day. Tostig and the Viking leader were slain along with thousands of their troops. Harold's army also suffered heavy losses and the unpaid survivors, for the King was destitute, were tired and had little enthusiasm for another forced march and probable battle. A call by the King for volunteers proved unsuccessful and, after resting for two days, he began his journey southwards, accompanied only by his house-carls. Somewhere en route to London Harold received the news that, after being delayed by bad weather, William had finally landed in

Sussex and his army was busy ravaging the county.

The Battle of Hastings

William sailed with his fleet on the evening of 27 September and, after an uneventful crossing, landed at the Roman fort of Pevensey in the late morning of the following day. William was reported to have stumbled when disembarking. This could have been seen as a bad omen for the forthcoming campaign, but the slip was immediately turned to his advantage with the remark that he was only grasping land that was rightfully his. Differing accounts attribute this observation to either the Duke himself or one of his servants. After disembarking a section of his army, William despatched the rest of his vessels eastwards to Hastings where it made another unopposed landing.

Both Pevensey and Hastings were good defensive positions, but, as the latter possessed a better harbour, it was here that William decided to make his temporary base, building a small fort within the existing town. The contingent that was landed at Pevensey also improved the Roman fortifications, an inner rampart was added and the width of one gate reduced.

While William remained at Hastings, planning his campaign and overseeing the replenishment of supplies that were arriving from his homeland, the army was encouraged to ravage the surrounding countryside. Not only was there plundering and stealing of effects, but houses were burnt down or their occupants evicted. William knew that Sussex was loyal to Harold for he had inherited large estates in the county from his father and it was the Duke's ploy that, by landing in the Englishman's shire and devastating his lands, the King would be provoked into making a hasty and ill-prepared attack. The ruse worked, for when Harold learned of the suffering of his peoples 'he did hasten his march'.

Harold arrived back in London with his mounted housecarls on 6 October, the journey of 190 miles (306km) taking just eight days. He remained in the city for five days, resting and recruiting for his new army. A number of his victorious cavalry arrived from Yorkshire but the majority of the new infantry were locally enlisted men with little experience of battle. It was during this short stay in London that Harold made the first of several strategic mistakes. A delay in engaging William would have allowed time for more of his previous forces to rejoin him, and to fight without the support of his archers would put him at a great disadvantage. Men from the southern shire counties did not favour the bow as a weapon and the remnants of the Stamford Bridges archers were still several days march away when the King left the capital. Harold also insisted that all the great names of Wessex and southern England accompany him

into battle, ignoring the fact that, should disaster strike, as it certainly did, there would be no remaining leader capable of continuing the fight. The King was impatient, and, believing that he would be able to surprise William as he had surprised the Norsemen, he left London with half an army of unknown quality for a 58-mile (93km) forced march through the Weald towards Hastings. After three days of marching they reached what was to be the site of the battle, only to find that the Duke was fully prepared and awaiting their arrival.

The battle site encompassed three hills. To the north was Caldbec Hill, this emerged direct from woodland and was the assembly point for the English army. The main hill to the south was twin-topped and dual-named, Telham and Black Horse. This was where William had organized his forces. Lying midway between the two armies was the traditional site of the battle. There is a strongly held opinion that the battle was fought on the northern hill, not where the commemorative Abbey now stands. The main argument for this view is the lack of military artefacts that have been discovered around this central rise. However, if the same criteria were to be applied to Caldbec Hill then it too would fail the test.

At first light on 14 October the two armies faced each other across the two valleys and the central ridge. William made the first move, sending his archers forward in an attempt to stop the English infantry from occupying the governing ridge. The infantry won the race for the summit but suffered heavy casualties in the process.

An unreal war occupied the next few hours. Both armies were evenly matched in numbers, 7,500 to 8,000 men on each side, but it was the Normans who had the experience and were better equipped. Harold held the superior position and was content to play a waiting game for reinforcements from London were due arrive overnight. The onus was on William to make the first move. This he did with a combined infantry and archer attack. Shooting up the slope, the archers were largely ineffective since their arrows were either easily parried by the English shield wall or flew harmlessly over the heads of the defenders. The infantry too had little success, and even when they were supported by the Norman cavalry the wall remained firm. The French were taking heavy losses, and one flank of their line which consisted mainly of Bretons, of whom William had a poor opinion, fled in disarray. It was during this period that the Duke was thrown from his horse; rumour soon circulated that he was dead. If that had been true then the Normans would have been leaderless and unlikely to have been able to contain the English advance. The Duke remounted and, through inspired leadership, managed to coerce his troops back into an effective fighting force.

It is one of the battle's mysteries why Harold did not press ahead when he held the obvious advantage. The most likely explanation is that the death of his brother, who was fighting at his side, somehow affected his judgement. Whatever the reason, the English were returned to their original hilltop position. Again a stalemate existed. William realized that he had only about three hours of daylight remaining in which to achieve a victory. Another frontal attack on the wall would be unlikely to make the breakthrough he needed, but a two-pronged attack could well be more successful. While his infantry continued to probe the English shield line, a unit of cavalry attacked the extreme right of the defences. From this point it would be an easier ride to the top of the hill. After a short encounter the horsemen made a feigned retreat, thus drawing the undisciplined defenders off their position. While the ensuing skirmish was in progress further cavalry advanced through this largely unprotected flank of the English line and made an attack from the rear.

William was now able to coordinate his horse and foot on a broader front. The archers were ordered to fire their arrows on a higher trajectory so that they fell like rain on the defenders. Instinctively shields were raised as protection against this nuisance attack. The strategy succeeded, for, as the shields were raised, the wall

The 1066. A daily reminder of the great Sussex battle.

automatically became less effective. Finally it was breached, then collapsed. Bloody hand-to-hand fighting followed with extensive casualties on both sides. Gradually the Normans gained the upper hand and many of the English defenders who were still able began to desert into the surrounding woodland.

It was during this late stage of the battle that Harold was killed. He was spotted on the top of the hill surrounded by a few of his remaining housecarls. Twenty of William's best knights were sent to seize the English standard and kill the King. Both objectives were accomplished after a ferocious scuffle. The Bayeux Tapestry depicts Harold with an arrow protruding from his eye; this is an instance of artistic licence for he was killed and then dismembered by the French hit squad.

The Bayeux Tapestry

The events of 1066 and the Norman conquest are well documented. The battle itself was quickly recognized as a major historical event and was treated as such by any writer of the period. The majority of the reports originated in France and the events were recorded with a Gallic leaning. One major omission in the reporting of Hastings is the lack of eye-witness accounts; at that time there were no war correspondents and the timetable and events of the day were probably chronicled several years later.

There are three main reports for the year, two from France and the well-quoted *Anglo-Saxon Chronicle* from England. The most comprehensive French account was written by William of Poitiers who was chaplain to the Duke. His hero-worship of William, who in his eyes could do no wrong, has led to many students of the period to consider that his position was more of a mouthpiece for William than his chaplain.

The Bayeux Tapestry is an illustrated account of the events of historical year. Tapestry is a misnomer for it is in effect an embroidered frieze, just 20in (50cm) wide and 230ft (70m) long. It was commissioned by Bishop Odo of Bayeux for display at the dedication of his cathedral in 1077. After the conquest, the bishop was made Earl of Kent and it is believed that the tapestry was created by Kentish weavers working for him at Canterbury.

The first scenes show Edward the Confessor on his deathbed; Harold's coronation occupies the middle section, and the story ends with the flight of the English after the battle of Hastings. The last 9ft (2.8m) has been lost and it is thought that this part featured William's entry into London and his crowning as King of England. The portrayal of men, their equipment and actions may, perhaps, be likened to the characters in an early Disney cartoon, but careful study of the scenes gives a surprisingly accurate insight into the lives of the participants over the eleven months that the story covers.

Sussex is well represented on the tapestry. Harold is shown hunting in his estates around Bosham and again feasting on the upper floor of his manor house before embarking on his visit to William. As well as general scenes of the invasion, the construction of the Hastings fort is shown, with men shovelling earth on to the motte; this activity is overseen by a Norman knight (? William). The ravaging and burning of the Sussex countryside by the army is also depicted. The decisive battle occupies the last section of the tapestry. Charge and counter-charge are featured, the shield wall is shown, both standing firm and also when breached. The hand-to-hand fighting and the death of the King, all are graphically illustrated. One regrets the missing ending.

On the day following the battle, William returned to his base at Hastings, where he and

THE MALFOSSE

As the English survivors were attempting to make their escape, pursued by the French horsemen, the expected reinforcements appeared. The newly arrived housecarls took up station on the sides of a steep ghyll 600yd (550m) to the north of Caldbec Hill. This valley contained a series of deep ditches, their sides disguised by brambles and undergrowth. In the gathering gloom, decoy fugitives lured the Norman cavalry into the ravine. The horses fell or were killed and their riders were quickly despatched by the waiting housecarls. The following horsemen, unable to see what was happening to their colleagues, continued into the trap. Soon the whole was a pit of dying and injured horses and men. The slaughter ended only when the pursuers were brought up short by the sheer volume of dead in front of them. With the ambush complete, and feeling that in a small way they had avenged the death of their King, the English dispersed into the night. From that time the ghyll has borne the name of Malfosse — evil ditch.

BATTLE ABBEY

During the battle of Hastings William publicly vowed that, should he be victorious, he would build a religious house on the site. The traditional story confirms that, although he was kept fully occupied in quelling rebellions in both England and France, he kept his word. More probably the building was constructed as a penance because he was considered to have used excessive force in subduing the English. Building started around 1075 and six years later the eastern end of the church was sufficiently advanced to allow its consecration; its final completion did not occur until 1094. The Abbey sits on a narrow ridge and extensive terracing of the surrounding ground was needed before the building could begin. The high altar is said to be placed immediately over the spot where Harold was killed, but in the confusion that existed after the battle it is unlikely that the exact position of his death was accurately recorded for posterity.

William bequeathed that, on his death, several of his personal effects were to be given to the community and the Abbey was endowed several extensive estates, including all lands within a $1^1/_2$ mile (2.4km) radius of the high altar. This gift made the Abbey one of the richest religious houses in the country.

Battle Abbey. The imposing gatehouse built on the site of the early abbey.

his army rested and waited for reinforcements. His next objective was the capture of London, but he feared a direct approach through the Wealden forest for it was to him unknown territory and was controlled by anti-Norman residents. Instead he took his main force eastwards along the coast to Dover, thence to Canterbury and, after an isolated attack on the capital, continued south of the Thames, finally crossing the river at Wallingford. A secondary unit diverted westwards from Hastings and followed an underdown route to the Wessex capital of Winchester. After obtaining the submission of the town, it went northwards to rejoin the main army. William continued through the shires, his progress being marked by a trail of destruction. Any settlement that the army encountered on its march was ruthlessly destroyed. The defenders of London, realizing that they would be unable to contain the invaders and fearful for their own safety and that of their town, submitted to William and invited him to become their king. On Christmas Day 1066 William, Duke of Normandy, was crowned William I of England.

William was by title King of England, but his authority at first covered only the former province of Wessex. More battles were needed to enlarge his holding. Continuing problems in his French duchy led to his departure from Pevensey to his homeland. This enforced commuting between territories continued through the reigns of the succeeding kings and the periodic lack of authority gave rise to many of the revolts that occurred in the next two centuries. On his return after a nine-months' absence the Conqueror brought with him several of his close friends and supporters, from these emerged the future controllers and landowners of Sussex.

The Administrative Districts of Sussex

It took a further five years for the new king to gain what could be called control, of all of his English territory. In the early years of the campaign submission to William often meant that the incumbent retained his lands, albeit paying heavy taxes to his new master. As the number of rebellions against Norman authority increased, this privilege ceased and the land, together with any viable assets that remained after visitations from the ravaging army, were given to French supporters, although, in theory, all land belonged to the monarch and these installed tenants were subservient to him. Throughout the country the basic form of local government remained largely unchanged; Sussex was the exception.

King Harold held extensive estates in Sussex and one of the Conqueror's first acts was to confiscate all of these and those held by the former king's supporters. As he now had two cross-channel territories to administer, William needed a base in the southern counties that would provide a secure communication route between the two. He was already aware of the potential threat to his kingdom from former allies who held land to the east of his French duchy and he therefore committed the coast of south-east England to his most trustworthy barons. Sussex now saw the most radical changes to land administration that had ever taken place in the country, the system being adopted from a successful French prototype. The original Saxon estates had spread haphazardly across the countryside with scant regard to the shire boundaries. Now the county was divided into five, later six, roughly parallel strips called 'rapes', this name being retained from the earlier Saxon taxation unit. Each rape possessed a port and a fortified position, with the tenant-in-chief holding all the non-ecclesiastical land of his particular district.

In a show of nepotism, William gave the rape of Hastings to his second cousin, the Count of Eu. Pevensey was to be held by his half brother and two more relatives were given Lewes and Arundel with Chichester. Around 1073 a slight adjustment was made to several of the boundaries to accommodate the new rape of Bramber. Each port became the administrative centre for the district and, with the exception of Chichester, each defensive position was upgraded or rebuilt with a castle.

Parham. On lands once held by the Abbot of Westminster, this Elizabethan manor stands isolated below the western Downs.

Domesday

During the rest of William's reign (he died in 1087) Sussex continued at peace under the new regime. One of his last acts was to commission a survey into the land ownership and usage in his English territory. 'Ownership' is probably the wrong word to use since he considered himself to be the owner of the whole country and his appointed barons and prelates were only land-lords or landholders.

There is no surviving document to confirm why this survey was made; an account written a hundred years later stated that 'the Conqueror decided to place the government of the country on a written base. ... A careful description of the lands was placed in a book.' The survey may

also have been used for taxation purposes; the tenants considered that this was the primary rea-son for it was they who called the findings 'Domesday' or day of judgement. Although Domesday is the most famous English public record, the form in which it has survived makes for a misleading guide to the extent and charac-ter of rural Sussex. An omission from the book does not mean the non-existence of a holding or settlement. Many ecclesiastical lands and churches that were, in effect, tax-free did not appear in the relevant pages.

Domesday lists nearly 200 landowners for the English shires since some north country areas were not surveyed; for Sussex the total is just fif-teen. William held two areas, both taken from Harold Godwinson (King Harold): Bosham in the west of the county and Rotherfield in the east. The Bishop of Chichester was listed as a landholder and had his lands positioned mainly away from the city, although ten sites near to the cathedral were subleased to him from the King's manor of Bosham. Eight religious houses were landholders, of which only two, Battle and Chichester, were in Sussex. The Abbot of Westminster held the isolated downland pocket of Parham. Nearby Bury and the important town of Steyning were held by the only absentee landlord, the Abbot of Fecamp, who was also in charge of a small area in the rape of Hastings. The remaining lands were attributed to the barons of the individual rapes.

Norman New Towns and Castles

The building of new towns often coincided with the construction of castles. The castles not only provided protection for the immediate urban area but, when they housed a unit of cavalry, this 'rapid reaction force' could quickly subdue any troubles arising in the surrounding countryside.

Lewes, before the establishment of the forti-fied Saxon burgh, probably existed only as a convenient crossing of the River Ouse. Downstream the river became wider and inland was the dreaded Wealden forest. When the infant town was made the administrative centre for the rape, the landholder, who also held extensive lands in both Surrey and Norfolk, decided to make this his base and built the cas-tle. As with many of these early fortifications, little of the original building survives. A further boost to the developing town was the creation of a Cluniac priory; this was established in a joint venture between the landholder and his wife after a joint return visit to their home in Brittany.

Arundel saw another combination of town and castle. As with Lewes, this is another hill town, the development taking place mainly between the castle and the river. The Saxons cre-ated a fortified burgh 2 miles (3.2km) upstream, but this site did not find favour with the newly-created earl and landholder. The first castle was built of timber but then quickly rebuilt in stone.

Bramber. All that remains of the castle that belonged to William de Braose.

The structure was added to in the following two centuries and remained in good order until it was destroyed during the Civil War. The castle that is on view today is a modern replacement, scarcely more than a century old. Any remnants of the Norman building are largely covered by recently constructed walls.

Bramber was one case where the combination did not materialize; the castle was built over-looking the River Adur, but the accompanying settlement never developed into more than a vil-lage. Although remaining small, both it and neighbouring Steyning were granted borough status, each electing two Members of Parliament until 1832. The incumbent of the Bramber rape, William de Braose, tried to develop the village as a competitive port to the long-established Steyning and built a causeway into the river as a further deterrent to upstream traffic. His venture was not a success and in 1100 he established a new town and port close to the mouth of the river at Shoreham. The most visible remains of the original castle are a finger-like slither of keep and the adjacent church.

A great number of castles were built throughout the country in the early years after the conquest; the Sussex total hovered around the mid thirties. No doubt many more would have been constructed had it not been for the action of Henry II who brought castle building under strict royal control. The majority of the Sussex castles, apart from those on the coast or where river communication needed protection, were not built as defences against raiders but as a form of conspicuous consumption by the local barons. The general rule appeared to be that, the more important the landholder, the larger the building. Most early castles were constructed of timber on a design known as motte (French for mound – built from the earth extracted from the surrounding ditch) and bailey (the inner courtyard).

The defensive mound could be totally man-made, but, where possible, natural features or earlier earthworks would be adapted as required. As these castles were privately funded, their design followed no standard form. Similarly, the conversion from wood to stone was very much dependent on the baron's finances. Many of the castle sites today can be recognized only by the protruding motte. Aerial photography of the mounds does, however, indicate the extent of the above-ground defences. Two examples in the west of the county which are devoid of any masonry are Selham and Fulking, while at Knepp, which is adjacent to the A24 road, a finger of the keep still survives.

Two East Sussex showpiece castles, Bodiam and Herstmonceux, did not begin life until later, in 1380 and 1440, respectively. Bodiam was restored in the early twentieth century while Herstmonceux, like Arundel, is a rebuilding of the original structure destroyed in 1777.

William died in France two months after receiving a battle wound. His eldest son Robert considered himself to be the rightful heir to both Normandy and England. Although he was granted his father's inherited lands, the acquired territory passed to the second son William Rufus. This division of property gave rise to enormous problems for the succeeding English monarchs, more of their time was spent abroad protecting or regaining their French possessions than in their kingdom. This situation was not finally resolved until 1289 when Edward I became the last king of England to hold court in France.

Neither Robert nor Rufus was happy with his share of the inheritance. Finally, after many threats and verbal exchanges, Rufus became the sole beneficiary when Robert pawned the duchy to his brother. Rebellions by anti-monarchical factions were a common occurrence throughout the next two centuries. The first took place soon after the crowning of Rufus by pro-Robert barons, who were led by the incumbent of the Pevensey rape and his brother Bishop Odo. After a six-weeks' siege of the castle, the occupants of Pevensey Castle surrendered, not beaten in battle, but starved into submission. The site also saw two further sieges. In 1147 another anti-royal insurgence occurred, with a similar result. The final event took place in 1265 when it played host to a group of survivors from the battle of Lewes. This time the temporary residents were victorious and the castle remained unharmed. Later the castle was granted to the queens of England who were personally responsible for its upkeep and security. Arundel castle also featured in a rebellion against the crown. Henry I, after a successful attack and short period of ownership, granted both it, its estates and title, to one of his supporters.

The decentralization of the monarch's lands were of economic benefit to Sussex. Although taxes were continually increased to pay for the king's overseas commitments, much of the revenue raised from the county was indirectly returned by the use of the Channel ports. They offered the nearest and safest connections between the two territories. Shoreham, Seaford, Pevensey and Hastings all became thriving communities. This prosperity was not confined to

THE TOWN OF BATTLE

This town was one of the Norman 'new' towns; the sole purpose for its existence was to service the adjacent abbey. Before the conquest there was not even a hamlet on the site, but by the time of Domesday twenty-one peasants were shown as living there. In all probability these were outworkers of the religious house. The first cluster of buildings was built adjacent to the abbey gate; then, as the population increased, the housing spread northwards off the battle ridge. By 1110 the expanded settlement listed 109 householders; interestingly seventy-eight of the residents gave English names, twelve Norman and nineteen Anglo-Norman. This breakdown suggests that at this relatively early stage of French control a certain amount of intermarriage was taking place between the two peoples. A local parish church had been built and a market established on an edge of the town site well away from the abbey precincts. The town now began to develop independently of its founder, with a complement of traders unrelated to religious activities. By the time of the dissolution Battle was strong enough as a market town to survive in its own right.

Modern Battle High Street.

Knepp Castle. King John's favourite country retreat.

KING JOHN

John is usually remembered for his acceptance in Magna Carta of the barons' demands for reform and his ability to lose his baggage while crossing the Wash. But of all the Norman and Plantagenet kings it was he who had the greatest affinity with Sussex. On one occasion, after a campaign on the Continent, he disembarked at Seaford and, instead of returning direct to London, he stayed in the Sussex countryside. Thereafter, whenever his military commitments would allow, he would spend his days journeying from manor to manor, no doubt enjoying the hospitality of his supporters. One of his favourite retreats was Bramber and its smaller hunting lodge at Knepp. In 1208, after an altercation with William be Braose, whom he thought was plotting against him, he seized both castles and their estates and transferred them to his son. However, Knepp continued to enjoy his custom for, in the remaining years of his reign, he made at least four further extended visits to the castle.

At first many of the influential Sussex landowners supported him, but John had a penchant for quarrelling with all his friends and consequently his support in the county declined. In 1205 he lost Normandy, and until his death twelve years later, his main concern was with the protection of the coast against a threatened invasion. The Sussex lords, ever mindful of their own safety and inheritance, mobilized their forces and put their great castles in good order. A short-lived invasion did come but it was after John's death and had little impact on the county.

Cocking Church, of Saxon design but built after the Norman invasion.

the coast; the hinterland too found a ready market for its produce and industries. Once again Sussex had become the favoured area of the country.

In 1264 Sussex, her barons and castles again became embroiled in anti-monarchical action, this time the rebellion escalated into civil war. The king involved in this dispute was Henry III, and the opposition was led by a foreigner, Simon de Montfort. As often happened in these revolts, the conflicting leaders were closely related, in this instance Simon was the King's brother-in-law. Henry had made what the landowners considered to be unwise commitments abroad, and in 1258 they took all forms of government out of his hands. An uneasy truce lasted for five years before the conflict was rekindled. The decisive battle took place on the outskirts of Lewes,

which unexpectedly Simon won. The King was captured and the remnants of his forces found refuge at Pevensey. The barons finally lifted the siege; this allowed the royalists to regroup and the following year, at Evesham, Simon was killed and Henry's authority restored.

The Revitalizing of Religion

The Norman invasion brought to Sussex a resurgence of religious activity both economically and in a new style of architecture. A large amount of arable land in the county was granted to the religious houses of Normandy and the early lords built new priories and cells as dependencies of continental abbeys. The style of these new buildings also followed European design. The new church at Steyning was constructed under the direct supervision of the monks of Fecamp and bears a strong resemblance to the Romanesque buildings of northern France. The cathedral at Chichester was based on that of Caen and is much less ornate than the buildings of Lewes where William founded a priory *c.*1077 and gave it to monks from the Abbey of Cluny in Burgundy. This abbey was at that time in the forefront of European art and learning. Monastic buildings were later added to the complex, which was destroyed in the Dissolution of 1537.

In the early medieval period the church was the focal point of the community, housing and ancillary buildings radiating from it. Many of the small parish churches were rebuilt in the decades following 1066, but a cluster around Pulborough, in the west of the county, have survived on a simple chancel and nave design. There are also tiny, poorer churches of this construction that were built soon after the conquest, on the Downs or heathland where the population remained small. The so-called 'shepherds' churches' of the South Downs can be put into

CHICHESTER CATHEDRAL

The Anglican diocese of Chichester covers both sections of the county. The Cathedral Church of the Holy Trinity is not ideally placed geographically for it is but 7 miles (11km) from the western boundary of the see and 90 miles (144km) from the eastern. However, its spire is only yards from the traditional centre of the city, the market cross, and is a feature in the surrounding countryside.

It was William the Conqueror who brought about the transfer of the see from Selsey to Chichester in spite of Lewes being a larger and economically more important town, and the advantage of being more centrally situated in South Saxon territory. However, as most of the bishopric's estates were in the west of the county, financial factors took preference in the decision making.

It is unclear when building of the new cathedral commenced, probably *c.*1075 when the see was transferred to a temporary home at the Minster Church of St Peter. Originally, stone from the Isle of Wight was used in the construction. Progress was slow and it was not until 1184 that a scaled-down version of the original plan was finally consecrated. Three years later a city fire totally gutted the building. When rebuilding started, this time with Purbeck Marble, lack of finance necessitated the incorporation of sections of the original walls with the new. Over the next two centuries sporadic remedial work was undertaken, with various stones, including a stone spire modelled on that of Salisbury, until late in the fourteenth century when the cathedral was deemed to be complete.

In 1538 the shrine of St Richard was demolished and all the gold, silver and jewels purloined by Henry VIII. Later that century much-needed, but only partial, repairs funded by the sale of cathedral plate were made. These were mostly ineffective, for disasters occurred at regular intervals, the north-west tower falling *c.*1636.

At the beginning of the nineteenth century the building was in a very poor state. The first attempt at restoration took place between 1812–17, but this was only a cosmetic exercise and over a decade passed before significant repairs were started. These efforts continued throughout the early Victorian period but were unable to prevent the collapse of the tower and spire in 1861. These were quickly rebuilt (in five years), the replacement works being 6ft (2m) higher than the original.

A building of this magnitude requires constant attention. Repairs, restorations and the opening-up of new areas to the public are an ongoing process. One of the more interesting discoveries was made when underfloor heating was being installed in the south nave aisle: a well-preserved Roman mosaic was unearthed, confirming that the site has seen human activity for almost two millennia.

Fifty years ago a visual change occurred on the exterior of the building, when the lead coverings on the high roof were replaced with copper. As this material weathered and tarnished the famous turquoise green colour appeared. This 'green' phenomenon is not confined to Chichester, for the parish church at Harting has its spire shingled with the same material.

North Marden. A twelfth-century downland church constructed mainly of flint rubble.

this category. The eighteenth-century naturalist the Revd Gilbert White was scathing when writing about these diminutive places of worship, calling them 'mean' and 'little better than dovecotes'.

It was the Wealden area that saw the greatest upgrading and enlargement of the parish churches, reflecting the growth in population and increasing prosperity. The 'field' villages of the central Weald all received large numbers of settlers as the forest was opened up to agriculture, all of its churches receiving substantial increases in capacity.

Two other semi-religious groups that held considerable swaths of land in Sussex were the Knights Templar and the Knights Hospitaller. Both were founded after the first crusade to

Palestine and their members have been referred to as 'Christians with warlike tendencies' or 'mercenaries with Christian affiliations'. The original aim of the crusades was to restore the Holy Land to Christian rule; as time passed this objective became somewhat blurred with the participants looking on their journey as an adventure where they could gain both prestige and material goods. Richard I, as Duke of Aquitaine, was a great supporter of the cause and at one period of his reign was absent from his English kingdom for almost four years.

The Templars had a good publicity machine and their cause drew in many gifts of cash and land. These should have been used to protect the Christian enclave against the Muslims, but many of the donations seem to have remained in the local purse with only the interest going abroad. In 1125 the order was granted the manor and church of Shipley, then followed Sadlescombe and Sompting. Simon de Montfort in his war with King Henry at Lewes protected his troops with armour that bore the white cross of the crusaders; these suits were probably purchased with the proceeds of his earlier raid on the Templars' store of gold and silver.

In the early fourteenth century the Church conducted an orchestrated campaign against the organization. Torture, hearsay and concocted evidence were all used in a dossier of deceit. In 1312 Pope Clement V dissolved the order in Sussex and all their lands and property were transferred to the Knights Hospitaller who were based at Poling. This is now one of the smallest parishes in the county with an electoral role of only about 150.

The Opening Up of the Forest

The Weald was one part of England that was given an early identification as a distinctive region. When archers were recruited from these woods they were given the derogatory title of Wealdsmen. In the early medieval period it was still considered a backward area for land values there were low; this fact was accepted by the Exchequer because 'they were in the Weald'.

The main clearance of the Low Weald woodland took place between the late twelfth and the early fourteenth century by land-hungry farmers. The early settlements evolved from temporary summer shieling; permanent buildings were constructed only when the land came under year-round cultivation. It was the sheltered valleys, with the densest tree cover, that were the most favoured for grazing and swine foraging. Over time, this continual summer grazing and soil disturbance destroyed much of the emergent young growth and created pockets of open land. When much of the suitable, lower land was occupied new would-be farmers were forced up slope, building their homes around what were originally isolated hilltop churches. This form of development formed the nucleus for many of the Wealden hill villages, Mayfield, Heathfield and Wadhurst being typical examples.

The clearance of the High Weald was a long, gradual process. Before the mid thirteenth century there were only small, cleared patches where the trees had been destroyed. The residents in these were more backward and less affluent than the lowland farmers. Around this time an influx of pioneers arrived in the region. These entrepreneurs held their land from the landlords by a scheme of moneyed rents; no longer was the system of enforced periods of labour to the landlord implemented. These arrivals were know as 'asserters', from the old French word *essarter*, meaning to grub up trees. This fully describes their activity in the forest, but much of the mature woodland was unaffected, for their actions cleared mostly the scrub and brambles.

Increased pressure on the available land meant less-fertile marginal land had to be brought into cultivation. This led to the introduction of the artisan farmer, a smallholder who worked part-time on his holding and supplemented his income by other forms of self-employment. The piecemeal development of the Weald led to an irregular pattern of small, isolated fields joined by winding lanes. As the population increased and new farms and holdings were established, a dense network of these lanes developed. Many remain in the county's road system today, for, unlike other parts of the country where large open fields existed, this part of Sussex was little affected by the enclosures legislation.

Hunting Forests, Deer Parks and Chases

One feature of the Sussex countryside that developed indirectly from the woodland clearances was the establishment of the royal hunting forests and deer parks. To the Saxon kings hunting was enjoyment but with the Normans it was an obsession. The Saxons pursued the wild creature, parks of a type did exist but the idea of a fenced area that would house semi-domestic animals arrived with the Normans. The early captives in the deer parks were the red and the roe deer; in the twelfth century the fallow deer was introduced from the Continent and the number of parks increased dramatically for it was found that this creature was easier to retain in a park pale than the native types. The possession of a park now became a status symbol and, although a licence was needed before one could be established, they were no longer available only to the king and the great magnates. Ecclesiastical houses and the lesser gentry could now join society. The Earl of Arundel possessed twelve parks in Sussex; an out-of-county resident, the Archbishop of Canterbury, owned three and one of the county's lesser prelates, the Bishop of Chichester, could put his name to at least seven.

Deer were the main occupants of the parks and, since these are woodland animals, large areas remained tree-covered. Cattle and swine were allowed to summer graze in allotted areas but sheep and goats, which have similar eating habits to deer, were barred. A later introduction, again from the Continent, was the rabbit. These were encouraged to breed in artificial warrens constructed in fenced-off enclosures. Their destructive habits were soon recognized and young trees in the park had their trunks painted with tar to prevent coney damage.

A term that rarely occurs in the Sussex vocabulary is 'the chase'. This was an area of woodland and cultivation over which the landholder had the freedom to hunt 'beasts of the chase' that were normally available only to the king. These beasts and game included fox, hare, pheasant and partridge. The sporting Bishop of Chichester held two chases in the west of the county which today would encompass several parishes. In the eastern areas of the Wealden clay extensive sections of common and cleared land were highly prized chases, much to the annoyance of the tenant farmers.

The word forest did not exist in the Saxon tongue; to the Normans it was a legal term applied to land that was governed by a certain set of laws. This legislation was originally drafted for the protection of deer which only the monarch could hunt, but over time these laws became increasingly restrictive and related to the land as well as the wildlife. The boundaries of the forest were not normally defined on the

WINNIE-THE-POOH

The most famous resident of Ashdown Forest is the honey-loving bear 'Winnie-the-Pooh'. Although now well past retirement age, he first appeared in print in 1924 and has continued to delight children of all ages for the last seventy-six years.

The story of this character originated in Canada during the First World War. Winnie was a bear cub mascot of an infantry brigade. The bear accompanied the unit to England and, when it was posted to France, Winnie was presented to the London Zoo where it became the favourite animal of Christopher Robin, the son of the author A.A. Milne. Christopher's teddy bore the hardly original name of Edward, this was quickly amended to Winnie. The reason for the Pooh addition can be found in the introduction of another of the author's books *When We Were Very Young*.

Milne, who lived in the north-east corner of the forest, combined with a West Sussex illustrator Ernest Shepard to write a series of books about his son, Winnie and their friends from 100 Acre Wood. Eeyore, Piglet, Tigger, Kanga and Roo are all based on Christopher's favourite stuffed toys while Rabbit and Owl were natural residents of the wood.

This bear has found world-wide fame; his adventures have been translated into well over twenty-five languages (including Latin) and the character has been honoured by films, postage stamps and even telephone cards. Near to his home is the village of Hartfield; here at Pooh Corner you may buy memorabilia, refresh yourself at a Pooh café, then play Pooh sticks on his favourite bridge.

Fallow deer in modern Petworth Park.

ground, hills, rivers and other natural features usually sufficed. Occasionally, in sensitive areas, ditches or paling fences were needed. At their peak, the restrictions related to forests were calculated to cover about a third of English land. Once again, Sussex did not conform to this general rule, for its three largest forests totalled only 10 per cent of the Wealden land area. The Sussex forests were all situated on ridges of the High Weald. St Leonard's and Worth remain largely tree-covered, while Ashdown has been converted into the largest remaining area of lowland heath in south-east England.

Ashdown Forest covers almost 14,000 acres (5,700ha) and consists mainly of open heathland combined with small sections of retained and mature woodland. One report in the fourteenth century advised that the tree cover was so dense that guides were needed to convey travellers through the area. In all probability the author was referring to a much earlier period, for, just a century earlier, the forest supported over 100 deer, stocked over 2,000 cattle and fattened a similar number of swine. With this number of animals, and considering that it was relatively poor pasture, much of the forest must have already been cleared. The final act of deforestation came in the sixteenth century when much of the remaining timber was cut down to fuel the expanding iron industry.

It was climate change that had the greatest effect on the county in the medieval period. Early maps of the area show a deeply indented Sussex coastline, with each inlet having its own port or military base. In the second half of the twelfth century the English weather went into a marked deterioration. Floods became more common and Channel storms more severe. The old

Rye. These fortifications at one time provided protection for a secondary Cinque Port.

Winchelsea. An over-ambitious parish church for Edward's doomed new town.

THE CINQUE PORTS

In the century of Edwardian rule (1272—1377) Sussex remained largely immune from the domestic campaigns that occupied the attention of the three monarchs, but in 1339 the Channel ports became involved with the intermittent Hundred Years War with France; then several of the Cinque ports became victims of reprisal raids from over the water.

In medieval times there was no English navy; when the need arose the ports supplied both ships and crews to convey troops or supplies across the Channel. Even before 1066 there was a loose affiliation of the south-eastern ports, but after the conquest this grouping became more organized and, in exchange for providing a concerted defence strategy, the ports were given a degree of local autonomy and received certain fiscal concessions. These harbours were able to control completely the narrowest sector of the Channel until an unexplained breakdown of the system occurred in the mid fourteenth century. Originally there were five (*cinque*) ports in the confederation, only one of which, Hastings, was in the county. Later over thirty other south-eastern ports joined as associate members; Rye and Winchelsea joined before 1190 and were attached to Hastings, as were, but in a lower category of membership, Seaford and Eastbourne. The ports were at their most profitable and influential during the reign of Edward I.

The fourteenth century saw the decline of the federation; this was possibly due to the silting up of the harbours and also by changes in the methods of naval warfare. Larger ships with larger crews were emerging from both Southampton and the West Country ports; this reduced the contribution that was needed from the five. In 1569 the first national lottery was set up to secure funds to restore the ports, but the venture had little success since two decades later they were able to provide only six small ships in the defeat of the Spanish Armada.

town of Winchelsea was the main community to suffer; it received several inundations and, in 1288, a combination of storms and high tides completely changed the profile of the area. The town, together with a large part of Romney Marsh, disappeared under the waves. In preparation for this expected disaster Edward I had already planned for a new town to be built on a low inland ridge and totally safe from the sea. The town was to be laid out in a grid pattern with thirty-nine rectangular plots interconnected by right-angled streets. There was also to be good inland access and a deep-water harbour. But the planning did not take into account the fickleness of the Channel, for longshore drift, accelerated by storms soon isolated the town. Today the shoreline is a mile distant and the site was never fully completed. Drift also brought about the demise of other of the county's early ports: Seaford, Pevensey and Hastings all accompanying Winchelsea into oblivion.

Reclamation of the marshes inland from Pevensey took place in the twelfth and the thir-teenth centuries. It was a relatively simple operation to convert the levels into pasture. Improved drainage and the construction of a protective shingle beach were the basic needs. In 1287, a year before the Winchelsea disaster, the shingle was breached and the grazing again became saline.

The weather continued to worsen in the early years of the fourteenth century. Four times between 1315 and 1321 there were crop failures and in the years 1324 and 1325 thousands of sheep were drowned in neighbouring Kent. The report probably referred to Romney Marsh, where the majority of the county's sheep grazed; if this is so, then it is extremely unlikely that Sussex escaped the deluge. With non-existent harvests, grain prices soared and, with a society that had few long-term storage facilities, famine and disease followed. The bad years finally came to an end and the prospects for the county looked brighter. Then in 1348 came the arrival from the Continent of the plague or the Black Death.

6. LATE MEDIEVAL AND TUDOR YEARS

By the middle of the fourteenth century the population of England was at a level three times that of pre-Conquest times and, since 90 per cent of these peoples were rural dwellers, the countryside was existing above its realistic capacity. A succession of poor harvests and the arrival of the plague completely changed the situation.

The epidemic was not confined to Britain nor even Europe but had afflicted all the known world. The strain of the 'Black Death' that devastated Britain originated in China and Inner Asia. It was transmitted to Europeans (1347) when a Kipchak army, besieging a Genoese trading post in the Crimea, catapulted plague-infested corpses into the town. The disease was brought into Europe by Italian trading ships using the port of Venice. It quickly spread through the Continent and arrived in Dorset during the summer of 1348. The disease arrived on French ships and the fleas of the black rat. It was thought that the fleas passed on the bacillus either through their faeces (then inhaled by humans) or from their bites, this being a natural hazard for the population at that time. Recent research suggests that inter-human contact was the more likely agent, given the rapid spread of the disease across the country. The time from infection to death was usually less than a week and in his last few days the victim was highly contagious. Within eighteen months of the first outbreak over a half of Britain's population had succumbed.

There were repeat outbreaks of the plague in Britain between 1361 and 1396, each reducing the population yet further. Most of the graphic accounts of the deaths that occurred during these visitations relate to the larger towns, but the rural communities also encountered great suffering. Although the spring crops had been sown before the disease's first arrival, few hands remained to gather the harvest or control the livestock.

The Black Death has often been advanced as the reason for the 'lost' villages of the county, but more probably it only accelerated a decline that had been in existence for almost a century. A list of villages shows a predominance of sites on or near to the downland ridge. Originally these settlements comprised mainly arable holdings, but, with the large-scale introduction of sheep, this part of Sussex adopted a different form of agriculture. Sheep would provide two crops: meat for local consumption and fleeces, where the excess could readily be sold or traded. As the price of wool increased more areas were converted to sheep-rearing. The Downs were not the only area to be converted, for the landlords of the adjacent, lower lands soon realized that more profits came from the animals than from cereals. Fewer people were needed to tend sheep than were required in arable farming and this, in effect, created an early model for the later clearances in Scotland, where sheep replaced humans in the countryside; the deportees largely relocated to the towns or ports.

Much of the Sussex wool was exported to the Continent, but the duties imposed by Edward I on the fleeces to pay for his military campaigns lessened the overseas demand. The start of the Anglo-French wars finally killed the export trade and further depressed the market. The land- and the sheep-owners found it difficult to remain solvent, so the obvious first choice was to reduce the work force. This led to a further exodus from the country into the towns.

The Lost Villages

The plague was instrumental in the break-up of the traditional village community in Sussex. With the death of half of their tenants, the holdings became vacant and provided no income or services to the lord. With this labour shortage

Herstmonceux Castle.

the survivors were in a strong position to negotiate an improvement in the terms of their employment. Rent for their land and wages for their employment now took over from the previous arrangement of services and payment in kind. The manorial lords were in no position to impose restrictive conditions and the enclosure of land by voluntary consent between tenant and owner began to be established. This system was almost complete by the Tudor period and pre-dates that of the Midland shires by almost two centuries. With a secure holding and cash in his pocket, the smallholder began to vacate the compact village to build his home on his own land. In several cases this left the church, which was previously the focal point of the community, remaining alone in complete isolation.

Lullington in East Sussex is a good example of such a church, although here it is thought that the post-plague survivors moved en masse from the hillside to a lower, level site.

There are over sixty recorded lost villages in Sussex, two-thirds of which may be attributed to the events of the mid- to late-fourteenth century. Many of the downland settlements succumbed totally to the changing agricultural practices and were abandoned; others were reduced to a gap-toothed cluster of domestic housing. One example of the former is Upper Barpham, in the Downs behind Worthing. Here an inspection of the site would reveal no trace of its buildings, but, when viewed from above, on a downland ridge the outline of several buildings can be traced showing through the turf. The village was

East Marden. The centre of the community, the village well.

Lullington. The sole survivor from a deserted village.

Coombes Church. This building and an adjacent farm are the only survivors of an Adur valley settlement.

important enough to appear in the Domesday survey and excavations of the church foundations have revealed a substantial building with varying types of architecture spanning several centuries. Nearby were found several shallow graves; these contained children's bones, indicat-

BUXTED

The medieval village of Buxted was a north–south linear development on either side of its thirteenth-century church. Taking its name from the place where box trees grow, it survived the troubles of the fourteenth century only to be abandoned 400 years later and then only on the whim of the landowner. Thomas Medley pulled down the old manor house and built the present Park House a little to the south of the church. To create privacy for his new home and for the scenic environment of a deer park, the village was moved almost a mile (1.5km) to the north-east. The arrival of the

railway encouraged further development around this relocated housing. There remain noticeable signs of house platforms on either side of the church, and it is believed that other ground features were destroyed when the churchyard was extended. In 1968 the old village well was discovered and a comprehensive search of the area a few years later produced a great amount of medieval pottery and other artefacts. A public right of way follows the line of the original village street and other connecting footpaths cross the deer park to the modern village.

Bodiam Castle.

ing that the plague had found its way to this isolated spot. The advent of aerial photography, showing the foundations of buildings not visible on the ground, has greatly assisted in the study of these communities. In the Downs to the north-west of Chichester lie the four Marden parishes. Today, North Marden is represented by a church, farm and undulations where former buildings stood; Up Marden a church and little else; East Marden has a church of similar date and is the only village to retain a nucleated settlement. The western village, ironically, lost its religious building in the sixteenth century but thanks to an influx of modern housing is now the largest of the four.

Several small communities on the Manhood peninsular disappeared during this period. Storms and tidal erosion accounted for Bracklesham and what remained of Old Selsey, while others that were protected from the waves either suffered from the common combination of agricultural decline and the plague or were unable to compete in the world of cross-channel trading.

There are only two instances of lost villages in the Wealden district: Isfield, where the whole community unexplainably moved away from the church; and a later departure, Buxted.

Sussex not only had to contend with the post-Black Death problems but also suffered from periodic raids from the French during the Hundred Years War. This conflict began in 1337 and, for the first twenty years, the English were largely successful. Two notable victories at Crecy in 1346 and at Poitiers ten years later saw large sections of France return to English sover-

Herstmonceux Castle.

eignty. English fortunes later ebbed and the Sussex coastline came under increasing attack from marauding French forces. These were not intended as invasions and could be likened to nuisance reprisal raids. At one period the continentals followed the old Viking tradition and based a flotilla at the Isle of Wight. The raids all took place during the summer months and no port nor coastal settlement escaped the harassment. Even after the war ended the Sussex landowners considered there to be a threat from across the Channel and this belief led to the construction of three of Sussex's best known castles.

Bodiam Castle was built in 1385 by a veteran of the French wars as a second line of defence for the Rother valley. Seven years earlier, Rye at the mouth of the river had been sacked and, although some distance inland from the coast, the river at Bodiam still had a width in excess of 300yd (275m). The castle was based on a French model and was one of the best designed defensive structures in England.

Herstmonceux was built by another war veteran in 1440. Officially it was created to defend the Pevensey levels against a foreign landing. Moated, and with only narrow approaches, technically it was a castle, but in spirit it was only a crenellated country house. Like Bodiam, it too was inspired by continental models and, being constructed of brick, it had the distinction of being the first large building in the county to use this material since the Roman occupation.

Sundial. Standing in the Herstmonceux Castle gardens, this timepiece is a reminder that the building was once home to the Royal Observatory.

Territories in France continued to be gained and lost and the apprehension of a French invasion continued well into the reigns of the Tudor kings. The monarchy considered the coastal lands of Sussex to be England's first line of defence. Many of the earlier castles and fortified houses were starting to show their age and so Henry VIII decided on a new chain of fortifications that was to stretch from Kent to Cornwall. Sussex received one prestigious building at Camber. In the early 1540s £23,000 was spent on enlarging and refurbishing a structure that had been built only three decades earlier. Designed to protect the Rother levels, it never repaid its building costs since later in the century the river changed its course and left the castle isolated among the marshes.

Rural Unrest

With the post-plague reduction in the available labour, the extent of land under cultivation followed a similar downward trend, the marginal lands in the High Weald being the first to be abandoned. Where the tenant or villein faced a choice, it was the most profitable holding that continued to receive the attention of the plough. The early bargaining power of the work force was quickly eradicated, rents were increased and wages reduced. The war against France was proving expensive and new forms of taxation were introduced to fund its continuation. Unlike the earlier taxes which brought a modest return of revenue through the increased use of the Channel ports, the populace of south-east England could see no benefits arising from these new impositions. The introduction of a poll tax, where a fixed levy was raised on every individual regardless of his wealth, led in 1381 to a rural uprising known as the Peasants' Revolt. Obviously a number of peasants did become involved, but the main organizers and participants were the villeins and landholding tenants. The revolt was confined to the south-eastern counties, but Sussex did not become involved; being ever mindful of the threat from France, the

leaders of the revolt declined the attendance of any Sussex resident living within 10 miles (16km) of the coast. After a confrontation with Richard II in London, the rebels dispersed, leaving behind their murdered leader. Repression duly followed.

In 1450 a further revolt occurred, into which Sussex was dragged. Led by Jack Cade, this rebellion started in neighbouring Kent and quickly spread into the county through a perennial hotbed of peasant unrest – the village of Brede. On this occasion major support for the cause came from the overtaxed upper classes and the clergy. The mayor and citizens of Chichester voiced their distaste of the punitive extractions, as did the Prior of Lewes. Cade suffered the same fate as the leader of the previous revolt, and when the inevitable reprisals arrived it was the lowly peasant who took the heaviest beating.

With its partial abandonment, the Weald once again became home for many types of undesirable. Law enforcement was undertaken privately by landlords and then it only covered their lands, property and work force. The control of unproductive land was considered to be uneconomic and unenforceable. This no-man's land helped, as in so many previous occasions, to isolate much of the county from the domestic unrest that was a feature of these times. Sussex survived the lean years of the mid-fourteenth century, and thanks to its industries and contact with the outside world, became largely self-contained and prospered.

For the next 200 years from the end of the century, the Low Weald enjoyed a boom economy. The supplies that were needed by the flourishing cottage industries could be obtained locally from the farming community. This trading pact ensured a fair return for both the supplier and the consumer. The wild lands to the north were no barrier to trade since the Channel offered unlimited opportunities for export. But these were also years of the heavy taxation that continued to be imposed by both the Crown and Parliament.

The Old Shop, Bignor, a typical country Wealden house.

The Arrival of the Noble Families

The great families of Sussex developed slowly through the decades, with almost all tracing their roots back to the knights that William brought over from Normandy. Originally landowners or holders, as their wealth increased, they were able to increase the size of their estates. These were usually purchased outright but occasionally a cheaper policy of leasing was adopted. Rewards for services rendered formed another avenue pursued by several nobles, titles usually accompanying the gift of these lands. If the recipient was lucky, he had a choice of titles to accept since land was not always given that was adjacent to his home estate. Wealth encourages wealth, as many of the nobility found. A profitable second income, that of money lending, was practised by many of the aristocracy, the beneficiaries including the lower gentry, the church, or in rare cases the Crown itself.

The Earl of Arundel, Richard Fitzalan III, who died in 1397, was typical of the wealthy nobility, although he was wealthier than most since he was considered to be among the six richest men in England. The Honour of Arundel was acquired in 1243 by one of his ancestors through marriage, and a century later Lewes was added from the de Warenne inheritance. His father concentrated on increasing the West Sussex estate and Richard inherited sixty-four manors, twelve forests, seven deer parks and over 23,000 acres (9,300ha) of arable and woodland. Arundel became the administrative headquarters for these and, although he spent time at Lewes, his attention did not live up to the expectation of the citizens of the town. A refusal to defend the castle unless the costs were met by the local community probably accounted for an isolated incident in the Peasants' Revolt when the fortress was broken into and damaged. Names of other Sussex nobility that recur throughout this period of history include the Sackvilles, the de Bohuns and the Etchinghams, all of Norman descent.

Domestic Housing of the Period

There are few houses, apart from the castles and large manors, that can accurately be dated back to the thirteenth century; those that can are almost always stone-built. There are many four-teenth-century homes that have survived the passage of time and remain in habitation today, albeit much improved and often completely disguised. These early domestic buildings may be roughly divided into three types: those that were home to the lowest stratum of the population, the peasants; the larger timber-framed buildings which accommodated the farmers and urban craftsmen; and the great houses of the nobility.

The dwellings of the peasants normally consisted of two rooms: a living area that was partitioned at one end for sleeping accommodation. These buildings closely resembled the long houses of upland Britain which were elongated in relation to their width. A later change of design added a third room which was usually used for storage. Animals may have at times been housed in this extension, but normally only as an emergency measure since no drainage channel was constructed. A mid-fifteenth-century survey recorded in the downland village of Alciston shows a further improvement in design. The buildings now comprised rooms on two floors, which substantially increased the space available for the living accommodation and storage. It is only through such surveys that a picture of these primitive homes emerges, for in no way could they be regarded as permanent structures.

The Wealden House

There was a continuous programme of improvements made to farmsteads both before and after the Black Death; this was noticeable in the Weald where the plentiful supply of timber led to the construction of more substantial and durable buildings. By far the commonest design was the timber-framed jetted structure. The idea of jetty-ing, where the upper storey extends over the lower, is believed to have originated in Scandinavia and is only practicable in a timber structure. In towns the jettying of buildings provided pedestrians with some protection against the weather. This was not effective in the countryside but the design was popular with the rural builder, the first houses of this type arriving in the county in the fourteenth century. The basic design, with local derivations, soon became universally accepted and, by the end of the century, the 'Wealden' had not only captivated the area bearing its name but had extended over the Downs and into Hampshire.

These buildings were the acme of medieval house design and were found in isolated farms, villages and market towns. They were built largely for the middle classes, the yeoman farmers, the craftsmen and traders, and there are few parishes in Sussex that have not retained an example of the design. They have suffered from improvement more than any other form of medieval building, the most common form of restructuring results in the space below the jetties being obliterated by additional facades. In the towns many were converted and used as inns, while others were extended to enclose a courtyard. Rye holds two examples of the converted inn: 'The Mermaid' and 'The Flushing', while the house of St Mary's at Bramber is believed to be the remaining arm of a courtyard building.

The original infilling between the timbers of wattle and daub was slowly superseded by the use of bricks, but the general appearance of the building changed little for it was normal practice to limewash the complete exterior, infill and

Mermaid Street, Rye.

Rye. A 'magpie' form of an urban Wealden.

THE WEALD AND DOWNLAND OPEN AIR MUSEUM

This museum is situated in the village of Singleton, 6 miles (10km) to the north of Chichester, and was founded in 1967 with the aim to establish a centre where traditional homes and workplaces from the south-east of England could be exhibited. The buildings have all been rescued from destruction, dismantled and re-erected on the site.

The exhibits, which number around forty, range from a charcoal burner's hovel, through barns and sheds, to farmhouses and urban shops. The earliest buildings date from the thirteenth century and one of the latest is a local school from the early 1800s. Probably the showpiece of the collection is a Wealden farmhouse of the early fifteenth century. This particular example came from Kent, but it is typical of the style of many farmsteads in the Sussex Weald. The characteristic feature of this Wealden type is the recessed front wall of the central, open hall. The rooms on either side are jettied out on the upper floors; but, as the hall has no upper floor and consequently no jetty, it gives this section a recessed appearance.

A later timber-framed home from Midhurst illustrates the building design that had arrived by the end of the following century. This is a typical yeoman's small farmhouse; gone is the central hall and in come two storeys, plus an enclosed fire and chimney that provide part of the house with heating. One feature that remains unchanged from its medieval predecessor is the unglazed windows. Another exhibit from Sussex is a pair of shops from Horsham; again fifteenth-century, they come from the market area of the town and together are probably a second- or third-generation building that was originally introduced as a replacement for temporary market stalls.

Midhurst. A stand-alone building with brick infill.

frame. The magpie appearance that is popular today is a relatively recent cosmetic addition. The windows were unglazed and usually sited high up on the north and the east wall. There was no standard roofing material; in the corn-growing areas, where straw was freely available, thatch predominated. Where this material was used, by-laws insisted that this too was lime-washed as a deterrent against fire. Clay tiles appeared, but mainly in the east of the county, while along the coast imported slates from Cornwall or Brittany were installed. In the central and the northern Weald, although heavy, Horsham slab limestone was often used.

Towards the end of the Middle Ages there was a marked shift in the economic and social life of Sussex from the coastal lands into the Weald. It was this area to the north of the Downs that saw the greatest building of country homes. Much of this building can be attributed to the resurgence of the iron industry. A few were commissioned direct by the iron masters; Bateman's at Burwash, which was once home to the writer Rudyard Kipling, is a prime example. Others came from the profits made by the associated sale of timber, or families who held shares in the burgeoning iron trade. Rich London merchants were also now beginning to seek a country retreat not too distant from their workplace, an invasion that has continued to the present day.

Unlike the basic design of domestic architecture for the middle ranks of society, where the Weaden house ruled supreme, there was no uniformity in the buildings of the gentry. Many of the manor houses developed from smaller

Wakehurst Place. An Elizabethan truncated mansion.

dwellings, enlarged and improved to the owner's or builder's whims. For new buildings, timber and stone were the materials most commonly used, for it was not until late in this period of great rebuilding that brick construction became more common. Although Sussex had a plentiful supply of suitable clays, bricks were shunned by the local builders.

Many of the earlier manor houses were moated. It is not known whether this was originally done as protection for the house and stock, for the waters corralled more than the dwelling; or whether the feature was used as a status symbol. A few of these moated sites still remain, but of the majority only detailed investigation based on local names and documentation, assisted by aerial photography, reveals their previous existence. The *Victorian History of The English Counties,* *Sussex*, published in 1905, lists fifty-seven known sites. a local historian claims a private list of over 230, which may be excessive. The Low Weald, as one would expect, contained the greatest concentration, for here surface water was usually available and the impervious clay acted as an ideal retainer. The upper Arun was one river that spawned a chain of houses with this feature. The names of Pallingham, Harsfold, Lee and Okehurst are today just farms recorded on maps of the area; in Tudor times they were not homes of yeoman farmers but non-ecclesiastical outliers of the Bishop of Chichester.

In the Tudor period the 'renaissance' style of architecture became the vogue, with the conversion of older buildings into a more flamboyant form. This change of style largely affected the interior furnishings, leaving the exterior to follow a slow progression into brick. The last timber mansion to be built in Sussex started its life in 1612; by then the demands of the iron and shipbuilding industries had greatly reduced the stocks of suitable timber and by necessity other materials had to be used. The Elizabethan type of building with its symmetrical 'E' plan was often a reconstructed section of an earlier house where the whole enclosed a central courtyard. A good example of this later form may be seen at Wakehurst.

Tudor Towns

In the early sixteenth century only one Sussex town, Chichester, was listed among the top forty towns of England, with a population of around 1,500, which equated to that in Domesday; it managed to creep into the lower end of the list. This dearth of sizeable towns indicates that the county's economy remained based on the agricultural produce from estates and farms. In the Subsidy Rolls of 1524 upwards of twenty market towns appeared, but few were of any size, a population of 500 taxpayers being extremely rare. The listed communities could in no way be described as centres of wealth, their prosperity only equalling that of many smaller villages. East Grinstead and Uckfield, both founded about 1250 on opposite sides of the High Weald forest, were, almost three centuries later, little more than short streets of intermittent housing. Certain towns such as Horsham, Cuckfield and Petworth, whose increased wealth was due to the adoption of the cloth trade, began to flourish. However, their gain was to the detriment of other older centres, and, overall, the county remained primarily dependent on agriculture.

The Sussex ports also went into decline. Mention has been made of the storm damage

COWDRAY

Cowdray was the greatest Tudor mansion ever to be built in Sussex and was also one of the first. The original residence was a Norman castle built on a hill overlooking the western Rother and adjacent to the town. In the fourteenth century the castle was abandoned for the moated house that stood a little to the north and on the opposite river bank. This second house is believed to have been built towards the end of the thirteenth century and remained the principal residence of the de Bohun family for over 150 years. The earliest beginnings of the present building may be dated to between 1520 and 1530 and were inaugurated by Sir David Owen who, through marriage, had inherited the de Bohun estates. The old house became the nucleus for the new mansion and, although the extent of his work is uncertain, it is thought that he was responsible for the quadrangular courtyard design.

In 1529 the house and the estate were sold in dubious circumstances by Owen's son to Sir William Fitzwilliam, Earl of Southampton. He and his successor, his half-brother Anthony Browne, were responsible for completing the transformation of the property. Permission was received in 1535 'to build walls and towers ... and to battle and fortify'. Henry VIII paid the first of several visits to Cowdray in 1538, the royal tradition continuing after his death with a visit in 1552 by his son Edward VI to the Browne house. Reports indicated that on every occasion the visitors were well entertained by their host. The house was largely completed by 1550, with small alterations being made later in the century. These were mainly enlargements and changes of design to the existing windows. The tall window in the great hall was one of the earliest examples of the extensive use of glass in a domestic building. Another innovation for the house was the installation of a piped water supply. This was gravity-fed from a pump house sited above the main house and about 100yd (90m) distant. This 'round house' has been converted into a unique residential unit and remains occupied today. Sadly, this cannot be said of the main building, for in 1793 the house and much of the furnishing were destroyed by fire.

and drift problems that affected the Cinque Ports, but others further to the west also suffered. Shoreham, after an early period of prosperity when a substantial church was built in anticipation of a population explosion, became the victim of the River Adur. Sea floods and erosion continually forced the river eastwards, a sand and shingle bar finally blocking the port. The river responded by submerging the southern half of the town. It was not until centuries later, when the estuary was canalized, that Shoreham once again became a thriving port.

Newhaven town and its port were born in the 1530s, thanks to a new channel that was cut through the shingle bar that was blocking the mouth of the River Ouse. This new town was the only one to be created in the south-eastern counties in over a hundred years, and superseded the silted Seaford. With the decline of these ports came the associated downturn in shipbuilding, but the Chichester Harbour ports continued to thrive and Itchenor, in the seventeenth century, brought about a rejuvenation of the industry. At one stage plans were made to enlarge the port to rival that of Southampton. Thankfully for the area and for West Sussex the idea was shelved. The development of the Hampshire port as a distribution centre for the south of England took most of the export trade away from Sussex, effectively forcing the county's merchant fleet to operate as coastal traders.

Medieval Industries

The processing of iron had existed in the Sussex Weald from the time of the Celts, but until 1496,

Cowdray House.

when the blast furnace arrived from the Low Countries, the industry was small, unorganized and largely family-run. For centuries the base metal was obtained by layering charcoal and iron ore in a simple furnace. After ignition air was forced into the furnace by bellows. Two or three days later a plug of semi-molten metal formed at the bottom of the structure; after cooling the plug was extracted and shaped at a forge. This 'bloomery' process, as it was known, was slow and unable to guarantee a continuous supply of metal.

Along with the blast furnace came a wave of migrant workers from northern France; they oversaw the construction and operation of the new technique. Put simply, the process involved a permanent structure with a long furnace chamber and wide chimney. A series of bellows projected into this chamber; these were compressed in turn by a rotating wheel, forcing a continuous stream of air into the furnace. The wheel could be worked by oxen or horses but more commonly water-power was used. With the increased draught the process occurred more quickly and at a much higher temperature; this allowed the molten metal to be drained from the bottom of the chamber into moulds. As the furnace was top-filled the process could be maintained almost indefinitely. When in full production the output from one blast furnace equalled that of thirty of the earlier bloomeries.

Another boost to the Sussex economy came in 1543 with the successful casting of a cannon. Previously these were made by banding together straight strips of metal to form a primitive and inefficient barrel. The Weald now became the 'Black Country' of England, a position it did not relinquish until a shortage of fuel resulted in its loss to the Midlands where there were unlimited supplies of coal to fuel the furnaces. In 1574 there were 110 recorded ironworks in Sussex; seventy-five years later this number had declined to eighty and by the beginning of the eighteenth century there were fewer than twenty remaining in operation.

In the boom years little thought was given to replacing the felled timber. Cash-hungry landlords felled indiscriminately and even the Crown was complicit, for large swaths of Ashdown Forest fell to the axe. The potential fuel crisis was realized in 1574 when a licence was required to manufacture or sell cannon. A few years later an Act was passed that prohibited the cutting of timber for processing into fuel for ironmaking within 14 miles (20km) of London. This was soon followed by a further restriction, this time to protect the local shipbuilding industry, with the ban to operate just 12 miles (17km) from the coast. In 1585 an embargo was placed on the construction of new ironworks in the east of the county; the iron masters soon circumnavigated this by an expansion centred on Fernhurst and the upper Arun valley.

The rapid expansion of the industry was matched by an equally sharp decline. Although the shortage of fuel was the primary reason for its demise, the Civil War in the seventeenth century and poor transport links played their part. Many furnaces were controlled by the supporters of Charles I, these became the target for Parliament and were decommissioned or destroyed by the army.

The roads in medieval Sussex were no worse than those in any other clay-based county; but by the seventeenth century they were notoriously bad. Ironworking was a year-round operation and tracks that were able to support a light farm cart in winter were totally unable to accommodate the loads of timber and iron that were imposed upon them. As early as 1585 another Act was passed, this time compelling the iron masters to contribute to the upkeep of the roads: for every ton of iron carried, 'one load of sinder, gravell, stone or chalke' should be laid on the highway. The Act proved to be unenforceable and there was no improvement until the arrival of the turnpike system two centuries later.

The fifteenth- and sixteenth-century iron workings had more impact on the Wealden landscape than the industrial activities of any previous period. The short-term reduction of the tree cover was undoubtedly a negative legacy, but one that was more than compensated for by the

Furnace Pond, Slaugham. A wider example of an Iron Age reservoir.

creation of hammer ponds in numerous valleys. These brought, when their active life was over, an attractive new feature to the area.

A small, localized industry was founded in the north-west corner of the county, again by immigrant workers. Glass-making needed three primary ingredients: the right type of sand, timber for fuel and bracken that could be burnt to provide potash. A small area on either side of the Surrey border was able to provide all three. As early as 1560 small manufacturers of bottle glass had been established at Kirdford and the adjacent parishes. Into this area came French entrepreneurs, introducing new, green glass consumables and an improved product for window glaz-ing. It was a small work force that made the goods and, although prices were high, this proved no deterrent to the Elizabethans. Business was buoyant, so much so that glass-making was in direct competition with iron for the available timber. In 1615 a protectionist Act was passed prohibiting the further use of wood fuel for glass-making. Two years previously a monopolistic patent for coal-fired furnaces had been granted to a Staffordshire company. Together, these two killed the Sussex industry and by 1730 all production had ceased. This successful enterprise had lasted less than seventy years, doomed by outside protectionist interference.

Kirdford. The diamond of this village sign is made from fragments of locally-produced glass.

A cottage industry that once again developed with continental technology was the cloth trade. Cloth making, beyond the needs of the local market, had originated in the thirteenth century; this was boosted by the arrival of Flemish weavers. The hub of the operation was at Cranbrook in Kent, and a corridor of cloth towns, on an east–west axis, sprang up through central Sussex. All the towns involved were only a short distance from the source of the raw material, the downland sheep. Domestic out-workers were responsible for the carding, spinning and weaving, with the finishing and marketing controlled by a small number of merchants. After two centuries of prosperity the fortunes of this rural industry paralleled those of iron, disappearing completely by the end of the seventeenth century.

The Politics of Tudor England

English politics went through a hundred years of turbulence following the plague. Wars, plots, conspiracies and murders among the ruling classes continued unchecked. The Hundred Years War with France was finally lost, only to be followed by a thirty-years domestic squabble between the houses of Lancaster and York. Sussex, apart from some involvement in the two peasant revolts, remained largely unaffected by the confusion that existed in other parts of the country.

The crowning of Henry VII in 1485 introduced the house of Tudor into England. This was a dynasty that lasted for 118 years and is recognized as a period of cultural significance which gave the world, among others, the playwrights Shakespeare and Marlowe. Henry brought stability to the country and his marriage to the daughter of Edward IV largely resolved the antagonism that existed between the houses of Lancaster and York. The corruption that existed in the earlier Parliaments was ended, a small House of Lords was allowed to continue with a lower house, the Commons, created with its Members elected from the shire counties. Henry's foreign policy was based on trade and

alliances, not expensive wars. When he died he left his son a peaceful and united country with its treasury awash with funds. Henry VIII had a different outlook on life and the actions he took during his reign had a profound effect on the country and the monarchs who followed him.

Henry VIII and the Dissolution of the Monasteries

Whereas his father was a peace lover, Henry VIII, and particularly in the early years of his reign, revelled in war and it was only in his later years that his interests changed into an obsession to create a male heir. Successful campaigns were waged against Scotland and France. These costly excursions, plus the upgrading of the navy, quickly depleted the royal purse and by the mid 1520s England was virtually bankrupt.

In the late fifteenth century there was a growing feeling of resentment against the Roman Church. Over the centuries it had become extremely rich, with a landholding of over one-sixth of England's total. Its administration had become lax and it had lost touch with the leaders of lay society. At the local level, priests and monks remained in harmony with their congregations, but the dissatisfaction was felt towards the invisible hierarchy.

Henry's war with Rome was precipitated by his wish to divorce his first wife Catherine, who was his late elder brother's widow, and marry Anne Boleyn. Not unexpectedly the request was turned down by the Pope; Henry reacted by declaring himself to be the leader of the English Church. His position was confirmed in 1534 by the Act of Supremacy which entitled the king to be both head of state and head of the Church. This now nationalistic church received a further boost when the Latin liturgy, which few congregations could understand, was replaced by one in English. Many of the continental immigrant workers who were instrumental in the development of the iron, glass and cloth trades, were fleeing from Catholic persecution and they not only brought new skills but also radical ideas for the organization of this new church and its

Michelham Priory.

role in society. Theirs was a simpler form of teaching. Based on the Greek New Testament and honed by Lutheranism, it was a form of religion more easily understood by the masses. Henry was neither a Protestant nor a traditional Catholic and his inconsistency created a dilemma for many moderates who were undecided as to where their allegiance should lie; to the state or the Church? This rift in society proved to be a recurring problem for the next 150 years.

Henry saw the dissolution, or requisitioning, of the monasteries and other religious establishments as a two-pronged attack on the Roman Church. Not only would it eradicate or substantially reduce its influence in the country, but it would create a new source of revenue to replenish his much-depleted exchequer. The monaster-

ies and other religious houses were allowed to remain; it was their landed estates that were the king's target. These were then sold to the highest bidder or occasionally given to a supporter for services rendered.

The Sussex houses were greatly affected by the transfers. The first to suffer in the county was the house of Bayham. By 1525, although rich in land, it was deep in debt and had suffered from maladministration for many years. It was requisitioned by Cardinal Wolsey, a confidant of Henry, who was seeking funds for his Cardinal College at Oxford (now Christchurch). This seizure appears to have been the only time on which the residents and locals opposed a closure. To appease them the abbot was temporally reinstated, but the revolt was soon quelled and the ringleaders imprisoned.

Boxgrove Priory. Now an oversized parish church.

There was a lull in the closure programme until the mid 1530s when many of the Sussex houses surrendered. Lewes went in 1537 and was followed a year later by Battle and Robertsbridge. Although the buildings were not the target of the dissolution many did suffer. Lewes was gifted to the minister responsible for the closures, Thomas Cromwell, who, until he was executed two years later, after falling foul of the king, spent his last years demolishing as much of the building as possible. Battle was presented to the Master of Cowdray who immediately began a conversion from abbey to grand house. The transfer of many smaller houses from religious to secular status occurred county-wide. A well-preserved example is that of Michelham Priory; originally founded as an Augustinian priory in 1229, it was converted into a moated Tudor residence and now boasts the longest remaining water-filled surround in the country. A few establishments decided to convert to the new faith, as at Boxgrove, where the priory became an oversized parish church.

There is little record as to how the dissolution affected the occupants of the religious houses. The majority of the monks and nuns are believed to have transferred easily into the new order; those with a stronger conscience appeared to have received generous pensions to allow them to continue with a secular lifestyle. The tenants continued to pay and the servants continued to serve their new masters.

Before his death in 1547, Henry rekindled his disagreements with his old adversaries Scotland and France. These forays again proved costly and for a second time the king was forced to debase the currency. This action saw the return of inflation and a new round of labour unrest;

the uprisings had mainly an economic basis but they also allowed the workforce to express its concern with the changes in religious practices. The Catholic Earl of Arundel met the leaders of a local revolt and, after listening to their complaints, dispensed summary justice. This was accepted by all involved for it was his authority that they honoured, not that of the spendthrift monarchy.

Bloody Mary

Henry was succeeded by his frail son Edward VI. His reign and that of his half-sister Mary saw the country embroiled in a decade of religious extremes. Edward was a Protestant whose principal concern was to bring the country into his faith. The resident clergy were taken from their parishes and told to travel the shire counties as missionaries in an attempt to convert the masses into the new form of belief and practice. The rural economy was suffering from rampant inflation and, when further raids were made on church property, the proceeds were not used for the relief of the working classes but were channelled into the coffers of the privileged few. Surprisingly, apart from the single Arundel revolt, Sussex remained immune from further uprisings.

The arrival of Mary on the throne was largely welcomed by the English people; they had tasted Protestantism and it was not to their liking and were only too happy to revert to the position of five years previously: a Catholic country but independent of Rome. This was not to be, for the new queen was a headstrong, devout Catholic who believed that she had been called by God to save England from heresy. Her marriage to Phillip II of Spain was not popular since it not only meant that England returned to the subjugation of the Pope but that the country was now a province of Spain.

Mary decided that the erring Protestants needed to be taught a lesson. Her Christian beliefs did not encompass forgiveness, only the burning of the miscreants would suffice. The bishops were the first to suffer, then folk of hum-bler rank followed. Between 1555 and 1558 over 300 souls perished in the flames, of those twenty-seven, men and women, came from Sussex. The greatest massacre in the county took place in the market place of Lewes where ten were despatched. This act of barbarism strengthened the resolve of the residents and ensured that the town remained a Protestant stronghold. Chichester, Brighton and Steyning were other centres to supply victims. There was one section of the community that escaped persecution – those who had made fortunes from the spoliation of the church remained silent. Martyrdom was not for them; the retention of their estates was their foremost objective.

A decade earlier England had been poor but proud and independent, now she had been dragged by Spain into a losing war with France. Not only was the country facing an external foe but large sections of the people were being attacked by their own monarch. It is little wonder that when Mary died the country celebrated and toasts were raised to the new queen, Elizabeth.

The Elizabethans

Elizabeth was twenty-five when she inherited from her sister a poor, divided country surrounded by enemies. The first ten years of her reign were spent repairing the damage that had been inflicted upon England by her predecessors. A new Act of Supremacy was passed, again severing relations with Rome. This act was less draconian than the original and was accepted by the majority of the people. A few hard-line Protestants, now known as Puritans, showed their resentment in varying ways. In Sussex the parish church at Hailsham was one building that suffered. The majority of the county's parishes took the oath of allegiance to the new Elizabethan order, their ministers publicly modifying their practices even if privately remaining sceptical of the new teaching. Over the next forty years, as Puritanism spread, a split developed in the ranks of the Sussex leaders; those who retained their Catholic faith were viewed

Cowdray Park. Queen Elizabeth's Oak, the tree where she is reputed to have sheltered or rested while hunting deer.

with suspicion by their friends who were unable to understand a dual allegiance to Church and Crown.

Initially over a half of the Sussex nobility were Catholic, but, with increasing pressure from central government, their influence in the county slowly lessened. The Masters of Cowdray were one family that remained true to the Tudor cause and at the same time retained their Catholic beliefs. This apparent division of loyalty created no problems for the queen because in 1591 she visited the mansion, enjoying life and shooting deer in the surrounding park land. This visit is remembered locally in two ways, one upper room in the now ruined house is traditionally known as Queen Elizabeth's room and the shell of an ancient parkland oak also bears her name. Opinions differ as to whether it was a commemorative planting to celebrate her killing of an animal or where she sheltered during a rainstorm.

Although the authority of the Sussex aristocracy was on the decline, their wealth continued to increase. This prosperity was not confined to the nobility since a second layer of wealthy landowners emerged, the tier commonly referred to as 'the gentry', a term that continued in use well into the twentieth century and comprising smaller-scale landowners, often controlling only a handful of farms. They formed an adaptable clan which readily accepted newcomers into society, especially when arrivals took over the lands of declining families. The final stratum of wealth belonged to the yeoman farmers. They were the descendants of the late medieval farmers; their holdings were small, often family-managed on land that was their own or rented from someone higher in the social pyramid.

Who lost in this age of expansion? As always, it was the common people who suffered. The inflation that followed Henry's interference with the economy hit them the hardest; their work was cash-based and they were regarded by their employers only as work horses that were completely expendable if the need arose. Those that worked for the great estates did receive a living of sorts; their brothers who occupied the High Weald were dependent on a crofting form of existence, subsidized by casual labour when available. There was also a large migrant workforce around the forests and these undoubtedly added to the area's reputation for lawlessness.

The general prosperity enjoyed by rural property owners was not always mirrored by the urban community. In general, the smaller towns that provided a full range of services for the surrounding countryside, thrived. Lewes, as a larger town, also became a success. The presence of a port almost within the town and its access to the coastal marshes, the Downs and the Weald were instrumental in its development into the trading centre for the east of the county. Throughout the Tudor and the Stuart period the town grew, with the three communities of Lewes, Cliffe and Southover merging into one. Chichester, however, went through a period of stagnation, the dissolution of the religious houses had removed patronage from the city, funding that it was unable to replace. The port was reasonably successful, but a large fleet of privateers decided to use its facilities, creating difficulties in the collection of harbour dues. Located adjacent to a prime agricultural region, the regular markets and fairs should have been beneficial to the city but little revenue appears to have found its way into the local coffers.

As Elizabeth moved into the middle years of her reign, England, abroad, continued to prosper. Drake and his privateers were engaging in patriotic piracy, forever taunting and raiding Spanish possessions. For centuries Britain was on the edge of the known world; now with the opening up of the American continent it found itself in the centre of two trading areas. Drake, Raleigh and their companions took every opportunity to prove that at last the country was indeed mistress of the seas.

These halcyon years saw the expansion of the arts in England. In the theatre the names of Marlowe, Shakespeare and Ben Johnson came to the fore. Poetry was invigorated and, for the first time in recorded history, England could claim the title of the 'the musical centre of Europe'.

It was a prosperous and contented country that relaxed in the remaining decades of the century. However, two vaguely interconnected issues could not be ignored: religion and Spain. In 1577 the central authorities began a country-wide crackdown on recusants, non-attendance at Anglican churches resulted in the levying of substantial fines. In 1580 several leading Catholics were imprisoned for non-compliance with the order. This persecution quickly led to a religious underground movement which went largely undetected, for the Puritan gentry found it difficult to betray fellow members; religion still came second to clan loyalty. Three members of the Sussex community were unlucky; in 1588 Edward Shelley of Warninghurst was executed for harbouring a priest, and in the same year two priests from Chichester met the same fate. This religious divide continued throughout the remainder of the queen's reign, with the Puritan element of Protestantism slowly gaining support and influence.

When Elizabeth came to the throne England was a Catholic country subject to Spain. Its northern neighbour Scotland was also Catholic, but a province of France. Within two years both had broken free and established national, Protestant churches. Spain, partly in retaliation for naval raids by the English, decided on a series of political plots to rid England of its queen and reinstate a Catholic monarch. When the Spanish ambassador in London was found to be involved in this intrigue he was expelled and an undeclared war commenced, a conflict not resolved until after the queen's death. In 1588 the Spanish Armada was defeated by a combination of the English navy, the weather and good fortune. As noted earlier, Sussex, once a great maritime county, could on this occasion supply only six small ships for the defenders. Inland, the county forgot its religious differences and the combined factions were able to raise over 4,000 troops for the defence of their country.

In the spring of 1603 the Tudor dynasty came to a close when Elizabeth died with no close relative to succeed. It fell to the Privy Council to choose the new monarch. The leader at the time was Robert Cecil, whose family had greatly benefited under the late queen, and it was to his credit that he managed to obtain a peaceful transition from the Tudors to the Stuarts. Thus James VI of Scotland became James I of England.

7. STUARTS AND HANOVERIANS

When James VI of Scotland became James I of England he was the first monarch to rule over four British countries. But it was not yet a United Kingdom for Scotland and Ireland retained their own Parliaments, a division that had an influence on the future civil wars when the northern territory switched allegiance between the Crown and Parliament.

James seemed unable to adapt to English life and one of his first actions was to antagonize the Puritans, a rift that was continued after his death by his son. Charles had strong Catholic sympathies and his marriage to a French princess further alienated the largely Puritan Parliament. He continued his father's belief that he had a divine right to control all things, both religious and political. He dissolved the chamber in 1629 and for eleven years the country existed under a virtual dictatorship. Severe financial demands finally forced the King to reconvene Parliament. He hoped that this action would release funds to clear his mounting debt, but animosity between the two sides continued unabated and in 1642 Charles withdrew from London. The first of the civil wars had begun.

The Civil Wars

The years leading up to the war were, for Sussex, a period of an increasingly strong religious divide. During the reign of Elizabeth there had been a loose compromise on the form of the faith, but Charles along with Archbishop Laud attempted to impose High Anglican practices throughout the country. A growing number of Puritans were diametrically opposed to these; in East Sussex, and particularly at Lewes and Rye, there was an increasing tendency to follow the latters' teaching. Other royal actions caused the Sussex gentry to question their allegiance to the Stuarts. One such incident concerned a notable

eccentric, Thomas Lansford of East Hoathly. He had been prosecuted and fined for two of his escapades; first, he shot at his neighbour's deer, and then at his person. Before the punishment could be imposed Lansford fled abroad, only to be recalled by Charles and promoted to colonel in the army. This promotion did not guarantee a trouble-free life, for in 1649 he sold his estates and emigrated to the New World.

There was no clear dividing line in the pattern of support in the county between Crown and Parliament: towns, communities and even families all showed split allegiances. There were thirteen county boroughs in Sussex, each returning two Members to Parliament; five were divided, three stayed true to the Crown and the other five were against. It was thought that the coastal towns would have royalist tendencies, given that taxes raised inland were needed to bolster their defences, but only Hastings was strongly for the monarch. Throughout the county it was the upper strata of society that were interested in the continuing politics. The local economy was the prime concern for the smallholders and villagers.

Sussex was an important player in the struggle between Crown and Parliament; not only was it the arsenal for the country, providing cannon and to a lesser extent gunpowder, but it had a multitude of small ports and friendly beaches through which Charles could be expected to receive assistance from his French associates. It was therefore essential for Parliament to stop the Royalists from gaining control of the county. There was the potential for widespread damage to the county's infrastructure but this did not happen. No major battles took place within its boundaries and, particularly in East Sussex, daily life was largely unaffected.

The city of Chichester was a good example of the split allegiance of a community. For three

Lake at Petworth.

REMEMBER, REMEMBER

'Remember, remember the fifth of November' is the first line of a well-known poem that is beloved by children, but it is the second line: 'Gunpowder, treason and plot' that is more relevant to Lewes. There are few places in Sussex that do not celebrate the 1605 event when Guy Fawkes and his group of fanatical Catholics attempted to rid England of its king, ministers and Parliament.

Lewes is the bonfire capital of the southern counties, offering a series of celebrations that annually draw thousands of spectators into the town. Although commonly regarded only as a celebration of the thwarted attack on Westminster, public bonfires were a common occurrence in Elizabethan times where the working classes were able to break free from their drab existence and express joy at the ending of Bloody Mary's oppressive regime.

A year after the gunpowder incident an Act proclaimed that the discovery of the plot '... should be held in perpetual remembrance ... for the deliverance from the Papists'. The fifth of November was declared a public holiday, but the Lewes celebrations did not start until 1679. There are few records for the early years but from around 1800 the event began to get out of hand and cause concern to the local authorities. By the 1840s the custom of rolling blazing tar barrels around the town was well established. The rollers, the so called 'Bonfire Boys', many of whom chose to appear in disguise, regularly clashed with the town officials and constabulary. In an attempt to keep order on the night, the year 1847 saw the importation of London police; these, along with a hastily recruited constabulary and a troop of lancers from Brighton, successfully curtailed the festivities. In an act of revenge the

Bonfire Boys continued to celebrate throughout the month, thus creating more disruption and aggravation to the community than in previous years.

Ironically, it was the actions of the Pope that gave the celebrations a justification that has survived to the present. His restoration of the Catholic hierarchy in England and the appointment of a Bishop of Westminster was not appreciated by the Protestant town. The Bonfire Boys now had a new target to attack. They also realized that, in order to gain respectability, they needed to control their more ebullient members, and therefore individual societies were created, each to control the events in its own area.

These societies have been modified over the years and new personalities have found their way on to the fires, but the aim remains the same, to provide enjoyment and entertainment for participant and spectator alike. Today five independent societies, each with its own territory, after parading individually, join at the top of the High Street to form a Grand United Procession. The grand parade can be over a mile in length and be accompanied by up to twenty bands. After entertaining the town each society returns to its own area to continue the festivities.

This annual spectacle draws crowds from all of southern England. In recent years, ever mindful of of the damage that vast crowds could inflict on themselves and on the ancient town, efforts have been made to control the number of visitors. There is, it seems, but one authority that can achieve that aim, the weather. But even if the night is wet and murky, the enthusiasm of the locals will ensure that the town continues to remember 1605.

months after Charles had raised his banner in Nottingham, supporters of the opposing sides drilled daily, at different times and in different areas of the city. This civilized arrangement ceased when the gentry from the surrounding countryside made a surprise raid and took control. The Royalist occupation was only temporary, for, when Parliament learned of the situation, it immediately sent a force of 600 men from Hampshire under Gen Waller to retake the city. This it did after a six-day siege, when con-

siderable damage was done to the eastern suburbs. A supplementary force continued to Arundel which was believed to be a Royalist stronghold. At the time the town contained only a handful of defenders and it surrendered at once. Parliament had easily achieved its first objective, the control of Sussex, and the following year passed uneventfully.

Chichester took no further part in the conflict since a Parliamentary force remained garrisoned there until the end of hostilities in 1646.

Arundel Castle. The present building is a comparatively recent rebuilding to resemble a medieval castle.

Arundel was less lucky, for early in December 1643 a strong Royalist company entered the county from the north-west. Aided by a frost-hardened ground, it made rapid progress, Stansted and Cowdray were captured, then Arundel surrounded. The local Parliamentary leader for East Sussex, Col Morley of Glynde, managed to raise a small group of men and appealed to Gen Waller for assistance. This was immediately forthcoming and on 19 December the combined force of over 1,000 encircled the royalist fortifications. The siege lasted over the Christmas period with the capitulation of the garrison taking place on the morning of 6 January. Extensive damage was done to both the town and castle, but it was the failure, or sabotage, of the castle's water supply that brought about the surrender. A contemporary account reported that on their release from their prison half of the survivors transferred into Waller's army.

This second siege of Arundel was the last military incident of the wars that involved Sussex. Small disturbances continued, mainly in the west of the county, but these were usually expressions of dissatisfaction by the working classes against the Cromwellian regime. The majority of farmers and villagers held no strong political views; they would ally themselves to either side provided they were allowed to live and work without interference. As the war dragged on their resentment increased, both on the levies imposed on food and the billeting of troops upon them. Protest meetings were organized, the largest of which took place in September 1645 on The Trundle and attracted over 1,000 protesters. The local army commanders were quick to clamp down on these dissident meetings which they regarded as a movement of non-cooperation. The imposition of another governmental 5 per cent tax on food, when combined with a series of poor harvests and low agricultural wages, brought about another series of protests, this time the centres of unrest were at Horsham and Pulborough. This pattern of protest by rural workers continued spasmodically for the next 200 years.

The formation of the New Model Army in 1645 took some pressure off the working classes. Throughout the centuries armies found their supplies as they moved about the country, often impressing local labourers into an unwilling force. Now the lower classes had a choice of who or whether they wished to serve. The Parliamentary army found few enthusiasts among the Sussex rustics; one of Cromwell's officers suffered the indignity of a beating while attempting a recruiting campaign at the West Hoathly fair.

As noted earlier, many of the iron foundries were decommissioned or destroyed by the army;

those that were at the greatest risk were where the owners had been outspoken in the support of the Royalist cause. The estates of the dissidents were also targeted by Cromwell. Heavy fines were imposed or, in extreme cases, as at Ashburnham, the complete estate was sequestered; other houses whose owners supported the Crown were destroyed. There was no fixed pattern to the destruction, houses across the county succumbed, from Bodiam in the east to Blackdown on the Surrey border.

The first civil war ended in 1645 with Charles I surrendering to the Scots, who immediately handed him over to Parliament. Although offered generous terms by Cromwell, which he rejected, Charles continued to promote a policy of dissension among his opponents. A short second war erupted, this time the army defeated an amalgam of royalists, Scots and dissident English Presbyterians. Cromwell dissolved the House of Lords, decimated the Commons and tried and executed the King.

The killing of Charles alienated the country against Cromwell and he was forced to retain his control by force. England almost descended into

THE MONARCH'S WAY

The year 1651 brought West Sussex back into the war zone. The future Charles II, after his defeat at the battle of Worcester, planned an escape route to the south coast in order to reach his allies in France. His first escapade in the journey involved hiding from his pursuers in an oak tree. Whether fact or fiction, this incident spawned a plethora of local hostelry names, many of these 'Royal Oaks' being many miles from his presumed route.

A semi-official long-distance path purports to follow his journey through the southern counties. The rambling of this path does little to confirm its authenticity, although the final section through Sussex is probably close to the route he took. When travelling through the county he disguised himself as a servant of Col Gunter of Racton; the modern recreational path passes within a mile of Gunter's former house before veering inland towards the first of two river crossings that had to

be negotiated before he reached relative safety. The crossing at Houghton was less than 3 miles (5km) upstream from Arundel, which housed a large Parliamentary garrison, when Charles's party stopped for lunch at the local inn, which overlooked the river bridge. Charles accepted refreshments but declined to dismount, arguing that this action would save him precious seconds should the enemy appear.

The second crossing was of the Adur at Bramber; this involved a night stop before he continued the following morning. A room in the medieval house of St. Mary's claims his occupancy for the night. Once over the river it was an easy ride to a safe house at Brighton, from there he backtracked to the port of Shoreham and safety in France. His departure from England is a fact, but the Sussex incidents, like the oak, could be fact or fiction; most probably a combination of both.

A 'Royal Oak' at Midhurst.

both religions, he was unable to produce a legitimate heir. This failing led to his succession by James II whose short reign further increased the religious problems and culminated in his ejection.

Nonconformity in Sussex

Religious intolerance started to develop after the compromise that existed during the reign of Elizabeth. The civil wars could be called battles – not between holders of differing beliefs but between extreme schisms of one faith. As early as the 1620s perceived religious persecution resulted in emigration to the New World, one well-documented exodus was that of the 'Pilgrim Fathers'.

The extremes of Puritanism as practised during the republican period received many of their ideals from Huguenot refugees. Deserting their French homeland, they arrived at Rye, stayed for a while then found new homes in London and East Anglia. It is no coincidence that for years this port remained a Puritan centre for rigorous public morality, accepted by the populace on the surface but conveniently ignored when it was likely to affect their enjoyment. Other sects were also 'imported': Calvinism and Presbyterianism were two that needed only a short journey to England. The Church of England was the main

a state of anarchy; sections of the army mutinied, some ships of the navy deserted and his actions were not accepted by the colonies. Swift action was needed to prevent a disaster, the man was up to the task and control was regained. However, in 1653 Cromwell quarrelled with Parliament and, unable to agree with it, he assumed the role of dictator, euphemistically calling himself Protector of a United Commonwealth. Rule was maintained by army generals with draconian police powers, the whole organization funded by taxes levied on the Royalist community.

Cromwell died in 1658 and a subsequent 'free' Parliament invited Charles II to return from France. This he did, landing at Dover in May 1660, to great acclaim. The period of the republic was a depressing interlude in English history, but the arrival of the dashing Charles promised better times ahead. The new King was a ladies' man and, although taking mistresses of

The 'George and Dragon' at Houghton. The inn where Charles enjoyed a 'swift half'.

sufferer in the seventeenth century; it appeared to drift rudderless with no fixed aim and became an easy prey for stronger forces. In mid-century the structure of the Church was abolished, the Prayer Book and all religious festivals were outlawed. In the larger centres the cathedrals were secularized with many being converted into barracks or prisons. In the rural communities the old services continued, but, as the clergy died or deserted, they were not replaced and the village churches played host to diminishing congregations.

Two of the biggest sects in Sussex were the Baptists and the Society of Friends (Quakers). In 1669 a survey of nonconformists in the county listed six gatherings of Quakers, eleven of Baptists, four of Presbyterians with twenty-four being unspecified. Many of these were probably small village groups attempting to continue with their traditional worship. The great families of Sussex mainly stayed loyal to their Roman Catholic faith and after the Toleration Act of 1689 they were no longer forced to practise their beliefs in secrecy.

The founder of the Quaker movement, George Fox, first visited the county in 1655 and 'many times I met with opposition from Baptists and others'. The Quakers' rejection of formal worship brought them into conflict with the gentry and authority, and, as the movement was particularly strong in the corridor between Steyning and Horsham, the latter town's gaol was home to almost 200 members in the twenty years after 1665. Many of the early meetings were accommodated in members' homes, since, having a mainly rural following, the numbers attending would not be unduly large.

One of the leading members of the Society in Sussex was a man who became better known nationally as the founder of a New World colony, Pennsylvania. William Penn lived for twenty-five years at Warminghust, an isolated settlement 10 miles (16km) from a town of any size, and it was here that the idea of a safe haven for persecuted Quakers was born. Such was his enthusiasm for the movement that his farmhouse often received congregations in excess of 200.

The 'Blue Idol'. William Penn's meeting house at Coolham.

When a meeting house, the 'Blue Idol', was established at Coolham, Penn and his wife made the weekly journey on horseback, the children following in an ox cart. The Coolham house retains its function today, doubling with that of a guest house, but Penn's home was pulled down shortly after his death.

The religious divide continued throughout the reigns of Charles II and James II, with the monarchy being closely aligned to Catholic France and Spain, while the Protestant faction showed their friendship towards Holland. The English Parliament and Church were mainly Protestant and, when James introduced Catholics into the army and seats of learning, the ruling classes became concerned. When his son was born, who would have continued the Catholic line, the Bishop of London and six high-ranking laymen invited William of Orange to England to protect English Protestantism. Cleverly evading the navy who expected him to land on the east coast, William sailed to Torquay. After a few skirmishes James had no stomach for a fight and fled to his friends in France. Three years later he had a change of heart and left France for Ireland in an attempt to use the country as a stepping stone to regain power in England. His involvement in the politics of this island no doubt precipitated the north–south divide of the country which still exists three centuries on.

This period was one of enterprise and expansion. Abroad, new colonies were established and a few were lost, while at home it was a time of great achievement: Newton was deducing, Milton and Bunyan were writing, Pepys organizing the navy and Wren rebuilding London after the plague and the fire of London. It was now that the two great political parties, the Whigs and the Tories, came into existence. The eighteenth century saw another Hundred Years' War, for there were only a few years when Britain (Scotland joined the Union in 1707) was not involved in conflict. Although Sussex was in the frontline of defence against continental adversaries, it was not until the last decade of

the 1700s that the county noticed any large-scale change in its way of life.

The monarchy transferred into the Hanoverian dynasty in 1714 and remained in its hands until the death of Victoria almost two centuries later. An Act of Settlement passed in 1701 decreed that, should Queen Anne die without an heir, the house of Hanover would rule. George I was hugely unpopular with his people; he arrived unable to speak the language and had little interest in his new country. In spite of this early indifference, the Georgian period was an age of great rebuilding, both in buildings and the landscape. Encompassed in this century of development is the so-called Regency period, this lasted for only a decade, between 1811 and 1820, when the later George

Petworth House. Viewed across an example of Capability Brown's open landscaping.

IV was acting as Prince Regent during his father's madness.

The Redesigning of the Sussex Landscape

Much of the Sussex landscape changed radically in the eighteenth century. With the demise of the iron industry, nature was again allowed to reclaim its own, the regeneration of the native oak and mixed woodland often being assisted by planned reforestation. Large parts of the forest ridges were planted with softwoods; the descendants of these conifers remain today as the grouping of Scots pine on Ashdown. Beech again found favour on the chalk hills; the skyline clump on Chanctonbury, which, according to local legend, was nursed through its early years by the landowner's son, provided a landmark that was visible for 30 miles (48km). Sadly, it was to become a victim of the great 1987 storm. The lower slopes of the Downs were not ignored, designer woods appeared and, where a suitable pocket of soil was discovered, specimen trees were installed.

By 1700 many of the county's estates had been consolidated, either by marriage or acquisition into a select few families which largely retained control of the countryside for the next two centuries. At the beginning of the eighteenth century the landscaping of the parkland surrounding the great house was limited to the

Sheffield Park. An example of Capability Brown's garden design.

immediate environs of the building and was little more than an extension of the earlier Tudor gardens. The first attempts at designer leisure lands were influenced by the French model of Versailles and its English counterpart Hampton Court. Geometric patterns, right angles and long, straight avenues of trees were the order of the day. The best surviving example of this form of planting is at Stansted, close to the Hampshire border. The early plantings here delighted Defoe when he stayed at the house in 1724; those that remain today, and many are showing their age, are from a much later replacement planting.

Tiring of this austere fashion, the later designs for parkland were for areas more sympathetic to nature. The curve and the casual took over from the block and the straight line. If the designer could leave his project with a natural appearance then he considered it a job well done. Two of the greatest names in parkland and garden conversions of the period were 'Capability' Brown and Humphrey Repton. Brown's masterpiece is undoubtedly Petworth; here its rolling parkland with lake and seemingly naturally placed groups of trees make for an area of relaxing informality. Brown, in fact, was only in charge of four Sussex gardens although his influence is apparent in several others. Sheffield is another of his creations, where the natural forms of the landscape were enhanced by the addition of water features and connecting bridges, these also to his design. The original plantings were of native species but much was changed during the Victorian years when the garden's owners became obsessed with imported exotics.

Nine of the county's park and gardens are attributed to Repton. Born forty years after Brown, he was if anything more free-flowing in his plans than the earlier master. Entry lodges and other buildings away from the main house were ridiculed as 'childish symmetry'. Uppark was one house that felt the full force of his pencil and spade. Out went the old gardens and terraces and in came a landscaping of the surrounding Downs to bring lawns up to the windows of the house. This building was also improved with the addition of a Doric colonnade to the north wall. Brown created his woodland effect with new plantings but Repton's favourite option was to reduce the existing tree cover to the requisite size.

These two landscape artists, and their unnamed followers, combined to provide Sussex with some of the finest park and garden scenery to be found anywhere in England.

The Villages and the Towns

The expansion of the market towns which had begun in the previous century continued throughout the seventeenth and the eighteenth centuries. The population continued to grow and new housing was needed. It was the craftsmen and the traders who first felt the need for an improved standard of accommodation; add to this a buoyant agricultural economy and the reason was there for a change to the face of the high street. New construction and the renovation of existing buildings went hand in hand throughout the county. Where new buildings replaced existing structures many of the materials were cannibalized from the originals. The appearance of the new homes was largely dependent on locally available materials, for it was not until the coming of the railways that regional variations in construction began to disappear.

In the Downs and along the coastal strip flint in varying forms was often incorporated into the main material. Inland it was the knapped stone that was combined with limestone or brick, while on the shoreline rounded pebbles or cobbles faced the outer walls. Examples of this latter construction may still be found in the back streets of the coastal towns, but many of the buildings have been disguised by later alternative facings. To the north of the Downs local sandstone was used; the extent of the beds may be roughly determined by a study of the village buildings. Below the scarp of the Downs lies a string of villages and hamlets built from the belt of Upper Greensand. This is a coarse stone,

MAD JACK FULLER, 1757–1834

John Fuller was born in 1757 into a family that had made its fortune through the iron industry. He became squire of Brightling on his twentieth birthday and soon became a local celebrity. Sussex, over the years, had produced its share of eccentrics, many proving of little value to the county. Fuller was not of this ilk; he loved the county and it was not only his village that benefited from his philanthropic nature. In 1829 be bought the dilapidated Bodiam Castle when it was threatened with demolition, thus saving the building for the enjoyment of future generations. He also built the Belle Tout lighthouse, on the cliffs near Beachy Head, but this must be considered to be one of his follies for the chosen site suffered from sea fogs and was of little use to shipping. The arts also gained from his generosity with the artist J. M. W. Turner being a regular guest at his Brightling mansion.

He was a large man of 22 stone (140kg) who dressed in an old-fashioned style with his hair powdered and drawn into a pigtail, his ample girth earning him the nickname of 'Hippopotamus'. After a dubious election campaign he became MP for East Sussex, his antics in the chamber continually bringing him into conflict with the authorities. During one debate he was ejected twice from the House; on the second occasion his departure was only enforced by the Serjeant at Arms, ably assisted by several badge messengers. Parliament finally despaired of this character and offered him a peerage, which he rejected saying, 'Jack Fuller I was born and Jack Fuller I will die.' This brought forth a less derogatory nickname, that of 'Honest'.

It was after his retirement from political life that he started adorning his estate with a series of follies. The most prominent landmark is that of the Brightling Needle, a 65ft (20m) obelisk that stands on one of the highest parts of Sussex. It was erected to celebrate Wellington's victory at Waterloo in 1815, or was it for Nelson's at Trafalgar a decade earlier? No one is sure. The Temple, the Dome and the Sugar Loaf all have local connections, but it is the Pyramid that is the most remarkable. Situated in the village churchyard, it was built as his future mausoleum twenty-five years before it was actually needed. Local belief was that he was interred in the building in full evening dress and seated at a table with wine and a meal before him. As with many local anecdotes, this proved to be false for he was buried conventionally at the base of the tomb.

Although many of his activities appeared to be slanted towards the frivolous, the local community received regular largesse. The church was given a new organ and, on the celebration of its installation, the choir members received new outfits. In spite of his eccentricity he was a paternal squire who was ever mindful of his responsibilities to his subjects: a larger than life notable whose life brought great benefits to the village and the countryside around his estate.

unique to the county and the area where it was used was extremely narrow. Further to the north it was the local sandstones that were more commonly used, their colours and textures varying from quarry to quarry.

Brick was finding favour as a building medium and there were few parishes in the Weald that, by the eighteenth century, did not possess their own brickyard. The yards seemed not to work continuously, restarting production as and when the need arose. This interrupted supply line led to differences in the firing; this, when added to the fact that, like the stones, the Sussex clays were not of a uniform consistency, gave an individuality to buildings in the same locality. The variations of colour facings of a single brick gave the builders the opportunity to develop a local pattern of laying. In several towns the blue-hued ends of the bricks, when grouped among the red 'stretchers', made for a distinctive architectural feature.

Towards the end of the sixteenth century tile hanging was developed as a form of wall cladding; in common with bricks, the appearance of the finished tile changed with the location of its firing. As the transportation of these

Squire Fuller's Pyramid at Brightling.

lighter objects was easier, the range of an individual type was greater and there were fewer variants on offer. Later, as ornamental tiles were introduced, they vied with the bricks as decoration. Tile-hung facades were most common in the north and the north-west of the county, while close to the Kent border a further form of protection appeared. Painted weatherboard protected many rural farmhouses and cottages from the elements. Imported continental softwoods were most commonly used, normally painted white. The style spread haphazardly throughout Sussex, small pockets of it being found where the supplies could be obtained locally from a water-powered sawmill.

Many of the buildings of the county's towns and its two administration centres are living lies.

Terraces of plain-faced, Georgian frontages hide the timber frames of earlier buildings. From the exterior the rebuilds are indistinguishable from the new housing, and it is only when interior reconstruction is carried out that the true age can be determined. Lewes gives the impression of a comfortable Georgian town, for few facades are earlier than the eighteenth century. Many of the town's residents were professional people and, as the older buildings were demolished, there was money available for a complete rebuilding. Some homeowners, however, decided to remain in their original dwellings and, in order to match their neighbours, accept a modern refacing. Chichester owes much of its attractiveness to its early planners who divided the city into precincts, each with its own character and

Flint-walled cottages at Singleton.

function. For centuries the city had contracted, or at best managed only to retain its previous size; now the eighteenth-century developers brought a period of expansion unmatched since the Roman occupation. The Pallant district in the south-east quadrant was a town within a town, the street plan of Chichester followed a cruciform pattern; this form was miniaturized for the Pallants, even down to the provision of a market cross. It was in this sector that the major rebuilding took place; out went the cottages and nondescript buildings to be replaced with elegant residential housing. These 'palaces' had only a limited life, for less than a century later they were converted and the area became the city's professional quarter.

One market-town enigma that has never been fully explained concerns the larger town houses. Many of these were built for and financed by semi-absentee landowners. The wealthy gentry spent the winter months in town, when travel through the countryside was difficult, then returned, with the sun, to their summer manors. The unanswered question is: did the houses remain vacant for a period of the year or was it the beginning of the holiday accommodation industry, when they were available for short-term leases?

Changes in Agricultural Practices

The period from the restoration to the arrival of Victoria saw a dramatic change in the agricultural practices of Sussex. The industry now became more market-responsive, with production being standardized and always aiming towards cost-effectiveness; this was a process that imposed on the local work force and led to the renewed uprisings of the early 1800s. The population of the country increased rapidly from 1750 and, with the greatest concentration being in London, a short distance over the hill, there was always a ready market for the county's produce.

The increase in productivity was obtained in various ways. Improved husbandry of existing land, the enclosing of marginal wastelands and the conversion from pastoral to arable all contributed. More systematic crop rotation became possible, cereals alternating with grasses or legumes, the latter being grown for animal food. New types of grass were introduced from the Continent together with several clovers and trefoils. Mechanization was needed for more intense cultivation; this was assisted by the introduction of the seed drill in 1701, which, together with its companion horse hoe, combined to give a much improved distribution of crops over a given area.

Land enclosures in Sussex comprised mainly the conversion of wasteland margins. The fields obtained from these enclosures differ from the older, irregularly-shaped fields by their more geometric plan: those that were to be tilled annually by horse power needed a shape that was easy to cultivate. The evenly-shaped fields that emerged were now enclosed by hedges instead of narrow strips of unclaimed woodland. Profit-conscious landowners attempted to squeeze every small pocket of uncultivated land into production, even resorting to the theft of commonly-grazed water-meadows. Many of the Wealden commons had already been enclosed during the Tudor and the Stuart peri-

A West Sussex country cottage. The simple decorative tiling accentuates the off-level roof eaves.

East Sussex weatherboarding at Brede.

od and the only areas remaining as open land were the forests of the High Weald. Half-hearted attempts were made to contain and restock St Leonard's and Tilgate forest, but the only crop the land could support was rabbits, their catchers finding a ready outlet for them in the London markets. Attempts to convert the edges of Ashdown Forest brought opposition from the Commoners who were fearful of losing their rights of pannage and grazing. These altercations were destined to continue for many years.

In this period, as the market price for grain continued to increase, it was inevitable that the landowners would look for new land on which to grow cereals. With all the suitable lowland accounted for, eyes focused on the Downs. Unlike the destruction in the 1940s, when the

conversion was instantaneous, this was a gradual infiltration; each year a few more acres were stolen from the sheep. Surprisingly, this poaching of the habitat did not affect the numbers remaining on the hills. With the alternative food now presented to them and the practice of overwintering on the lower levels, their numbers increased. This conversion of the downland continued into the first part of the nineteenth century, when tumbling grain prices brought about the abandonment of tillage on the hills. In the eastern Downs, around Jevington, traces of this temporary cereal cultivation may still be found, the colonizing grasses showing as a coarse sward against the traditional close-cropped turf.

Local specialization of crops did occur, more especially the growing of hops in East Sussex, but a regional agricultural map of the county

Uncommon boarding at Wisborough Green. The Horsham slate roof signifies its position in the north-west of the county.

would have roughly followed geological lines. The central core contained the common grazing plus commercial rabbit warrens; surrounding this heathland were the mixed farming and cattle-fattening lands of the Weald. A narrow strip along the Western Rother featured fruit growing, a practice that precariously manages to survive in the twenty-first century. Below the Downs it was arable and livestock; on them, as noted earlier, it was a mixture of sheep and cereals. The relatively small area of the coastal plain could have been called 'the bread basket of south-east England', for more grain was exported through Chichester than the other Kent and Sussex ports combined. The marshlands inland from Pevensey were used for the breeding of livestock; cattle predominated, for, unlike

Romney where the drainage system was brackish and only suitable for sheep, the Sussex levels were fresh, making them more amenable to cattle.

The raising and fattening of cattle was widespread throughout the county and it was a rare smallholding that did not have a few of the beasts. The large landowners favoured the red or black local breed, but the general farmer used a motley collection of breeds that had percolated into the county from the north-west of England or Ireland. In 1747 an outbreak of cattle plague brought about a ban on the importing of cattle into Sussex, over 8,000 head being stranded on the drove roads awaiting clearance. Milk production and dairying seldom extended beyond the meeting of local needs for meat and hides,

Lewes High Street. A glorious mixture of house facings.

and for the Sussex breed its use as draught animals was the future facing the newborn calves.

The Downland Shepherd

The traditional folding of sheep on the Downs brought to Sussex a unique character, the downland shepherd. These men were self-sufficient, with a vast knowledge of their charges. Generally they were given a free rein by the farmers to produce the best possible product. Over the last century they slowly faded away, disenchanted with the 'improvements' that were being thrown at the industry. Previously the farmers would consult with them on the needs of the flock; now they were being ordered, told what and how to do it, by 'furriners' who were more interested in lamb prices than good hus-

bandry. Other types were introduced to the hills by these incomers, breeds that were expected to thrive in conditions that were totally alien to them.

Between the two World Wars many thousands of photographs were taken of these downland residents, by both snap-happy tourists and professional record keepers. With their beards and, for a fee, in their linen smocks, they certainly created a memorable photographic image. One of the last to depart, in 1989, was 'Shep' Oliver; he was a well-known and well-loved institution who in seventy-five years had never missed an attendance at the Findon sheep fair. By coincidence, a previously recorded interview with him was broadcast on BBC television the night that he died. Probably the definitive work on the Sussex shepherd was *A Shepherd's Life* by W. H. Hudson; a shorter essay on this lonely character appears in another book by Hudson, *Nature in Downland*, and it paints a classic picture of the Downs at the end of the nineteenth century.

Improvements to the agricultural industry brought greater prosperity to Sussex, but this increased wealth was not shared equally throughout society. Profits accrued to the few and for the majority came increased stress and a lowering of living standards. In theory, the expansion of cereal and sheep farming should have called for a larger workforce; in reality the reverse was true. With improved implements greater areas could be sown and harvested with no increase in labour demand. Many landowners began to keep only a minimal workforce, importing workers as required. 'Importing' was the operative word, for the immigrants were willing to undercut the local community when negotiating rates of pay. An increase in population from the 1720s meant that more were seeking employment; this gave the hirers another opportunity to lower the rate offered when work was available. As an alternative to the poorhouse many families adopted a migratory lifestyle, tramping the countryside. At certain times of the year work could be found, but the rewards from this casual labour was never sufficient to cover the barren periods.

A lowering of food prices in the mid-eighteenth century brought temporary relief to the lower classes; but when the Midlands and East Anglia adopted arable, Sussex with many irregularly enclosed fields and largely unsuitable soils was left behind. As the century closed grain prices rose again, bringing more cash into the pockets of the already rich, many of whom took

Georgian Chichester: Pallant House. Note the dodo on each gate pillar.

An East Sussex hopfield. This field is in the Rother valley near the Kent border.

the opportunity to raise rents annually or, in a few cases, biannually. Unscrupulous landowners issued rent increases verbally with no written contract. This state of affairs came to an abrupt end with the end of hostilities with France in 1815. Over the next few years a series of poor harvests, plus the demobilization of the redundant military, who were unable to find employment in the marketplace, added to the feeling of resentment by the working classes. This undercurrent of unrest finally erupted in the autumn of 1830.

Poor Law and Workhouses

The statuary basis for Poor Law administration came with a 1601 Act, and by the eighteenth century it was only a minority of parishes that

did not subscribe to this early form of social security. This first Act provided for parochial relief for individuals and families but did not cover the provision of accommodation; this shortcoming was rectified by an amending Act in 1834 which forced parish officials to provide 'convenient houses for the impotent poor'. Ambiguities arose over the definition of impotent, which led to the synonymous usage of the terms workhouse and poor house.

The 1601 Act was designed to cope with a small percentage of the population – the aged and unfortunates – and did not make too heavy a demand on the parish or principal landowners. Relief was occasionally given in cash but more commonly in kind. By the end of the eighteenth century the system was breaking down; not only were the numbers of the aged and the unem-

Float Farm, Udimore. Oast kilns, where the hops were dried, combine with traditional farm buildings.

ployed increasing, but those who still had work often came into the 'poor' category, for, with the lowering of the agricultural wage, their earnings fell below the subsistence level. The collapse of cereal prices, poor harvests and the explosion of those seeking relief put a heavy burden on local landowners. Most continued to pay their dues, feeling that they had no alternative and hoping for better times ahead, but a few tried other solutions. The Earl of Chichester reformed his estates at Falmer, denying relief to all but the infirm; his ultimatum was: work or leave. The second choice would conveniently switch the problem elsewhere. A more sympathetic land-lord, Egremont of Petworth, set up a voluntary emigration policy. In the first five years of oper-ation no fewer than 1,456 persons accepted his offer to start a new life in Canada.

A small economic revolt took place in Battle in 1821. A group of labourers from Bexhill tried to obtain an increase in their wages from the local justices; when this was refused they stormed the George Hotel in an attempt to make the gentry meet their demands. This disturbance was easily quashed but it provided a foretaste of the troubles that were to come.

Many of the Sussex parishes had agreed to the 'convenient houses' well in advance of the 1834 Act. Some accommodation was rented by the parish, some purchased and adopted, and some was even purpose-built. The majority of the homes were small, usually housing less than fifty inmates; one exception was that of Eastbourne Borough which bought a redundant barracks and at a stroke took 200 unfortunates off the streets.

THE SOUTHDOWN SHEEP

If the martletts had not been chosen to adorn the Sussex pennant then this sheep would have made an eminently suitable substitute. Thanks largely to intelligent marketing in the twentieth century, the Southdown has become the county's most recognizable animal.

Up to the end of the seventeenth century agricultural practices had hardly advanced from those of the medieval period. With the cultivated land bereft of winter fodder, most livestock was slaughtered in the autumn and those that remained were, of necessity, hardy and thrifty in their eating habits. The ability to survive the hungry months was more important than productivity, and breeding was a matter of natural rather than artificial selection. With the introduction of root foods and clover grazing, more sheep could be overwintered. When the animals were community grazed it was almost impossible to practise selective breeding, but the increased winter food supply allowed for folding into enclosed areas where breeding stock could be selected.

The development of the Southdown can be attributed to John Ellerman (1753–1832), although his original stock continued to be further refined by other downland owners. He was born at Hartfield, in the north of the county, and the family moved to Glynde in 1761. His father had established a sound stock-keeping practice in both sheep and cattle, and even before his father's death John was experimenting in the improvement of the local downland sheep.

These 'locals' were a small, short-woolled, heathland animal that had run on the Downs for centuries, some claimed even before the Roman invasion. Their territory was the downland to the east of the River Adur; they were largely free-ranging during the day and folded at night. This daily enclosing ensured that the flocks became familiar with their shepherds and accustomed to regular handling; this attribute earning the breed the title of 'the original easy care sheep'.

The traditional Southdown is the smallest of the Downs sheep and its wool the shortest and finest. Beneath the fleece is a sturdy, straight-backed animal with thighs and rump that truly are a butcher's delight. Its general attitude has been described as 'with the carriage of a gentleman and walk of a thoroughbred'.

As early as 1780 Ellerman was exporting his new breed to East Anglia and the Midlands. Two decades later it arrived in the North, Scotland and Ireland. Over the following two centuries the basic breed or its crosses have been exported to Russia, the Americas, the Antipodes and, nearer to its home territory, France. Many other English breeds are Southdown crosses; the Suffolk, which was first known as the Norfolk Southdown, the Hampshires, the Dorsets and the Oxfords all have part Sussex parentage. This little downland animal has certainly been a good ambassador for the county.

The rising relief costs forced the parishes to seek ways of increasing income or of reducing costs. One idea was to have an in-house manufacturing unit added to the accommodation and the resulting goods sold to the public. Possibly because of the poor quality of the finished merchandise, the scheme had only limited success. As the nineteenth century progressed, several parishes were on the brink of bankruptcy; in order to remain solvent they were allowed to unite with neighbouring parishes, sharing provisions and costs, and controlled by a board of governors. This arrangement proved popular in West Sussex; in the east of the county several parishes, notably Rye and Battle, experimented

with contractors, paid on a per capita basis for their charges. A private enterprise initiative was introduced by inmates in the parish of Framfield, where the 'house' operated independently as the village brothel.

The 1834 Act not only forced the universal provision of workhouses, it also made radical changes to the eligibility of those seeking relief. Not an enlightened beginning for the new queen's reign.

The Napoleonic Wars

The people of Sussex had little interest in the French Revolution, but a few years later when war with France began they once again found themselves in the front line. As early as 1778 a policy of enforced recruitment was attempted but abandoned when local riots broke out. The mid-eighteenth-century European wars saw a revival of military activity in the southern counties; those in the county who were considered conscript material accepted the need to defend their country on their native soil but had no wish to lose their lives on a foreign field. This semi-patriotic feeling continued during conscription for the Napoleonic Wars; in 1805, at the height of the troubles, 14,000 locals were considered liable to serve of whom 9,500 claimed some form of exemption. Several ploys were used in order to opt out, self-mutilation, such as chopping off the top joint of a finger, was probably the most dramatic. Bribery by substituting a member of a lower social class or intervention by a high-ranking employer often succeeded. This last excuse was used by the Duke of Richmond when he cited the possible spoiling of his harvest.

Another problem for the county's infrastructure came with the wholesale billeting of troops and militia in the towns. As well as the difficulty in provisioning this army, accommodation was not available in existing houses and inns. Brighton was at one time asked to house over 15,000 men. This shortage was overcome by the extensive building of barracks. With one problem solved, another emerged. Controlling large numbers of men who had time on their hands was difficult; the county police forces were still far away in the future and although the communities could cope with small outbreaks of drunkenness and brawling, when large numbers were involved the towns suffered. The camps also created problems for the health of the county; in Battle in 1809 a severe outbreak of typhoid was traced back to the town's barracks.

Barracks were not the only buildings to arise: coastal forts were renewed and a series of towers were constructed along the south-eastern coastline. A hundred and three of these for-

tifications were built, of which Sussex received forty-seven, the majority of which arrived after the war had ended. They were spaced at intervals of 600yd (550m) so that the cannons which were mounted on top could provide crossfire. Their name, Martello, is an Anglicization of the original Italian, and those remaining are instantly recognizable by their shape. The design, although smaller, closely follows that of their Channel Island relations, built a decade earlier and for the same reason.

The Royal Navy was the first line of defence against attack across the Channel, and in order to both maintain contact with their ships and provide manned lookout posts, the Admiralty established sixteen signal stations along the Sussex coast. Inland, on the higher parts of the Downs and forest ridges, fire beacons were built, enabling a visual warning to be passed back. A more elaborate mechanical semaphore system was set up to operate between the naval centre at Portsmouth and London. This line of communication clipped the western edge of the county and it is here that the maps identify the Telegraph Hills; Beacon Hills are more widely spread among the uplands.

In 1804 work was started at the eastern edge of the county on a defensive dyke to be built around the Romney Marshes, for it was thought that this area was at the greatest risk from a French invasion. Following a centuries-old tradition, it was considered that a water-

The Royal Military Canal, Rye.

filled ditch would be the greatest deterrent. It was never planned as a commercial venture but still received the grand title of the Royal Military Canal. The Sussex contribution to this waterway was a little under a mile in length; it left the eastern Rother above Rye, through one of the only two locks on the system, and quickly crossed the county border.

After the Battle of Waterloo and the final defeat of France, the greater part of the military presence in the county was withdrawn. Sussex men returned to their homes and joined the ever-increasing numbers of the unemployed. Small garrisons were retained in the larger towns, partly for ceremonial duties and partly to act as a response force against any future domestic troubles.

The Turnpikes

The road system in lowland Sussex in the first half of the eighteenth century was in an atrocious condition and for almost half the year roads did not exist as means of communication. Deep rutted and with an undefined base of mud, the only traffic to attempt to use them in the winter months was the individual rider. In the worst areas even these doughty souls were, in order to make progress, forced to trespass on to adjoining farmland. The cessation of transport links in the winter created problems for the rural economy. Defoe on one of his journeys through the county in 1727 described the situation perfectly, 'corn in the Low Weald was cheap at the barn because it couldn't be carried

Toll House on the Findon to Clapham Turnpike. The tariff for users was posted within the shield on the wall facing.

out, and dear at the market because it couldn't be carried in.'

There were two primary routes in southern England linking London to the naval bases at Portsmouth and Dover; these roads largely followed more resilient terrain where flint, chalk and gravel were easily available to rectify any deficiencies in their surfaces. Sussex had just one comparable track, the southern ridgeway, fine for individual riders but inaccessible for wagons.

The first road map of the county was published in 1723, the compiler picking out sixty-three routes, the majority having a market town as the origin or destination. Significantly, the condition of the roads was not noted. Only four roads left the coastal settlements, aiming vaguely for the capital. Some 700 miles (1,130km) were listed as primary roads, suitable for the through traveller. That description was a trifle

optimistic for the upkeep of the roads was the responsibility of the parishes, which had little interest in assisting the vistor to pass through.

The development of the seaside towns gave a boost to road improvements in the county. These resorts brought fashion and income to the coast, but without easier travel from London and their hinterland the opportunities for future expansion would be limited.

The first turnpike road in the county was inaugurated in 1749, 'from Hindhead Heath through Fernhurst Lane and Midhurst to the city of Chichester'. Their lifespan was only around 100 years, ousted by the railway which began to infiltrate the county in 1841. The term 'turnpiking' referred to the metalling of major roads by local trusts who paid the costs involved from tolls collected from road users. The original capital for the trusts often came from local landowners who used some of the profits from

RURAL RIDES

William Cobbett was a farmer turned writer who published his impressions of the rural scene under the title of *Rural Rides*. Between 1822 and 1825 he made four visits to Sussex; on three occasions he travelled the county alone on horseback. His first visit to Battle was somewhat different: adopting the role of professional agitator, he spoke at crowded meetings in support of the dissident movement that was emerging. Throughout his writings his farming background was apparent; he saw the landscape through the eyes of a farmer and his at times exaggerated reporting contained a strong element of the 'them and us'. But, in spite of these shortcomings, his writings give a reasonable picture of Sussex rural life in the depression years that followed the Napoleonic Wars.

His account of his summer ride of 1823 is the most informative of his journeys through the county. He deplored the attempted enclosure of St Leonard's Forest: 'this forest is now enclosed, cut up, disfigured, spoilt with all the labourers driven from its skirts.' Nearby Horsham, however, won his approval, as did the majority of towns, they being both 'neat and tidy'. In general, he compared the

county favourably to others in the south, the cottage gardens and attire of the agricultural workers gaining accolades.

His journeys were made after most of the turnpikes had been completed, but the system did not fully meet with his approval. He appreciated the improvement in the quality of the roads, but felt that the benefits went to the wrong people. Toll charges discriminated against the farming community and favoured 'the commercial gentlemen who travelled the countryside by gig instead of horse'. He also regretted the way that traffic was canalized into the turnpike system to the detriment of the non-toll roads. On one occasion, in the west of the county, he had extreme difficulty in obtaining directions for a non-turnpike ride from Petworth to Lavant. The general opinion was that he was mad to attempt a route away from the traffic even though it was the more direct.

Rural Rides remained the definitive work on Sussex country life for eighty years until Hilaire Belloc wrote his semi-fictitious account of a walking tour of the Weald and the Downs under the title *The Four Men*.

their estates. Returns from these ventures were slow to materialize and in certain cases the original costs were never recovered. After fifteen years the turnpike had networked the county and only two market towns were not connected to the system. The majority of the improved roads were on a north–south axis and, as expected, Brighton became the hub of the coastal routes. After these were completed thought was given to upgrading the cross-country roads; there was less enthusiasm for these plans and any that were built were of a local nature. The first stage of turnpike mania was over by the 1770s and interest was not renewed until the early years of the nineteenth century. It was during this lull in the improvement programme that proposals were made to extend the county's waterways.

The turnpikes had the effect of dividing land values in Sussex. In districts well served by the new roads rents were increased substantially, but land adjacent to unimproved byways remained depressed owing to the difficulty in transporting bulky goods. County-wide the returns from commercial goods traffic never came up to expectations, the frequency of toll gates made the conveyance expensive. In all 640 miles (1,030km) of the county's roads

Wey–Arun Canal. A restored section of this canal at Loxwood.

were turnpiked and these contained 238 gates, giving one gate for every $2^1/_2$ miles (4km) of road. One notorious 23-mile (37km) stretch from Mayfield to Wadhurst contained no fewer than nineteen gates. It was leisure travel that benefited the most from the new roads. By the 1820s, thanks to the resiting of several roads, the journey from Brighton to London took less than five hours, bringing the capital into commuting distance. At the height of the turnpike age, just before the arrival of the railways, thirty-six coaches left Brighton daily for London; the logistics for this operation needed 1,200 horses to be stabled en route. Other coastal towns gained from new coaching runs, but Hastings remained isolated until 1821 when a coach and mail service finally made contact with the town.

Although the turnpikes did bring significant changes to travel in the county, one figure cannot be ignored: by 1837, when the programme was virtually complete, only 22 per cent of the roads had been improved and many rural communities were still subject to annual isolation.

The Waterways

Work on the Sussex waterways, both creation and restoration, took place mainly in the years when Napoleon threatened. As early as 1732 the Arun had been improved below Arundel, and new cuts were made to give the town direct access to the sea at Littlehampton. Over the centuries, the once navigable lower reaches of the other rivers had been neglected, making it difficult for even a small boat to negotiate the vege-

The Chichester Branch of the Portsmouth and Arundel Canal.

tation and the sandbars. With the realization that other parts of Britain were successfully using water as means of transporting heavy and bulky goods, a series of Acts were passed with the aim of bringing the county's waterways back into production. The Western Rother was the first river to benefit in 1791; this was followed by its eastern namesake, then the Adur (1806) and the Ouse (1812). The improvements to these rivers technically converted them into navigations; if necessary, locks were inserted into the stream and new cuts made to shorten a wandering loop, but wherever possibly the original course was followed. One exception was with the upper Ouse where a series of locks enabled barge traffic to extend into the Weald.

Apart from the Royal Military Canal, the only other true canals to be built in the county were the Wey–Arun and its offshoot the Portsmouth and Arundel. For many years schemes had been put forward to link both Chatham and London to the naval base at Portsmouth, all with the aim of bypassing the Dover Straits where the threat from France was at its greatest. The Wey–Arun was the only one to come to fruition. Construction began in 1813 and traffic was first carried three years later. The waterway was a fusion of two interests: the true canal, the Wey and Arun Junction Canal, left the river Wey above Guildford, entered the county at its highest point near Loxwood, then descended through a dozen locks to join the Arun Navigation at Newbridge, where there was a large transhipment depot. Although great things were expected from the waterway, it suffered from a perennial problem, shortage of water and it was no surprise when it succumbed in 1871. The lower section continued to trade until 1887; its offshoot, the Rother Navigation, was still carrying coal in the early years of the twentieth century.

The white elephant of the Sussex canals, the Portsmouth and Arundel, was the last to be built (in 1823) and the shortest and the first to expire (in 1853). It connected to the river Arun, 2 miles (3.2km) inland from the coast, crossed the coastal plain and discharged into Chichester Harbour just to the south of the city. There were several reasons why this speculative project went ahead, one was to complete an inland route to Portsmouth and another was to provide employment in the post-Napoleonic years. The third Earl of Egremont financed both this canal and the Rother Navigation, the latter servicing his estates at Petworth. Unlike the Rother, which was profitable, in no year did the Portsmouth manage to cover its running costs.

Shelley

Most of the great names of Sussex literature were born in the following centuries, but one maverick son was writing in the early decades of the nineteenth century. Percy Bysshe Shelley was born at Field Place, Warnham in 1792 and spent the first years of his life in the place he later described as paradise. 'This scene of earliest hopes and joys' was not to last; the village schoolmaster who introduced him to the classics was superseded by Eton and Oxford. It was during vacations from these institutions that his rebellious temperament began to show itself. It was his unwillingness to accept the Christian faith of his family and of society in general that led to his exile from Field Place and eventually England. Expelled from Oxford and banished from his home, he formed a covey of like-minded, nomadic individuals including Mary Wollstonecraft and Lord Byron, who wandered at will throughout Wales and the Continent.

He did return to Sussex in 1815, after the death of his grandfather. Forbidden to enter Field Place, he abandoned any claim to the estate in return for an immediate legacy. This was his last visit to his native county. He continued his writing in several homes in England, interspersed with continental travel. It was during one of his visits to Italy that he was killed in a boating accident. His was a short life, 30 years, but eventful, and his free-thinking spirit is commemorated in Horsham, the town near to his birthplace, by a rather obscure memorial.

The controversial Shelley Fountain. Hardly a fitting memorial to Horsham's famous son.

The Smuggling Industry

The golden age for Sussex smuggling was the eighteenth century, although the illicit industry had been active since Saxon times. Wherever there is a levy or tax on the free trading of goods smuggling will occur. The greater the tax and the more goods that are involved the bigger the incentive to operate outside the law. In the thirteenth century a localized dispute arose between the merchants of Shoreham and their Lord of the Manor over the amount of levy he could impose on each cargo. Lives were endangered on more than one occasion when the lord's agents confronted the townspeople and smugglers. Small, similar disputes regularly took place along the coast, but it was a governmental tax on wool that made smuggling into an organized industry.

For nearly three centuries wool was the basis for smuggling in the county; at the same time as a tax was imposed on it a further embargo was placed on the importation of base coinage. This dual imposition gave the smugglers a cargo for both legs of their journey. The arrival in the county of coinage necessitated a distribution network with wide contacts; this was quickly set up and the underground organization was able to move into other commodities whenever new restrictions were introduced. Before the arrival of income tax the national purse relied heavily on customs and excise duties for the bulk of its income; at one time there were over 200 items on the restricted list. Not all of these could be called luxury items – tea and tobacco coexisted alongside spirits and fine wines; this anomaly brought all sections of the community into the market for the black imports.

Hundred of men were involved in this highly organized trade, the leaders finding a ready supply of casual labour from both the employed and the long-term out-of-work. When a night's smuggling gave the same reward as a week's labour it was little wonder that the gangs had no difficulty in finding willing accomplices. In comparison, the preventive operations against the gangs were inadequate and inefficient. Many of the excisemen were, for a fee, willing to turn a blind eye to the nocturnal activities; those who were more conscientious were always under threat from the gangs who had a Mafia-like grip on the countryside. Occasionally arrests were made and justice done, as in 1747 when members of the notorious Hawkhurst Gang went out of county and first laid siege to, then broke into the customs house at Poole. Two years later seven members of the gang were apprehended and sentenced to death at Chichester Assizes and their bodies hung in chains at several prominent locations in the county as a warning to others.

All the coastal settlements, as well as many inland villages that had direct contact with them,

The River Cuckmere at Alfriston.

became involved with these nefarious activities. The little town of Alfriston was one of the main distribution centres, lying 2 miles (3.2km) inland on the River Cuckmere, for there was hardly a house in the town that was not in involved in the trade; indeed, the economy of the area depended on the smugglers. A typical example of the precautions the local gang took to avoid detection could be found at the Market Cross Inn. This was a maze of corridors and staircases, its twenty-one rooms boasted forty-five doors, with everything designed to assist the gang members to escape should the excisemen call.

Two main incentives were needed to bring the widespread smuggling activities under control: an effective policing system and the lowering of taxation on essential commodities. Both were initiated at the end of the French Wars; the govern-

ment now needed to take less in taxes and the navy had an excess of men. These redundant or retired seamen formed the nucleus of a highly organized coastguard authority. A chain of lookout stations was established along the southern coastline, each unit within signalling distance of the next and connected to its neighbour by a path which was patrolled each night. Within a decade large-scale smuggling had been eliminated.

The Birth of the Sussex Resorts

Brighton

The Sussex resorts owe a vote of thanks to a Lewes doctor, Richard Russell, who in 1750 published *A Dissertation Concerning the Use of Sea Water in the Diseases of the Glands*. In this

Alfriston. A tourist-oriented reminder of the earlier industry.

essay he claimed that sea water could prevent or even cure a variety of ailments. His teaching opened a new branch of medicine and, as his reputation grew, he decided to relocate his home and practice to his nearest seaside town. Brighton (originally Brighthelmston) in the 1750s was a run-down community that had retreated to the cliffs in order to avoid the winter storms. Although in itself not in the best of health, the town serviced a wide inland area through its maritime activities. The absence of a harbour was not a problem for the large fishing fleet and the coastal trade, the foreshore proving adequate for the types of vessel based there.

It was the local aristocracy who had time to spare and money to spend who were the first visitors. The spa towns had been 'done', and the opportunity to sample new health-giving plea-sures proved irresistible. These early visitors were mainly of the day-tripper variety, but, as the marketing of sea bathing increased, it was not long before the developers arrived. There was little thought given to the planning of these first buildings: wherever there was a strip of level land near to a beach up went a row of cheaply constructed houses. Towards the end of the century the Regency style buildings began to appear. The majority of these faced the sea or were erected in squares, terraces or crescents, all in a single architectural design. These well-proportioned homes reflected the resort's rising tastes and affluence. In 1760 the population of the town was about 2,000 and it welcomed only 400 visitors each year. Sixty years later the visitor numbers had risen to 11,000 and they were serviced by 25,000 residents. The majority of

Eight miles to Brighton. Ancient milestone in Lewes High Street.

these new servants arrived in the depression years that followed the Napoleonic Wars; the countryside could not provide them with a future, but Brighton might. To house these new arrivals a ghetto of simple cottages were thrown together in an area beneath the Downs. Often with no basic facilities, they quickly degenerated into slums, some streets having to be demolished after a life of less than ten years.

To develop as a successful resort a town needed three attributes: ease of access, approval of the medical profession and royal patronage. Brighton easily met all three challenges. It was the nearest south coast town to London and could be reached by coach in under five hours. Its reputation was slightly tarnished by the claims of suspect practitioners immediately after the death of Russell, but it quickly recreated itself by promoting its sea-bathing qualities and 'quality air'. The royal patronage came from the Prince Regent, later George IV, who, in a span of forty years, hardly missed a season's residence in the town. In the early years of expansion Brighton was the premier packet port for France, the steamers bringing many European patrons eager to sample the Sussex Experience.

There is a limit to the amount of bathing and

THE ROYAL PAVILION

In 1783 the Prince Regent made his first visit to Brighton; three years later he purchased the site of the present Pavilion and the following year work started on the first building. This was a simple Georgian-style villa that was to become the nucleus of the palace that is on exhibition today. In 1808 new stables and a riding house were completed in the grounds. This new structure dwarfed every other in the vicinity, and its most striking feature was a dome of wood and glass over 80ft (24m) in diameter. Around the covered courtyard were two tiers of Moorish arches, the lower ones leading to stalls for the horses with the upper tier to ostlers' quarters and tack rooms.

The Prince was now becoming interested in oriental design and he had the interior of the building redecorated and refurbished in the Chinese style. Plans were made to convert the exterior into a pagoda, but a further bout of fickleness, this time towards India, saw the architect responsible for London's Regent Street, John Nash, engaged to begin a project that would extend the building into a form resembling a small Taj Mahal. The final result, an Indian building with Chinese decor, did not find favour with either the local residents or the visitors. Many commentators considered the building to be in extremely bad taste, likening it to The Kremlin, an enlarged china shop or a Turkish Harem. The Reverend Sydney Smith suggested that the dome of St Pauls must have come down to Brighton and pupped.

In 1827 George IV, as the Prince had then become, tired of both his palace and Brighton, never to return. Neither his successor nor Queen Victoria favoured the resort and in the mid 1840s many of the interior fittings were removed to Buckingham Palace. The Pavilion was offered to Brighton for £53,000 and in 1850 the town became the owners of this extravaganza. Much of the original furniture has found its way back into the building and today it is a tourist attraction that is the envy of other English resorts.

The Royal Pavilion: onions and all.

promenading an individual can endure; to succeed a resort also had to offer after-hours entertainment. In the town legitimate interests were
catered for by the theatres, concert halls and
assembly rooms, where a variety of activities
could be enjoyed. More dubious pleasures were
available for both sexes, often offered by ambi-
tious individuals of the less well established
members of the landed class.

Brighton reached its first zenith in the 1820s,
then the squalid conditions of the inland town
began to edge seawards. What was a well-
designed seaside town degenerated into an unat-
tractive one by the sea. Fashion deserted, and it
was not until the arrival of the railway, which
brought a new type of visitor, that the town's
fortunes as a resort began to recover.

Other Sussex Resorts

The other resorts were late developers and were
designed so that they complemented but did not
compete with the premier resort. Hastings in
1800 comprised not much more than two
streets. Little improvement was made to this
area, the Old Town, all new building being concentrated to the west. Work on the new town of
St Leonards commenced in 1828 but progress
was slow and it was well into Victoria's reign
before the project was completed. An attempt
was made by Seaford to entice the less wealthy
to set up residence around its one inn. To cope
with the expected influx a terrace of elegant
houses was built. As they were separated from
the sea by an area of rough grassland where cat-

THE LEWES SNOWDROP

One tragic incident occurred in Lewes a few months before the coronation of the new Queen, an event which is typical of the problems endured by the county over the previous two decades: mention the word 'avalanche' and immediately one thinks of the skiing areas of the Alps or Pyrenees. Yet one of the worst tragedies attributed to snow in these islands took place in December 1836 at the county town of East Sussex.

December was a bitterly cold month; throughout the country were reports of closed roads, stranded stagecoach passengers and deaths from the sub-zero temperatures. In Brighton a stableman and a milkman became victims of the frost. Animals suffered too, over forty sheep and a horse died at Lewes and the town was isolated with only the river route remaining open.

On Christmas Eve it began to snow, the storm continued throughout the night and all of Christmas Day. Above the appropriately named suburb of Cliffe, where the Downs drop almost sheer into the river valley, high winds had forced the snow into thick drifts almost 20ft (6m) high. Along the rim of the perpendicular cliff, which overhung houses in South Street, there appeared a continuous rim of frozen snow. The residents of the street were not unduly concerned for in a similar situation fifty years earlier only slight damage was done to the properties.

The area most at risk contained a row of workmen's cottages known as Boulder Row. An old local bargeman, with a long memory, tried throughout Boxing Day to get the residents to evacuate their homes and seek safety elsewhere. He had no success for the safety haven was in the local workhouse, an institution dreaded by the county's residents. Early the following morning came the first avalanche, a small fall that still managed to demolish a timber yard. With the increasing daylight the temperature eased a little and ever-widening cracks appeared in the drift. Further small falls occurred, breaking open doors and cracking windows. At last the inhabitants of Boulder Row took heed of the warnings, not immediately, but only after they had transferred their possessions into a nearby warehouse. Time was not on their side, for at 10.15 a.m. the avalanche dropped; it first hit the base of the houses then, like a giant wave, carried them bodily into the street. Where the houses once stood there was now only a pile of snow.

Rescue volunteers were soon on the scene, seven people were found alive but eight had perished; if the fall had occurred twelve hours earlier when the residents were in bed the death toll would probably have been greater. Lewes was given a further reminder of the tragedy a few weeks later when the melting snow revealed broken and useless personal possessions, plus remnants of a festive season that was so tragically terminated.

The events of that day were commemorated by naming a local hostelry 'The Snowdrop'. Sadly, this is no more – as with many of the county's pubs, conversion has claimed another victim.

Cliffe High Street. South Street is squeezed between the High Street and the Downs.

tle were grazed, plus the local rubbish tip, there were few enquiries for occupancy. Eastbourne had only scattered pockets of development before 1850 when the Duke of Devonshire began his building of large estates. Bognor was the first resort to be promoted by one man. It was created by Sir Richard Hotham and was designed for those seeking seclusion but with the same luxury and ambience that was found in Brighton. He obtained the necessary royal patronage from Princess Charlotte, and the town found favour with both the English and the French upper class, these high-spending guests being accommodated in distinguished villas. Somewhat surprisingly, the planned resort was never completed.

Worthing was designed to be a smaller and cheaper version of Brighton. The development, which did not start until the 1780s, was centred on an old fishing village and so quick was its progress than in thirty years it offered all the facilities of a complete resort. The downturn in visitor numbers during the depression years was felt more severely than in Brighton for the town was not as accessible and had less of a reputation, be it good or bad. For several decades new building was put on hold and from then on it was never able to mount a serious challenge to its eastern neighbour.

Riots

'Riot' is possibly too strong a word to describe the events that took place in the county in the early 1830s. For a decade there had been a simmering of unrest throughout the country. In the south-east the so-called 'Captain Swing' troubles, named after an anonymous leader who signed orders under that pen name, spread quickly across the border from Kent. In the first two months of this activity 103 incidents were recorded, two-thirds being in the east of the county. There was little violence in the early disturbances, arson on newly collected cereal stacks being the commonest form of protest. The later troubles were mainly local events with the objective of obtaining a modest increase in wages. These demands were mostly met, but a small minority of landowners panicked and wrote to the Home Secretary with a highly coloured and largely inaccurate account of the events that were taking place in the county. As had happened before, any advantage gained by the working classes was smartly followed by repressive action against them. In a hastily arranged Assizes at Lewes fifty-three men and women were charged, the punishments varied from death, to transhipment to Australia and jail sentences. Surprisingly, eighteen were acquitted.

In 1832 a Royal Commission was set up with the aim to amend the existing Poor Law. Two years later the Poor Law Amendment Act became law. Two sections of it were not popular with the Sussex poor and led to increased unrest. The payment of relief in cash was to be ended, at least in theory, and relief was to be refused outside the workhouse. Those parishes that had not adopted the earlier reforms were now to be grouped into unions. This combining of parishes also led to problems when residents of one were forced into a house of another. The most serious incident happened at Steyning; when the authorities proposed moving several families to Henfield, fighting broke out which was stopped only by troops drafted in from Brighton.

No doubt influenced by the Tolpuddle Martyrs from Dorset, East Sussex saw the arrival of several pseudo-trade unions. Mass meetings were held outside Eastbourne and Rye where demands were made for substantial wage increases during the critical harvest period. These unions were in their infancy and the movements collapsed when the farmers threatened to lock out any individual who joined. Small protests continued for several years, but the formation of a rural police force for East Sussex in 1839 was a deterrent to organized activity. That, and the reluctance of the Sussex labourer to be pressed into actions he did not fully understand, led the workforce into an introverted acceptance of their position.

8. VICTORIANA

Victoria was born in 1819 and was only eight months old when her father died. Her childhood and teenage years were spent under the 'protection' of her mother, the Duchess of Kent, and it was a stubborn and rather immature individual who came to the throne in 1837. Within two years she had met and married her German cousin Albert. Throughout the marriage Victoria relied heavily on him for advice, since he was her intellectual superior. Although the coronation and the wedding were occasions for pomp and splendour these celebrations could be seen as a lull before the storm, for the country as a whole was destined to move into a decade of decline, a situation already experienced by the shire counties.

Richard Cobden and the Anti-Corn Law League

In the first few years of her reign Victoria's government faced problems from two independent protest groups. Both were based in the industrial north; the Chartists obtained their name from the six-point charter they adopted (1836) which demanded, among other objectives, manhood suffrage, annual Parliaments and the payment of Members. The Anti-Corn Law League (1839) had an agricultural base, in spite of its being based in the north. One of its principal leaders was a Sussex man, Richard Cobden. He was born in 1804, the son of a yeoman farmer and spent his early years in West Sussex. After moving to Manchester he became involved in politics and was elected Member for Stockport. The Corn Laws of 1815 forbade the importing of grain until its price had risen above a certain level; the League believed that this embargo kept prices artificially high, causing great hardship to the poor. Against the League were the landowners who foresaw bankruptcy and ruin should the

laws be repealed. After intense pressure from the League, ably assisted by their own elected abolitionist MPs, the legislation was repealed in 1846. The farmers' fears were unfounded for there remained a healthy market for all the country could produce and Cobden's home county, in common with the rest of rural England, enjoyed two decades of prosperity. Cobden remained a thorn in the side of government until his death in 1865. Three small parishes wish to claim the credit for Richard Cobden: Cocking, into which he was born, Heyshott,

The Richard Cobden Memorial at West Lavington.

Arundel castle.

where he worshipped as a boy, and West Lavington, where he was interred in the family grave. A recent inter-parish boundary dispute shows that the animosity over their son has yet to be resolved.

The Fortunes of Rural Sussex

With the repealing of the Corn Laws the county embarked on another upward cycle of the 'boom and bust', a situation that it had experienced many times over the previous centuries. With the increasing population in the Midlands and the North, the price of corn remained at a satisfactory level. This prosperity enjoyed by the country areas enabled the population of Sussex to steadily increase without creating excessive unemployment, until a peak was reached around 1870. Twenty years before then, Sussex agriculture employed directly one in six of the local people; if marginal activities were added then the ratio would have been higher. At the end of the century farming still accounted for one in eight persons, this figure being twice the national average. Throughout this 'golden age of agriculture', as the period has been called, more of the county's land was under cultivation than ever before.

In the early 1870s the British bubble burst, thanks mainly to the importing of cheap wheat

A village commemoration of Queen Victoria's Jubilee. The downland planting commissioned and funded by the local inhabitants of Street

from the USA and Russia. Large areas of the country suffered in the ensuing depression, but Sussex in general was able to survive thanks to its recent diversification into a range of alternative crops. Hop growing had spread from Kent into the east of the county, and, although not a great money spinner, it provided direct employment and in related woodland industries. The spreading of the railways into the county assisted the establishment of market gardens and orchards; with easy access to local stations fresh fruit and vegetables had but a short ride to the London markets.

There were two Royal Commissions on Agriculture sitting during the slack years. The first in 1873 gave only a cursory treatment to Sussex; the second, twenty years later, gave the county more consideration and enthused over one local, and unusual, industry set up around Heathfield. Chicken fattening was the basis for this enterprise and, with the middle classes of the resorts and south London the target, the scheme was soon in profit.

As the demand lessened for home-produced grain, it was the marginal lands that were the first to be converted from arable to pasture. The chequerboard of fields that changed their hue according to the season became a swath of unvaried meadowland. This change in farming practice continued well into the twentieth century; detailed field maps that had survived from the sixteenth century show that there was then more land under the plough than in the 1930s. Census figures for the latter date also show a similar drift away from the rural parishes into the market towns.

Only one new town was born during Victoria's reign, Haywards Heath, and it was the railway that was instrumental in establishing it. The main line to Brighton passed through an area of scrubland 2 miles (3km) to the east of Cuckfield; here a station was built to service the market town. It is unclear why a community grew up around the station but, once established, its development was rapid and by 1900 it was home to the largest cattle market in the county.

In many of the market towns gaps between the existing buildings were infilled by suburban housing, sometimes just a single 'semi', but, where there was a larger gap, a terrace of Victorian brick appeared. In times of buoyant trade the local shopkeepers took the opportunity to upgrade the facades of their Georgian premises with brick in an attempt to disguise their age and merge with the newer residential units. East Grinstead was one area that became an early commuter community: the dissolution of the Sackville estate provided the opportunity for row upon row of uniform housing to be built on the outskirts of the town.

The lifestyle of the Sussex rural worker changed little in the second half of the nineteenth century, the fluctuations in the income of his employer meant little to him, his wages and living conditions remaining constant throughout the years. An import from the Midlands, a trade union, arrived in the county in the 1870s; it was active for about twenty years but found difficulty in interesting the Sussex rustic; if anything, it drove him into an even deeper torpor.

Rural daily life was still governed by the established hierarchy; through consolidation, more of the countryside was being governed by fewer 'names'. These landowners often imposed themselves on the land by house decoration in the estate villages. Once again, the numbers of the country elite were swelled by an influx of financiers and industrialists. With money to spare, they wished for the life of a country squire – hunting, fishing and shooting to be enjoyed without the disadvantages of farming. The Wealden house was the prime target for these incomers, a bijou residence that was quickly improved by gas lighting and a water closet. Surprisingly, these newcomers integrated easily with their long-established neighbours and had little difficulty in acknowledging the few responsibilities that their position entailed.

The Victorian Resorts

The early years of Victoria's reign saw the fortunes of Brighton in steep decline. It had already bid farewell to many of the free-spending aristocracy and the loss in 1845 of royal patronage was a further blow. The Queen, unlike her royal predecessors, made only a few visits to the town. On her first visit every effort was made to

---

RICHARD JEFFERIES

Jefferies was famous for his detailed writings on the natural world but it was not until his later years that his essays dealt with the Sussex countryside. He was born in 1848 in Wiltshire and made early connections with the county through spending his holidays, both as a child and a young man, at Worthing. After several nomadic years he set up home at Hove believing that the better air quality would grant him an improvement in health. In spite of being a great naturalist, he found the lure of Brighton irresistible, possibly because of the abundance of young women in the resort. In one of his writings he observed 'there are more handsome women there than anywhere else in the world'.

After a stay of just two years his restlessness returned, departing from the county for Kent then returning, via Rotherfield, to the forest town of Crowborough and an aptly named house, The

Downs. Between recurring bouts of illness he was able to enjoy the nearby Ashdown Forest, then when confined indoors he continued with his descriptive writings, *The Hours of Spring* vividly recalling the harsh winter of 1885–86.

In the following summer, with his health continuing to deteriorate, he made his final move back to the coast, to Goring, adjacent to his childhood holiday home; to honour the town he named the heroine of his novel *The Dewy Morn*, Felise Goring. Even when too ill to enjoy the surrounding countryside he continued to write, dictating his words to his wife. He died in 1887 from consumption at the early age of thirty-eight. His links with Sussex continue for he was buried in Broadwater cemetery at Worthing, to be joined decades later by another of the county's natural history writers W. H. Hudson.

impress, with a stage-managed entrance through a floral arch. On her final visit, accompanied by Albert, she attempted an informal, early morning walkabout. She was not amused with the attention given to her presence on the streets and left for London the same day, never to return.

A through rail service from the capital began in 1841 and, after the expected teething troubles, it delivered a revitalizing boost to the town and its economy. Within a couple of years of its opening the railway brought the first load of day-trippers. These early trains were not much faster than the stagecoaches but they were able to carry a much larger number of travellers. The first excursion train ran at Easter 1844, comprising fifty-seven carriages (or trucks); it needed six engines for its motive power. The town retained its blowzy attractions for these short-time visitors, but it was a different type of clientele that was needed to provide a solid base for the town's economy.

Brighton was the premier resort, and where the leader went the other towns tried to follow, not always successfully. The increase in visitor numbers required a larger workforce to service them, the coast seeing the largest population increase in the second half of the century. Brighton doubled its number of residents. No longer were the earlier slum hovels acceptable; at the end of their short life they were replaced *in situ* by standard working-class homes. These

replacements could not cater for the demand and streets of identical form were soon constructed. Interspersed among the houses were the essentials needed to make the area self-contained: shops, stables and, of course, a public house. These new properties were built by private developers and, since many of the workers could not afford the rents, house sharing became a common option, so continuing the problem of overcrowding.

Hove, ever the more refined partner, adopted a different form of development. In the 1850s a group of local speculators built three self-contained streets of semi-detached villas intermixed with terraced houses. They were an immediate success, and the following years saw a flurry of similar estates built. An attempt to create a 'showpiece' centre based on the Grand Avenue failed, for the residents chose the town for its peace and quiet; if they wanted entertainment then Brighton was only a walk away.

The other resort towns, which started from a very much smaller base, saw a greater percentage increase in their population. At both Worthing and Hastings the rise was fourfold; at the top of the list came Eastbourne, which climbed from 3,000 in 1850 to 44,000 by the turn of the century. Hastings gained its increase by continuing with a policy of piecemeal, disorganized planning, Eastbourne must thank the seventh Duke of Devonshire for the solid

---

SQUIRE GOREHAM OF TELSCOMBE

Telscombe was one village that benefited from its new squire, Ambrose Goreham, who arrived in the village late in the nineteenth century. He was a London bookmaker who, at thirty-nine, and having accumulated what he considered a reasonable fortune, decided to retire and follow his other passion, that of breeding race horses.

Telscombe is little more than a Norman church and a cluster of houses at the end of a downland valley. There is only one road leading to the village. The new squire refused to allow any new development to take place, concentrating instead on improving the cottages and restoring the

church. He set up a training establishment for his horses on the local Downs and was reasonable successful, for one of his charges won the Grand National in 1902. Throughout his residency he continued to improve the village infrastructure, installing mains water and, just before his death, bringing electricity to the community. He bequeathed all his lands to Brighton Corporation on trust; his will stipulated that this gift was to preserve the rural nature of the village. Seventy years on the peaceful atmosphere remains, a fitting tribute to a forward-thinking man.

appearance of its streets, a design that was copied on a smaller scale by neighbouring Bexhill. Seaford, after the railway reached the town in 1859, tried to emulate Brighton; the theory was fine but no schemes ever came to fruition, for, although five separate companies were formed to build the town, none was willing to take the risk.

As the century progressed a new leisure group emerged to fill the void: the commercial and professional middle classes. These could afford to bring their families to the coast for a week's vacation and, as their numbers increased, two new forms of accommodation developed. The boarding or lodging house, run by wives or single women, arrived, usually outside the resort centre. To cater for the 'plutocracy' who considered themselves to be above lodging and were looking for a non-luxurious, country-house style of living, into Brighton came the Grand Hotel in 1865 and the Metropole in 1890. The town now had two seasons: spring and autumn remained devoted to pampering the well-established gentry who had refused to desert the town in the time of its troubles, while summer accommodated the new arrivals where vacations were often interrupted by regular, short invasions by the working classes.

The other coastal resorts had less direct rail links to London and the increased journey times made them less attractive to the day-tripper. Their absence was appreciated by a section of the moderately prosperous middle classes who were seeking a peaceful, respectable holiday that was reasonably priced. A relaxing walk along the promenade, perhaps a boat trip around the

Brighton seafront. Victorian facades mix with twentieth-century steel and glass.

A Victorian seafront terrace at Hastings.

bay, and sedate evening entertainment were all they asked. Worthing, Eastbourne and other similar towns were happy to oblige. What the railway bringeth so shall she taketh away. By the end of century the moneyed visitors were again deserting the Sussex resorts, this time for the coast of northern France. Ironically, the journey across the water had to be made by a railway company steamer.

Leisure

The working classes, which included the rural labourer and those who serviced the fledgling tourist industry, had little leisure time. The working week normally comprised sixty hours spread over six days. Any spare time was usual-ly spent, when funds allowed, drinking in the local public houses. In 1875 the average annual consumption of beer per person in Sussex was over 33gal (150ltr). This apparently high figure owed a great deal to the fact that, apart from its more wholesome taste, it was safer to drink than many of the local waters. From the mid century onwards, the pub became totally working class; besides its original function to provide refreshment, and at times oblivion, it became the social centre for artisan life. From small villages to the larger towns, the number of licensed premises continued to grow: by 1900 the total for the county was in excess of 1,300. Two decades earlier the number was probably higher, for, as more leisure facilities became available and especially for the urban dweller, beer drinking declined. To keep their share of the trade, the local brewers were forced to adopt a new strategy: welcome to the 'respectable' pub and a double handshake for the houses that offered a choice of bar. The workers and their bosses could now enjoy their pleasures under the same roof, segregated yet united.

Enterprising Brighton

If there were a league table of the English counties affected by the Industrial Revolution then Sussex would appear near the bottom. Apart from gasworks and the railway little was introduced to disrupt the lives of its residents. Any manifestations that did come south were leisure-orientated and concentrated on the premier resort.

In 1831 work began in Hove on a giant glass and metal dome known as The Athenaeum; it pre-dated both the Crystal Palace and the reading room of the British Museum. Sadly, the public were not able to enjoy the spectacle for on the day before its official opening the edifice collapsed. The design errors were realized and not copied into later, similar projects.

The chain pier was opened in 1823 to provide a berthing point for cross-channel steamers. This was a pioneering structure to demonstrate the feasibility of a suspension system operating in open water. By mid century it became fashionable to promenade along its length. For 2 pre-decimal pence (rather less than 1p) it was possible to visit the saloon and reading room, listen to the band and enjoy the refined amusements – activities that were soon offered by the newly

Drunkenness: a warning to all imbibers at Kirdford.

Brighton Pier. Known to millions as the Palace Pier, it has recently undergone a name change.

opened, downmarket Palace Pier. The chain pier did not survive into the twentieth century for it was destroyed in 1896 by a combination of storm-force winds and heavy seas.

The Devil's Dyke is a north-facing coombe in the Downs above Brighton. The area has always been a popular tourist attraction for both residents and visitors alike, and it was from here that another short-lived experiment was constructed. In the 1880s a cable car was suspended across the Dyke and a complementary funicular climbed from the underdown village of Poynings. Both of these attractions were among the earliest examples of these forms of transport, but little thought appears to have been given to their positioning. Traffic arrived from Brighton on the opposite side of the hill and there was little incentive for potential passengers to begin their experience with a down-slope journey.

The final two innovations belong to a local inventor, Magnus Volk. In 1883 he installed electricity in the Royal Pavilion and opened the world's first electric railway running along the undercliff to the east of the town centre. This has survived the years and remains a summer attraction for today's visitor. His second invention was less successful. He built a unique railway on the shore just above the low-tide level. At high tide passengers were carried, at a giddy speed of 2mph (3.2km/h) on a platform, raised high above the waves on an elongated framework. Its odd appearance earned it the nickname of 'Daddy Long Legs' and is believed to be the inspiration for H.G. Wells's *War of the Worlds*. Over five years this original contraption carried thousands of adventurous customers.

Education

One social change that, in theory, benefited the working classes of Sussex as well as throughout the country was the introduction of education for all children. Two Acts of 1870 and 1876 created this new system, a change of direction and compulsion that needed many years before its advantages became apparent.

The education of the sons of the middle classes had traditionally been divided between those families who chose to go out of the county and those who remained true to the remnants of the old grammar schools. The latter often offered only a substandard classical education. This deficiency was seized upon by a group of devious characters who set up in the resort towns a series of 'private academies'. To counteract these charlatans the curate of Shoreham, Nathaniel Woodward, with substantial financial backing, created the College of St Mary. This was part of a scheme to offer the middle classes a combined education at an affordable cost. Over the years a chain of schools were established, the elaborate buildings of which proved difficult to maintain from the income generated by fees from local pupil. Although originally founded for the sons of Sussex, their popularity soon drew more pupils and income from beyond the county. In the 1860s the remaining grammar schools, assisted by new colleges at Brighton and Eastbourne, were reformed to offer to any interested party a much improved curriculum.

Female emancipation did not arrive until late in the century when what was to become Roedean was founded. Before this the girls were at the mercy of private or dame schools. These were mainly small establishments with fewer than twenty pupils and where formal education took second place to the teaching of social graces. The preparatory schools were another late arrival. These tended to be clustered around the coastal resorts and were usually linked to a

---

H.G. WELLS

Wells first became acquainted with Sussex in 1883 when his mother was appointed housekeeper at Uppark, an isolated, downland mansion a few miles from the Hampshire border. Although her stay at the house was not of the happiest (she was sacked for gossiping), her son revelled in both the house and its environs. It was the library which offered most to the young Wells. One winter when the area was snowbound and he was forced to remain indoors he inaugurated his writing by producing a simple newspaper, *The Uppark Alarmist*.

Several times he was despatched from the house 'to seek his own life'. Each time he returned; on one occasion after recuperating from an illness he 'read, wrote and thought abundantly'. The little market town of Midhurst had been home to his grandparents and its ambience appealed to the teenager. An enjoyable period of employment with a local chemist came to an end when the funds could not be found to cover the expense of his qualifying. While at work, the headmaster of Midhurst Grammar School coached him in Latin, and later on his own he managed to obtain the qualification he needed both to teach and to continue his studies at the school. His hard work finally paid off when he won a scholarship to the Normal School of Science (later known as the Royal College) in South Kensington. It was here that he developed his scientific interests and began his serious writing.

Wells spent most of his adult life in London, but he was forever grateful for the happy years Sussex gave him. In several of his novels people and situations are based on personalities and events he encountered there. Two extracts from his later writings illustrate the depth of feeling he had for Sussex:

> I came to Midhurst a happy but desperate fugitive from servitude; I left it in glory' and 'I know no county to compare with West Sussex. It has its own colour, a pleasant colour and a warm flavour of open country because of the parks and commons and pinewoods about it.

higher establishment, offering the sons of the Sussex gentry their first step towards entry into a so-called 'public' school.

Education for the working classes grew in the early Victorian years in a haphazard and piecemeal fashion. Before the 1870 Act each village, town or community was responsible for providing and managing its own school, the government confining itself to offering aid to local funds. Some villages had parochial schools and, if they were fortunate, their own buildings. Others were less lucky and had to accept whatever accommodation was available. In 1851 Sussex had 359 of these schools, administered with either Anglican or Nonconformist supervision; despite their countywide spread, they attracted only one-third of their potential pupils. In the following decade they did succeed in doubling the number who attended. In 1851 it was also found that there were over 800 'private' schools in the county, most being run by uncertified teachers and with only a handful of pupils.

Regular attendance by pupils was a forlorn hope for the majority of rural schools, for, despite regular visits by inspectors, there were always outside demands that took precedence over education. Up to the turn of the century it remained vital for the children of rural workers to absent themselves in order to supplement the family income. These unofficial holidays were most often taken in the late summer in harvest time. The weather too played a significant part in attendance records; besides governing activities on the land, a singular wet or, in winter, snowy day would drastically reduce the num-

The original Tudor buildings of Steyning Grammar School.

bers in school. One can sympathize with these truants for it was not uncommon for pupils to make a 3 mile (5km) trek from home to school. How many of today's children would attempt – or be allowed to make – this daily trudge back and forth?

The two Education Acts of the 1870s committed all parishes to providing education for all school age children; any that were unable or unwilling to accept their obligations were placed under the control of a local school board. These boards reported direct to, and were centrally funded by, the national Board of Education, and were responsible for the financing and management of their buildings. Many of the rural boards were slow in taking up their duties, but when moneys arrived from central government a semi-standard type of school building emerged. It was usually built of stone, not of uniform size but had one distinguishing feature: a rooftop bell tower. Many of these schools have been made redundant and their buildings now converted into dwellings, but almost without exception the bell tower remains as evidence of their original usage. In 1902 the local boards were abolished and the county councils became responsible for education in their areas.

As Victorian England changed from a rural to a predominantly urban country it was natural that the legislators and central government should view basic education in an urban setting, and it was the town schools that received the greater funding and assistance. Being a largely rural county, Sussex suffered from this two-tier system that was not standardized until the county councils were given control.

Many of the village schools were one-man establishments where the only teacher taught all subjects to all ages. The standards were allowed to deteriorate even further in the 1890s when the smaller schools were no longer required to employ a certified teacher. Throughout Victoria's reign the standard of education for the county's rural children was less than satisfactory, governments preached but did not practise. With the arrival of the new century and a locally-controlled system things could only improve.

Victorian school buildings, complete with bell tower. These classrooms still form the nucleus of Easebourne Primary School.

Religion

The Victorians had a growing obsession with statistics; as well as the 1851 census for education the same year saw a probing examination of religious provision and attendance. Sussex fared badly in this; in spite of an increase in church building over the previous forty years and a programme of 'improvements' imposed on many of the earlier buildings, less than half of the county's population could be accommodated in a place of worship at any one time. The triple Sunday attendance so favoured by Victorian publicists attracted only a 56 per cent following, nearly half of the residents not crossing a church threshold on the Sunday that the count was made. Perhaps significantly the exercise was never repeated.

The Church of England, not unexpectedly, with two-thirds of the total attendees, came top in the survey. To bring more sheep into the fold new brands of Anglicanism emerged; these tended to follow traditional theology and ritualism. Anti-Catholic feeling remained strong in Sussex and these new directions were to many a first step towards 'Popery'. As noted earlier, the re-establishment of a Catholic hierarchy in 1851 brought a county-wide orgy of riot and protest. Lewes was the main centre of revolt and, although the uprisings were well-organized, one suspects that many of the participants were there only for the fun of demonstrating.

It was in the 1880s that the Salvationists appeared. Their combination of uniforms and music caused new riots in both Brighton and Worthing. Two local councils, Battle and Eastbourne, invoked long-forgotten by-laws that banned Sunday concerts in an attempt to stop their services. In spite of these early problems, the movement survived and in a decade their iron and brick citadels, along with their incumbents, became as respectable as any other denomination.

The Victorians tended to adopt a narrow attitude to religion; this was emphasized when they were unable to understand or tolerate a teaching that did not follow their own strict guidelines. The word forgiveness was often missing from their vocabulary; an instance of this bigotry is shown in the events that unfolded in the rural parish of Shipley.

The late Victorian period did bring to Sussex some outstanding examples of religious architecture. The humble Anglican church continued to be converted from what was now considered a medieval treasure into an image of what community religion should be, rather than of what it was. Gothic was in vogue: Arundel was blessed with a fairy-tale cathedral, while Lancing College, one of the Woodward Foundation schools, gained the edifice that now appears to control the lower Adur valley. The imposing building at Parkminster, south of Cowfold, owes its existence to foreign immigrants. Exiled French monks from the closed Carthusian order arrived in the county and built what at a distance appears to be a tall, isolated, church spire; a closer look reveals the grandeur of the whole building.

The Railways

The arrival of the railways was the greatest single event to affect the life of Sussex since William's invasion eight centuries earlier. No longer was the county dependent on horse power for its transport requirements.

Theoretically, the railways brought a cheap and convenient form of travel to the masses; in practice the charges that the companies made for some services did not always find favour with their passengers and held back many of the working class from using them. The trains did, however, liberate rural Sussex from its isolation, for, by the end of the century, no-one was more than 10 miles (16km) from a rail station. No longer were residents imprisoned in their local community.

Passenger travel was from the beginning a two-way traffic, a new class of tourist was now able to enjoy the county's resorts and countryside, while Sussex people had a direct channel to London's pleasures, since all of the first lines went to the capital. These same lines also introduced to Sussex the daily rat-run of the London commuter, an individual who has proliferated throughout the years.

The railway network eased the movement of goods throughout the country, although the start-up costs of its construction did not allow for cheaper distribution. Long-distance, cross-country carriers were now no longer viable; many changed their work into that of a local carrier, depositing their loads in the local station for a quick onward journey. To cater for this business even the smallest country stations

The Gothic Chapel Buildings of Lancing College. The college is the home school of the Woodward Foundation.

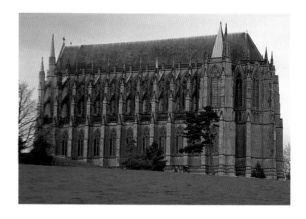

WALTER BUDD

Walter was born in Shipley in 1867. White of hair and pink of eye, this albino lad also had to endure occasional epileptic fits. These afflictions caused him to be shunned by the village, but he was the idol of his family and all their lives were disrupted when he was wrongly accused of petty theft. These allegations were later proved to be unfounded and his innocence confirmed. The events, however, so preyed on his mind that he took his life by drowning.

After his burial in the local churchyard his parents, Alfred and Charlotte Budd, had a cross erected in remembrance. Below the usual words of dedication they, perhaps unwisely, expressed their indignation against those whom they felt had contributed to the death of their son. When the vicar saw the inscription he took it as a personal affront to his ministry and ordered the memorial to be removed; for 'a symbol of sacrifice was not applicable to the remains of a sinner who had committed suicide.' The parents did not want his life to be remembered only by a nameless plot of earth and so moved the stone and its inscription to the garden of the local public house. Luckily this was a free house, not tied to any brewery, if this had not been the case the acceptance of the memorial could have caused further problems. When a new vicar took over the parish he incomprehensibly continued the church's vendetta against the Budds and ordered the removal of all wreaths and flowers from the now desecrated grave. This action caused his name to be added to the roll of honour at the base of the stone.

The memorial still remains close to the doorway of the 'George and Dragon' and is a reminder of the bigotry that could exist in the Victorian church.

The Walter Budd Memorial. Positioned at the front of the 'George and Dragon', Dragons Green.

found room for an adjoining goods yard. On the forecourt of the larger stations it was a different form of horse-drawn conveyance that was to be found. For journeys into town an omnibus waited, and for individual travellers, where there was less traffic, a lightweight trap would provide for the passenger's needs.

As the railways became established they looked to the local workforce for their staff. The construction of the lines was done largely by immigrant navvies, but the permanent staff needed to be local and loyal. In exchange for a disciplined effort, the companies offered job security, a uniform and a wage substantially above that of a farm labourer. The jobs were not unlimited but there was no other, single, comparable employer in the county. By 1910 over 5,000 men were working on the operating side of the London, Brighton and South Coast Railway and a further 3,000 in the locomotive

King's Head, Horsham. A coaching inn than did not succumb to the railways.

and carriage works at Brighton and Lancing where railway estates were built by the company to house their employees.

Where the railway was unable to make a close connection to the main community, a secondary cluster of houses often grew up around the station. One building that was rarely missing from this new settlement was the 'Station Inn', or Hotel, or just 'The Railway', these premises hoping to capture the trade lost by the deserted coaching inn.

The 'iron horse' killed off its rivals: the stage coach, the canals and the turnpikes and reigned supreme for over a hundred years until it too was severely wounded by the contraction of the national system under the malign guidance of Dr Beeching, formerly of Imperial Chemical Industries, and the private motor car.

The first railway south of the Thames opened in 1803, this was the horse-drawn Surrey Iron Railway and ran from Wandsworth to Croydon. It was a public railway copied from the mineral railways of northern England. The fact that it was public meant that anyone with the necessary wagons and horse power could use it; the tolls charged were dependent on the type of goods, their weight and the distance they were to be conveyed. An extension, opened two years later, found a gap in the North Downs and arrived at Merstham, still short of the Sussex border. Destined to proceed no further, traffic on the line was always light and its final closure came in the 1840s. A proposal to use the trackbed and a connection with the South Western at Earlsfield to the London terminus at Waterloo was not pursued.

Proposals for a railway line from London to Brighton and the south coast were first made in the 1820s. A few years later no fewer than six companies were each championing their route and seeking financial backing. A compromise scheme, at its third attempt, won the day: the authorizing Act of Parliament stipulating that the line should run 'from a junction with the London and Croydon Railway, at or near Selhurst Farm, straight through the Surrey and Sussex Weald to the sea.' This direct line needed significant engineering works, two main tunnels through the downland ridges and a long viaduct over the Ouse valley. The surveyors completed their work and construction began in July 1838.

The line was to be extended from Brighton to Shoreham, where the substantial port facilities could be used for the importing of construction materials. Priority was given to the completion of this extension and the inaugural train, carrying 230 passengers, left Brighton on 11 May 1840, it took just twelve minutes for the $6^1/_2$-mile (10.5km) journey. The local evening paper that day correctly forecast that Brighton was about to enter a new era of prosperity.

Progress continued on the London end of the line, Haywards Heath was reached in June 1841 and three months later, on 21 September, a through service began between Brighton and London Bridge. To begin with, there were six trains daily in each direction, the 'fasts' took 1 hour and 45 minutes and ran non-stop; the 'slows' took nearly an hour longer. The later introduction of excursion trains, on which the passengers paid a much reduced fare, had running times double that of the expresses. After some apprehension by the public, passenger traffic on the line increased and soon exceeded expectations; this led in 1845 to another innovation by the company: the introduction of season-ticket facilities.

The success of the Brighton line gave the incentive that other schemes needed. Each required an authorizing Act of Parliament, and, although initially operating as an independent company, it was soon taken into the LBSCR empire. From the core line, expansion continued both to the east and the west. Hastings and Chichester were connected by mid century and in the next two decades most of rural Sussex was

covered. Two invasions from out of county companies were attempted, the South Eastern built a line from Tunbridge Wells through Battle to Hastings, and the LSWR joined Midhurst to its network at Petersfield. In the first case the Brighton line did lose revenue because the Battle line gave a shorter and quicker ride to London. At Midhurst it is difficult to understand the South Western's intention; not only did it build its own terminus but it operated a policy of non-cooperation with its neighbour. The Brighton extended its line to the town from Chichester in 1881, but the feud between the two companies continued until amalgamation into the Southern Railway in 1923. The final years of Victoria saw only a few additions to the network; the Cuckoo Line extended southwards from East Grinstead to Lewes, Bexhill joined the SER at Crowhurst and the tourist line to the Devil's Dyke arrived from Brighton. Then there were the Colonel Stephens's railways.

Colonel Stephens's Railways in Sussex

In the last few years of the century, after the passing of the 1896 Light Railways Act, there emerged a significant number of usually rural light railways. Countrywide, seventeen of the enterprises were built by, or at one time managed by, this man. Sussex had three such.

The Rye and Camber Tramway was the second of the Colonel's lines. It was less than 3 miles (5km) in length and built to a gauge of 3ft (1m). The first section opened to Rye golf links and was later extended to Camber. Essentially a tourist line, it was popular with summer visitors and provided a year-round facility for the local golfer. In the 1930s it was decided to extend the line to a new holiday camp that was in the course of construction; the extension was completed only a few days before the outbreak of the Second World War and all services ceased at the end of the 1939 season. The army effectively killed the railway, for sections of track were concreted over during the war and restoration would have been too costly for the small company.

THE OUSE VIADUCT

The Ouse viaduct is undoubtedly the best known feature on the Brighton line. Emerging from the 1,141yd-long (1,043m) Balcombe tunnel, the line faced a crossing of the Ouse valley. A surface track was out of the question for the gradients involved would have been unworkable; a viaduct was the only option. The architect was David Mocatta, vice-president of the Institute of British Architects, and the engineer in charge was John Rastrick. Together they designed a structure to bridge the gap. The experience they gained in building this viaduct no doubt helped them when they encountered a similar problem on the line from Brighton to Lewes, only on this occasion it was streets that they had to override not open countryside.

The Ouse viaduct is 1,145ft (350m) long and uses thirty-seven arches. Apart from the stone parapet, it is built entirely from bricks, no fewer than eleven million were needed to complete the structure. One local historian claimed that it 'is the largest building in the world made only of brick'.

The Ouse that now flows through the arches is hardly more than a trickle, but in the 1830s it was navigable up to the site. In the early years of the century over £25,000 had been spent on improvements to the upper reaches of the river and for fifty years it was the principal carrier of goods from the surrounding area to Lewes and beyond. A new wharf was constructed to service the railway and for two years the river was busier than ever bringing up materials for the viaduct. As late as 1847 a local newspaper advertised that the most convenient way to transport of goods from Newhaven to London was via the river to Balcombe thence by train. River traffic above Lindfield ceased in 1861 and seven years later navigation downstream to Lewes was ended.

The total cost for the viaduct was only £38,500; this had to be an all-time bargain for in the next 150 years the structure needed no major repairs, despite a vast increase in the number and weight of the passing trains.

Arches over the Ouse. The view illustrates the height of the brick viaduct.

The Hundred of Manhood and Selsey Tramway, usually shortened to the 'Selsey Tram', first opened for business in 1897. Its official title adequately describing the area it served. The line was built on private land without any formal parliamentary approval and existed successfully until 1924 when it became legal, with a new company taking over its running and assets.

From the beginning economy was the primary consideration; slightly under 8 miles (12.5km) in length it boasted eleven stations, several with no accompanying buildings. A signalling system was not thought necessary and, where the line met a road, the crossings were gateless. In spite of its deficiencies and slow journey times the Tram was held in great affection, the public only

THE CLAYTON TUNNEL DISASTER

Clayton Tunnel. The castellated northern entrance was until recently a residential dwelling.

The Clayton tunnel, which bores its way through the South Downs, was in 1861 the scene of an horrific accident that changed for ever the slap-dash signalling procedures of the Brighton railway. Three trains played their part in the accident, although only two were involved in the collision. There was a signal box at each end of the tunnel, both were equipped with signals, hand flags and interconnected by telegraph. The signals were often unreliable in operation and another factor that may have contributed to the accident was the practice of the south box signalman to work, through choice, uninterrupted twenty-four-hour shifts. The Brighton Line, in common with many others in the country, worked its trains on a time-interval system where the only regulation was that successive trains on the same track should be given an interval of five minutes between each. On

that fateful morning even this simple procedure was ignored.

The first train was an excursion from Portsmouth; it passed the south box and disappeared into the tunnel. If working correctly, the passing of a train should have tripped the guarding signal back to danger; this did not happen and the signal remained at clear. Three minutes later, not five, a second excursion from Brighton approached. Concerned at the malfunctioning of the equipment, the signalman telegraphed the north box. Failing to get a reply, he frantically waved a red flag from his window. A second attempt on the telegraph received the reply 'Tunnel clear'. This he interpreted as referring to the second train; in fact, it related to the first. The driver of the Brighton excursion, seeing the red flag, stopped his train in the tunnel and started to reverse towards the entrance. A third train, again with less than the stipulated interval between it and the one that had preceded it, was allowed to proceed unchecked into the tunnel since the south box signalman thought mistakenly that both the previous excursions had cleared. In the resulting crash twenty-one people died and 176 were severely injured, making it the worst accident that had occurred on the country's railways.

The consequent Board of Trade enquiry castigated the Brighton company. Every one of its operating procedures was found to be lax and inefficient. The report recommended that the absolute block system that used the electric telegraph should be installed immediately. Reluctantly the Brighton board agreed to the experiment on a short section of line. This was so successful that by 1880 the block was in universal use over the whole system. Another first for the LBSCR.

deserting it when a faster omnibus service arrived on the peninsula. In the early 1930s no maintenance was carried out on either the track or the vehicles and it came as no surprise when the line closed in January 1935.

The Kent and East Sussex Railway was the third of the Colonel's lines in the county and had the longest lifespan. The Sussex section from Robertsbridge to Tenterden opened in 1900 and was closed by British Railways sixty-one years later. The extension through Kent to the South Eastern main line opened later and was closed to passenger traffic in 1954. Throughout its existence the line considered itself to be two separate but connecting companies; this was especially noticeable in the later years when through running was discontinued. This line is the only one of Stephens's enterprises that may be visited today, for the section from Tenterden to Bodiam has been restored by a preservation society and its train has more passengers in the summer months than the line ever managed to carry in its busiest years.

The Final Years

Towards the end of Victoria's reign Sussex was again becoming increasingly alarmed by events across the Channel and this time the villain was not France. Britain had aligned itself with its near neighbour in the Crimean war of 1854–56, and other disputes in which the country became involved were in far-flung territories of the Empire. Napoleon III had vaguely threatened us in 1859 and this led to the revival of local coastal defence volunteers, but it was the attitude of Germany in the 1870s that stimulated an increase in pseudo-patriotic activity. Long-established ports at Newhaven and Shoreham were rebuilt to protect the harbours, these being manned by an early uniformed Home Guard. This playing at soldiers became infectious and volunteer infantry and artillery battalions were formed countrywide. The units comprised mainly the gentry or tradesmen who seized every opportunity to display their eye-catching uniforms.

The Kent and East Sussex Railway. A potted history of the line.

The Kent and East Sussex Railway. Modern motive power? A Norwegian locomotive pulls away from Bodiam station.

True patriotism arrived with the second Boer War. The men of Sussex were eager to serve, but few were chosen. Seventy volunteered from Eastbourne, Seaford and Newhaven, but only twenty-seven sailed on a one-year contract. The survivors returned as heroes to a civic reception and the gift of a silver rose bowl. A hundred and sixteen regulars of the Royal Sussex Regiment went to South Africa; sixteen did not return. At the turn of the century Germany began to increase the size of her navy; to Britain this was provocative. Sussex was again in the front line but its regular and volunteer defenders had to wait a further fourteen years before the conflict began.

In 1861 Victoria lost her husband Albert. The Sussex people had not forgotten her premature departure from Brighton years earlier; this action, her disinclination to revisit the county and now the self-proclaimed extended period of mourning all combined to alienate the local population from the monarchy. By the time of her diamond jubilee in 1897 the county was willing to forgive and the celebrations were as enthusiastic as anywhere in the country. Every town and village discovered a means by which to commemorate this special occasion. The small community of Street proposed a novel undertaking: possibly inspired by the hilltop clump at Chanctonbury, the planting of trees on the slope of the Downs in the shape of *VR* (*Victoria Regina*) was envisaged. Money, however, was difficult to find and the second letter never materialized. In 1901 the little old lady in black died, aged eighty-two and having reigned for sixty-four years.

9. THE FINAL YEARS TO THE MILLENNIUM

A new century and a new monarch. Sussex paid its respects at the death of Queen Victoria, but the coronation of Edward VII allowed every town and village to celebrate the arrival of a new age. Victoria, through her children and grandchildren, was the unofficial head of many of Europe's royal families and, with these connections, attempted to bind Britain into the Continent; Edward with his freer lifestyle and thinking, leant towards one country, France. In this respect his actions could be likened to those of one of his predecessors, Charles II.

Edward was in his sixtieth year before he succeeded to the throne. From an early age his playboy activities troubled his mother but he was popular with both society and the English public. He was appreciative of women and enjoyed horse racing. These two interests could explain the frequent visits he made to West Dean Park. This estate was the home of Mrs Willie James, a famous society beauty, and was adjacent to the Goodwood course. Goodwood was more than just a race course, its summer meeting was the Sussex society event of the year, where top hats and tails were the dress for the day. Edward, although still under the watchful eye of his mother, decided to abandon the uniform so loved by the Victorians, out went formality and in its place came the more relaxed lounge suit topped by a Panama hat.

In 1903 Edward made another visit to his favourite country France, officially in preparation for the signing of the *entente cordiale*. This treaty was more of a tidying up of old squabbles than an undertaking of mutual protection, but it did entrust the control of the Channel to the Royal Navy. His short reign came to an end in 1910 when he was succeeded by his son George V. The threat from Germany lurked throughout his years, but generally it was a time for relaxation between the dour years of his mother and the staid, conventional attitudes of his successors.

The Edwardian years brought the motor car into the county. The Motor Car Act of 1904 saw a speed limit of 20mph (32km/h) introduced onto the roads. In an effort to identify the speedsters, the West Sussex County Council introduced a register of all motorized vehicles. Ninety-one cars and 107 motor cycles were the totals recorded. The car was generally a rare sight on the roads and horse power was the commonest form of transport for several years to come. Other appliances now first made their appearance in the homes of the middle and the upper class. Electric light, the telephone and the gramophone had all overcome their early inadequacies and were ready to expand into an eager market.

The political scene in the last years of Edward's and the first years of George's reign was less serene. The Liberal administration was trying to reduce the number deemed to be living in 'poverty'. Sussex, being mainly rural, did not feature in the statistics, but the introduction of an old age pension and a basic National Insurance scheme were appreciated by the county's workforce. Less enthusiastic were the landowners and the affluent members of society for the funding of these measures was to come from higher taxes on the wealthy and their land. No doubt members of the House of Lords from Sussex were active in the first rejection of the Bill. An acceptable compromise was finally reached, but then the country had to prepare itself for what semed to be an inevitable confrontation with Germany.

The Great War

The county's own regiment was the Royal Sussex. Originally formed in Belfast in 1701 as

Bexhill on Sea.

the 35th Regiment of Foot, it continued with this title until 1804 when the county title was assigned to a sibling infantry regiment, the 35th being allocated to Dorset. In 1908 several volunteer forces that existed in the county were transferred into territorial units of the county regiment. At the height of the war the regiment consisted of twenty-three battalions, serving in India and the Middle East, as well as continental Europe.

Recruiting began several years before the declaration of war. As time passed, the patriotic posters became more demanding, some in 1914 implying that the war would be over by Christmas. That prophecy came true for many thousands, killed in the autumn battles at Mons, Le Cateau and Ypres. In mid August Lord Kitchener (Secretary of State for War) headed a national call for 100,000 volunteers; one million men responded, so many that conscription was postponed until early in 1916.

Well over 4,000 Sussex men had joined up by the beginning of 1915, the majority being steered into a separate contingent where the SD (South Downs) insignia on their uniforms distinguished them from their neighbours. They were first issued with a navy-blue uniform, but this was soon superseded by the standard khaki. The SD boys were led by Col Claude Lowther. A Southdown lamb was donated to become the unit's mascot, and thereafter the troops were affectionately known as 'Lowther's Lambs'. The Lowther family donated land at Cooden for their initial training and accommodation; when it was completed they were dispersed across the southern counties for further exercises before combining with other regiments and sailing for France in March 1916. Most of the 'Lambs'

Goodwood Racecourse. The modern grandstand makes for a focal point on the Downs' skyline.

THE BLOOMSBURY GROUP

In Gordon Square, in London's Bloomsbury, in the early years of the century lived four young members of the Stephen family. Vanessa, Virginia, Thoby and Adrian were in their early twenties, each artistic and forward thinking; they were what in future years would be termed 'bright young things'.

Thoby and some of his Cambridge colleagues were the founder members of the group. Forsaking their original name of 'The Apostles', they had little difficulty in attracting like-minded associates into their circle. It was a self-praising group who met in that Gordon Square house – writers and artists in a loosely knit, self-admiration society. Loose may be used in another context for they advocated a permissive and amoral code of conduct, anti-establishment and unpatriotic, theirs was to be the way forward.

Vanessa, the artist, was the promiscuous elder sister who first married Clive Bell and set up home in an isolated farmhouse under the Downs at Charleston. She then carried on the Bloomsbury tradition by bringing her lover – another painter, Duncan Grant – into the marital home. This *ménage à trois* was apparently acceptable to all.

Virginia was the outcast of the group; always dowdily dressed, she had a reputation for remoteness and her marriage in 1912 to Leonard Woolf came as a surprise. Throughout her life she had to endure periodic bouts of ill-health and always retained the romantic notion that her health would improve if she could leave London and spend her time in some idyllic country retreat. The Woolfs' first attempt at rural living was not a success; not despondent, they soon found Asham House in Rodmell. Rural housing at that time was still primitive, no electricity, pumped water and only an earth closet. In spite of these shortcomings, Vanessa and her husband divided the next thirty years between their houses in Sussex and London.

With the Stephen girls in close proximity, it was no surprise that the area became the objective for artistic types, imitating the Bloomsbury style, but only succeeding in alienating the local community.

As the years went by, Virginia's life was punctuated by recurring bouts of depression, but in spite of this she continued to produce, from the shed at the bottom of her garden, a series of highly-regarded novels, including *Mrs Dalloway* (1925) and *To the Lighthouse* (1927). In 1941, while working on *Between the Acts*, she became unhappy with it, fearing that the illness was affecting her writing ability. One March morning, after leaving a note for Leonard, she strolled down to the river Ouse, filled her pockets with pebbles and finished her troubled life. The unfinished novel was published posthumously to universal acclaim.

Throughout the thirties the Charleston farmhouse occupied by Clive, Vanessa and Duncan was transformed by their own efforts from an uninspiring building into an extravaganza of Bloomsbury art. All fabrics, carpets and furniture were designed by the trio, one of the most striking items being the self-portrait by Vanessa. The surrounds of the house were not ignored. A walled cottage-style garden was created complete with pools, statuary and mosaic paths. In the two decades prior to the Second World War Charleston was a magnet for artistic and free-thinking spirits, Benjamin Britten being one of the celebrities who enjoyed the hospitality on offer.

The church of St Michael and All Angels at nearby Berwick also received the Bloomsbury treatment. In 1929 the controversial Bishop Bell, soon after taking office, commissioned the group to paint a set of murals for the twelfth-century church. Several local celebrities and locations were featured in the paintings, all cunningly placed in a Biblical setting. Work was not completed until 1943 and in the latter years the artists were assisted by their children.

were country lads who were unable to comprehend the horrors that lay ahead, for their world did not extend beyond the boundaries of their home village. Their enthusiasm was to be commended but in reality it was a case of 'Lambs to the slaughter'. In the following two years the

Lambs suffered in many battles: Ypres again, the Somme and Passchendeale and each took its toll. By the end of the war in excess of 1,000 Lambs had been lost or died from their wounds and many hundreds more were returned for hospitalization.

The Chattri War Memorial on the Downs above Brighton. The memorial is dedicated to the Indian soldiers who died from their wounds in local hospitals during the First World War.

As well as the Lowther camp, the coastal downland suffered from the construction of other military bases. Eastbourne was blessed with a hutted convalescent camp; in its six years of existence 150,000 patients passed through its buildings. At times of peak pressure local stately homes were requisitioned to accommodate the overflow. Seaford was home to two camps; these originally comprised rows of white bell tents, but as the war continued this temporary accommodation was replaced by more permanent, wooden structures. Large tracts of the Downs behind the camps provided the training areas for the new recruits, and as this need diminished the camps themselves were converted into holding units for troops awaiting shipment to France. It was not only the coastal strip that was disfigured

by these transient buildings. Maresfield on the edge of Ashdown Forest became home to a large permanent settlement. This substantial camp was still active until after the Second World War, demolition of the buildings not taking place until the 1980s.

The aeroplane in 1914 was still in its infancy; struggling to remain aloft and with only a limited range, it was notably absent from the Sussex skies until late in the war. The protection of the county and the coastal shipping was entrusted to a fleet of airships operated jointly by the Royal Flying Corps and the Royal Naval Air Service. These were slow and cumbersome but were able to remain on patrol for long periods, a trip lasting twelve hours was quite common. To service these dirigibles a chain of stations was estab-

THE NAB TOWER

In the later years of the war Admiralty Intelligence became concerned at the ineffectiveness of the air-ship patrols and the ease with which the German submarines could enter the English Channel. A hare-brained scheme was evolved to close the Dover Straits by means of a barrier of sixteen inter-connecting towers. Linked by steel booms, netting and mines, the whole device was to be sunk on to the seabed.

Shoreham was chosen for the construction; each tower was to be built ashore and then towed from the harbour to the required site. By 1917 the project was employing over 3,000 men and, as secrecy shrouded the project, local uncomplimentary names were given to the slowly rising towers. Engineering problems beset the construction of

these 300ft (90m) monstrosities and, thankfully for both the designers and the engineers involved, the armistice brought a conclusion to their efforts. Those towers that were still in the course of construction were demolished and their materials used as landfill rubble.

The one tower that had been completed remained at Shoreham for two years and then was towed towards the Isle of Wight. Five miles (8km) offshore from Bembridge it was sunk near the Nab sandbank. As the Nab Tower lighthouse, its beacon has shone across the waters ever since. In 1999 a Liberian-registered freighter attempted to extinguish the light when it struck it a glancing blow. The structure survived the impact, a tribute to Sussex workmanship and First World War ingenuity.

lished along the coast stretching from Tangmere to Eastbourne.

In spite of an ever-present threat from German submarines, life along the Sussex coast was, at first, largely unaffected. On a still day the rumble of gunfire could be heard from across the Channel (England was a much quieter place ninety years ago). Pleasure boating from the ports and harbours was cancelled but the local fish were landed daily from boats now crewed by old men and pre-conscript boys. It was the arrival of the casualties that made the county aware that there were troubles abroad.

Thousands of eager, patriotic men sailed from the English shores; on the return journey came a multitude of the maimed. In just a few weeks this army had matured and suffered. The British wounded brought with them many Commonwealth colleagues. In the wards of the hospitals and convalescent homes the intonations of the Empire could be heard among the British dialects. Brighton appeared to be the casualty centre for the county; so great was the influx of patients that, along with requisitioned private houses, the buildings of the Dome and the Royal Palace were taken over. It is not

known whether the choice of these buildings was intentional or left to chance, but over 4,000 Indian soldiers found sanctuary there. The bodies of the unfortunates who died from their wounds were cremated at a sacred site on the Downs above the town, according to their individual religious practices. In 1921 a permanent memorial of white Sicilian marble was built on the site and dedicated by the then Prince of Wales.

Community memorials were erected on village greens or in church grounds in the years following the 1918 armistice. Often the memorial was placed on site and the names of the fallen added at a later date. There were few, if any, parishes in Sussex that were lucky enough to receive the 'blessed' title, this signalling that the parish had no need for a roll of honour. A feature of the 1914–18 rolls, that thankfully was much less common twenty years later, was the repetition of a surname: brothers, cousins or more distant relatives, all from the same village family, making the ultimate sacrifice.

Each year on 11 November or on the nearest Sunday to it the towns and villages of the county remember the fallen of the twentieth century; occasionally a community does more to honour

its sons. The memorial at Burwash has a light in its pinnacle. On the commemorative date of the death of the inscribed names one parishioner ensures that the beacon is illuminated.

In the early years of the twentieth century the suffragette movement had little success in obtaining voting rights for women. In the war years, with the male workforce much reduced by the call of the armed forces, female labour was vital. The women's liberation movement combined with the government to persuade the female worker that there were opportunities outside the home. The Sussex women found their emancipation in nursing, on the land and in clerical and administrative tasks that previously were available only to men. By January 1918 nearly five million women were in employment, a situation that had to be rewarded. Later that year the vote was granted to women over the age of thirty, a partial victory for Mrs Pankhurst and her associates.

The Inter-War Years

The men returning from the war were promised 'a land fit for heroes'. However well intentioned this promise it did not come true. There were early post-conflict give-aways such as extended health and educational services, plus a pension increase, but the country in the early 1920s was in a divided and unhappy state. The greatest suffering and unrest were to be found in the industrial and mining areas; Sussex and the rural southern counties could watch and sympathize.

The population of the county had increased steadily before the war, but the increase was not uniform. The coastal strip and areas adjacent to the railway saw the largest increases while in the rural villages numbers declined. It was the development of road transport that brought about a new pattern of land settlement; again the coast was the first to be occupied, the majority of green pockets receiving their share of new housing. The downland to the east of Brighton was desecrated by a shanty town that was to become Peacehaven.

During the war land prices along the coast hit rock bottom. A transatlantic speculator took the opportunity to purchase large parcels of the south-facing Downs. As troops were being released his advertisements appeared: 'Homes for Heroes, a Seaside Paradise, and Garden by the Sea' were some of the terms used to describe the proposed development. The public rushed to buy plots on the biggest seaside development ever seen on this side of the Atlantic and by 1921 the first settlers began to arrive. Dirt roads were laid out but there was no electricity, a suspect water supply and only cesspool sanitation. A smattering of standard housing appeared along the roads, but by far the old railway carriage was the favoured form of accommodation. There were no public services; this deficiency did not deter the sprawl of bungalows and non-traditional housing from spreading over the Downs. In five years the area boasted a population of over 4,000 and became a byword for tasteless development, a descripion that took it many years to eradicate.

Only a few towns and villages did not receive an allocation of new houses; these new houses came with all the modern conveniences: electricity for cooking and lighting, a piped water supply and an indoor toilet, facilities that in the 1930s were still denied to many rural dwellers. After the war there was an increasing proportion of the population which aspired to be middle class and it was these social climbers, civil servants and white-collar workers, who were eager to take up the new houses. The resident natives were seemingly destined to remain second-class citizens.

On the surface, little appeared to change in the Sussex countryside, farm prices fell and incomes were squeezed, but the hungry years of the early 1930s largely bypassed the county, ever thankful that it had a mainly agricultural economy. Incomes were depressed there too, but so were shop prices and in general the county remained quietly content.

Burwash War Memorial.

RUDYARD KIPLING

Kipling was born in Bombay in 1865 and his first literary experience was as assistant editor for the Indian *Civil and Military Gazette*. Between 1882 and 1889 he travelled extensively in the Far East where he developed a lifelong interest in all things oriental. On his arrival in England he found his first residence at Rottingdean where he established a form of militia under the name of 'Kipling's Rifle Club'. This troop of around forty men formed the basis for his two-part essay *Army of a Dream*, in which the author spends time in a private citizen's army. Several events led to the writer's exchanging the coast for inland Sussex. The Rottingdean house was easily accessible by Brighton sightseers and, after the death of a daughter in 1899, the constant attention of spectators was proving irksome, and especially to his wife who was not in the best of health.

Kipling's hunt for a new home introduced him to the motor car. After a week's house hunting across the county, in which he hired a vehicle and driver, he was hooked. His first attempt at ownership was a disaster for the steam car he purchased spent more time in the repair shops than on the road. Undeterred, his next car was a Lanchester; this was the heroine of numerous letters, magazine articles and general articles about Sussex. He was now living at Bateman's, an iron master's house near Burwash; *They* and *Steam Tactics* take the reader on a semi-fictitious journey through the county where place names are encoded to bemuse the reader. His passion for the car remained with him throughout his life, his final acquisition being a Rolls-Royce.

He was a prolific writer who continued to work up to his death in 1936. His most famous volumes were aimed towards the entertainment of children: *The Jungle Book* and *Puck of Pook's Hill* are typical examples. Less well known are his books on the causes and events of the Great War which had a particular significance for him, for, in 1915 he lost his only son, killed at Loos on 29 September. Lt Richard Kipling, 2nd Irish Guards, is commemorated on the Burwash war memorial along with over 100 other servicemen from the village.

With his move to Bateman's he fulfilled a long-held ambition to become one of the English gentry.

As so often happens, he was seen by the local community as an outsider and throughout his life in the village neither side made any great attempt to close the gap that existed between them. This coolness has been long forgotten and the county now feels honoured that one of the century's most celebrated writers chose to make his home in Sussex.

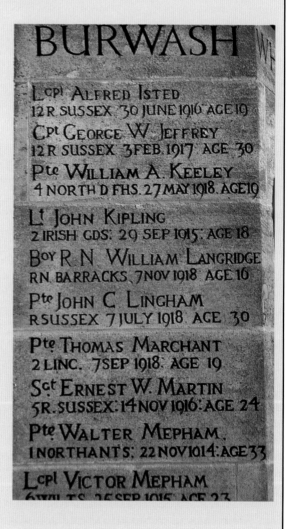

Names from the Burwash Roll of Honour.

Car, Aeroplane and Train

Although the internal combustion engine had arrived two decades earlier, it was not until the 1920s that its influence began to be felt in the county. On the farm the tractor arrived, and for £120 you could own 'a Fordson that does every thing but talk'. Slowly the horse was ousted as the primary source of motive power, but it continued to work on the smaller farms for a further twenty years. Increased power meant larger implements and accessories, and slowly the pneumatic tyre took over from the iron-rimmed, wooden cart wheel. A relaxing road noise of hoof and rim changed to a frenetic growl and thump as the attempt was made to complete tomorrow's work today.

The private motor car had not, before the Second World War, taken over the Sussex roads. In 1930 there were over a million privately-registered vehicles in Britain, most garaged or parked in the towns for it was not unusual for a village to have only a solitary car resident in the parish. Universal car ownership was still in the future, the labouring classes could not afford them, and, as they did not commute to their work, had little need for their own transport. The architects who designed the new housing estates obviously had the same opinion for few houses were built with an independent or integral garage.

Post-war public transport changed gear. The first powered buses were converted redundant ambulances operated by entrepreneurs and often with the backing of a local garage. Buyouts and consolidations were plentiful until one company, the Southdown, emerged as the premier contractor, with its green and cream vehicles. The railways had completed their network and the age of private motoring was yet to arrive, Southdown and its associates offered a reliable and affordable public transport service. A nucleus of routes was gradually extended until in the late 1930s its buses had found virtually every village. The company was very protective of its area and any other companies that tried to infiltrate the edges of its patch usually had to agree to operate with a joint route agreement where revenues were shared, not guaranteed equally. The countywide spread of Southdown allowed it to offer a local parcel service which threatened the viability of the village carrier. Express services and private hire complemented their bus routes, and in general Sussex was well served by the company. It was in the 1960s when the company became totally state-owned that problems began to arise.

LBSCR to SR

The railways continued to dominate public transport between the wars and it was the war effort and subsequent nationalization that started a spiral of deterioration and underfunding that has continued into the twenty-first century.

After the first post-war general election, held in December 1918, the coalition government began the process of handing the industry back to its previous owners. A newly formed Ministry of Transport was given the task of bringing an unwieldy number of companies into a more responsible grouping. The idea of nationalization was rejected; instead four large groups were proposed, still operating as private companies and reporting to their shareholders. The 1921 Act brought together the LSWR, the SECR and the LBSCR to form the Southern Railway. Fourteen subsidiary companies were absorbed; only one of those was in Sussex – the tourist-oriented Brighton and Dyke, a short line that wheezed its way uphill from the town to the Devil's Dyke.

The three constituents of the southern grouping relied heavily on passenger traffic for their income. Apart from the small Kent coalfield, Southampton Docks and mining interests in the south-west there was little heavy industry in this area. Transition from three into one should, on paper, have been a simple exercise but problems arose from the outset. One concerned the planned electrification of the suburban lines. Both the South Western and the Brighton were already operating electric services from their own London termini using non-compatible sys-

THE SOUTHERN BELLES

The naming of certain trains on the LBSCR–SR network dates back to 1899 when the name *Brighton Limited* appeared in the timetable. Eighteen years earlier the first all-Pullman train began a service between the Sussex resort and London Victoria. Changes were continually made to the running times but generally, with stops, the journey took 1hr 15min. The *Brighton Limited* was a Sunday-only train, operating for nine months of the year, October to June.

The *Southern Belle* was again an all-Pullman train; when it began in 1908 it had the distinction of being the first to have all of its stock home-built. Throughout its life it had an advertised journey time of 1hr, and in the last years of steam haulage the working timetable was for 58min but on occasion an unofficial time of 55min was obtained. The war and the general strike of the 1920s played havoc with the times, but when electrification was introduced the service had increased to thrice daily.

Friday, 29 June 1933 saw *The Southern Belle* become *The Brighton Belle*. On that day the world's largest sea-water swimming pool was due to be opened in the town and the opportunity was taken to combine the two ceremonies. The timings of the train remained unaltered until the outbreak of war when the name was discontinued; the withdrawal of the Pullman cars followed in 1942. Full service was resumed in 1947 to the pre-war times, these remaining unchanged until, in 1963, when a late-night departure (11.00 p.m.) from Victoria was added.

In the winter of 1968 the units were given a facelift, but the old lady was beginning to feel her age. Various proposals were put forward for a replacement train; these were rubbished by a manager's remark that 'the overriding factor ... was the economic one ... better utilization of stock' confirmed that the trains were run to suit the operator not the passenger. The last day of *The Belle* was 30 April 1972. So popular was this train that British Rail found a buyer for all fifteen cars, none had to suffer the ignominy of the breaker's yard.

tems; the Southern Eastern wanted to try a third way. Compromises were forced on the companies by the government and in January 1923 the Southern Railway was born. Its distinctive green livery remaining on its locomotives until nationalization twenty-four years later.

Throughout its existence the Southern Railway's constituent parts remained true to their pre-grouping territories. Sussex, on non-electrified lines, continued to work the Brighton locomotives, timetables too went largely unchanged. It was not until the privatization in the last years of the century that the county's traveller could enjoy direct services to other regions of Britain.

Electrification to the coast was first proposed in 1930; included was a doubling of tracks on certain sections of the trunk route, installation of colour light signalling and a new layout for Brighton station. Public services began on the first day of 1933 and in the next few years all coastal and Arun Valley lines were connected to the system.

The SR also had interests in other forms of transport. From the mid nineteenth century, the cross channel Newhaven to Dieppe sailing was a joint Anglo-French operation. From 1864 the ships were run in the LBSCR colours, although the cargo vessels were crewed by France and the Sussex company had only one-third of the capital. Most of the SR's interests were directed towards the short sea crossings from Kent and the Southampton complex. The company did, however, in 1926 take over the port of Newhaven and upgrade its facilities. New vessels, jointly owned with the French duly arrived: *Worthing* in 1928, to be joined five years later by a sister ship *Brighton*.

It was a forward-thinking board that in the early 1930s signed a charter agreement with Imperial Airways; this was followed by a joint venture with Imperial and the other railway companies. Sussex gained nothing from these initiatives for Shoreham was the only commercial airfield in the county and the railway air services decided not to operate from this coastal

SHOREHAM AIRPORT

Shoreham Airport occupies one of the few gaps in the residential strip to the west of Brighton. Bordered on the south by the railway and the sea, it faces inland to the river Arun. Always busy with flying schools, executive jets and private visitors, it still manages to exude the 1930s impression of relaxed informality. This appearance is enhanced by the 1936 art deco terminal building.

The first aircraft lifted off from the field in May 1910, when an ex-Lancing College pupil 'Piff' Pifford coaxed his home-built biplane into the air, just seven years after the Wright brothers had flown the first heavier than air machine. The airfield was officially opened the following year and in July the first British commercial cargo flight took off, carrying cases of light bulbs to nearby Hove. It quickly established itself and was one of the staging points for the 1911 round Britain air races.

In the 1930s several airlines operated from the field; most were domestic services, but Jersey and northern France appeared in the schedules. Immediately following the outbreak of war international services were transferred from Croydon, which was the original London Airport. The most exotic flight to leave Sussex was the Imperial Airways service to Alexandria, making two overnight stops en route and flying for fourteen hours – this survived until June 1940.

In the First World War Shoreham was a pilot-training school and in the Second its duties were centred on air–sea rescue. In the early years of this second conflict it was also home to a fleet of Lysanders which were used on anti-invasion coastal patrols. Although the airfield and the nearby power station provided attractive targets, both were largely ignored by the enemy and suffered little damage.

Shoreham Airport.

field. (Gatwick did not become Sussex property until after the war when the county boundary was changed.)

The high streets of the larger towns now began to change. The years between the wars were not a period of great prosperity, but among the family businesses came the first Sainsburys, Boots and, in the clothing sector, Burtons. Finding a space in the market towns, the Co-op arrived to sell its relatively cheap goods with a promise of a dividend at the end of the year. The village remained almost self-sufficient; individual shops were happy to concentrate on one product, the butcher, the baker and the general grocer believed there was trade enough for all and felt no need to tread on one another's toes. Public services in these rural communities were more than adequate; there was the school, the church, the pub and the post office – from where came, as late as the 1930s, three mail deliveries a day. Entertainment not provided locally could usually be found at the picture house of the nearest town, and there was usually a late bus to bring you home.

The writer J.B. Priestley, in his *English Journey*, published in 1933, describes his travels through three Englands. The one he called Old England was 'a country of cathedrals and minsters, manor houses and inns, parsons and squires'. Sussex in the 1930s would have been happy to be included in that category.

In the 1914–18 war there had been a significant threat to the English monarchy for George

V's family were of German descent; however, his many visits to the troops and his decision to adopt the name of Windsor endeared him to the British public. Christmas 1932 was a milestone in the relationship between the monarchy and the public, and Sussex was involved. In that year the BBC inaugurated the annual Christmas broadcast by the King and the script for his speech was by the county's own Rudyard Kipling. The jubilee celebrations of 1935 were quickly followed by his funeral the following year and a year later by the coronation of George VI. By the time of his daughter's coronation in 1953 television had arrived, changing the character of the nation's celebrations.

The Last Years of Peace

Leisure for the majority of workers was, in the pre-war years, largely confined to Saturday afternoon and Sunday. Paid holidays did not exist and annual breaks of more than seven days were a rarity. Family finances could seldom be stretched to accommodate a week at the seaside and so it was the middle and the upper class which filled the hotels and boarding houses of the resorts. Here the traditional seaside pleasures were being enhanced by more sophisticated entertainment, much of which had its origin in America.

On Sundays and Bank Holidays the resorts came alive with the day excursionists. Trains, and latterly coaches, disgorged thousands, all eager to enjoy their day of freedom. When the government proposed what was to most workers a holiday with pay, the holiday camp concept was born. Chalet-type accommodation with non-stop entertainment and a tightly regulated daily routine, all at a low and inclusive price, was utopia for the labourer with a few pounds in his pocket. A larger than average piece of land was needed for these compounds and the only

---

BILLY AND BOGNOR

In the early 1930s Bognor considered itself to be superior to the other Sussex resorts for George V had spent several months in the town convalescing and granted to it the title 'Regis'. His terse retort, 'Bugger Bognor' when asked whether he wished to make a return visit was still in the future – if, indeed, the remark were ever made. The town council did not encourage the day tripper with his need for cheap entertainment, they aimed to provide an ambience suitable for a better class of visitor.

Enter then Billy Butlin, born in South Africa to a fairground mother. He spent his early years wandering the world. He finally returned to England in 1921, short of funds and education but overflowing with self-confidence. For a few years he travelled the country as a fairground proprietor, but always in his mind was the idea of a low-cost, fully-inclusive, non-stop entertainment package for the masses, in short, the holiday camp. In 1936 he opened his first one on the east coast; another followed two years later. The war put all his future plans into storage.

Before the opening of his first camp he had purchased a parcel of land on the Eastern Esplanade at Bognor where he planned a zoo and funfair. In 1935 a lion was reported to have escaped from the zoo; over the next four weeks it was supposedly sighted around the area, culminating with 'the savaging of a sheep at Pagham'. In fact, there was no lion, just a well-orchestrated publicity hoax, staged to ensure that the people of Bognor remembered the name of Butlin.

Both in the pre- and the post-war years the town council was unhappy with the type of entertainment Billy was providing from his funfair and made several unsuccessful attempts to buy him off the Esplanade. The town itself divided, largely on age lines, into pro- and anti-Butlinites. So spirited was the debate that one one local paper referred to 'Civil war in Butlin Regis'.

Finally, a compromise was reached: in exchange for closing his funfair he was granted 39 acres (18ha) of land on the edge of the town where he could build a new camp. On 2 July 1960 the embryo South Coast World opened for business, attracting over 3,000 visitors in its first week.

parts of the coast where there was suitable space was in the extreme east of the county and around the Manhood peninsula. The camps had not long been established when they were requisitioned for military use in 1939.

In the 1935 election rumours of compulsory military service became an issue to be debated; but it was a further two years before the activities of Hitler and his followers gave rise to increasing apprehension. The celebration of George V's jubilee roughly coincided with Britain's realization that her defences were in a sorry state; the long-held view that there could not be another war in the next decade now began to have a hollow ring. The majority of British politicians adopted a policy of appeasement, always searching for an acceptable reason for Hitler's actions. The public originally wanted to accept their leader's line; however, as German greed increased, their fears grew. The Munich Agreement, bringing 'peace in our time', gave the country a breathing space. When the hollowness of this piece of paper were revealed then the country knew that war was inevitable.

As late as August the Sussex resorts were still receiving their quota of summer visitors, even though in places they were forced to share their beaches with workers filling sandbags Chamberlain's broadcast on 3 September 1939 saying that the country was at war was greeted in the county with both relief and fear. Relief that the months of uncertainty were finally at an end, and fear of the aerial bombardment which was was expected to follow.

1939–45

The county itself did not become too deeply involved in the First World War; there were air raids, both by airships and aeroplanes, and submarines skirted the coast. Of the conflict the county saw only the preparation and departure of the inexperienced for France and the return of the war-weary and wounded. This time the county formed the front line, although, thankfully, the expeience of 1066 was not repeated.

The predicted air attacks did not materialize, and the first winter of the war passed peacefully. There was an invasion, but that of children evacuated from London. To the Cockneys this was an alien lifestyle into which they were pitched, a few remained for the duration but the majority regarded it as a holiday and returned to the metropolis at the first opportunity. A few months later the evacuation process was reversed when children from the seaside towns were relocated to the northern Home Counties.

During the 'phoney war', which lasted through the first winter, the people of Sussex began to learn how to cope with rationing, shortages, the blackout and the loss of access to their favoured leisure areas. The beaches were sealed off by miles of barbed wire, the ever-familiar pier was isolated from the shore when a central section was cut away: to prevent its use as an enemy landing point was the official reason given. Vast tracts of the Downs and other open areas became out of bounds, remaining so until hostilities ceased. The cost of living rose by 14 per cent in the first year of the war; this increase hit the urban dweller the hardest, for the countryman could increase the amount of food he grew at home and the surrounding fields would provide something for the pot. The inhabitants of the great houses were not greatly inconvenienced by the rise, life for them continued much as before.

The 'Look, Duck and Vanish Brigade'

On 14 May 1940 the Secretary of State for War, Anthony Eden, made a radio appeal for non-committed male British subjects, between the ages of seventeen and sixty-five to join a force aimed at protecting the home country should Germany invade. In the first six weeks almost 1.5 million men agreed to join the Local Defence Volunteers (LDV) – hence the facetious 'Look, Duck and Vanish Brigade'. The LDV was only a temporary title: at the Prime Minister's insistence it became the Home Guard. The aim of the government was for ex-soldiers from the 1914–18 war to provide a nucleus of experience, and so the upper age limit had a degree of flexibility (birth certificates need not be presented). In 1943 the *Brighton Herald* reported that seventy-eight-year-old George Lyle was still an active member of his local unit. At the lower end of the scale, 'mature for their age' lads of fifteen were also allowed to enlist.

Several books have been written about the force and a classic BBC television series of eighty episodes highlighting the exploits of this ultra-keen but untested auxiliary army ran from 1968 to 1977. If the comedy is ignored, then *Dad's Army* gave a surprisingly accurate portrayal of the Home Guard in its early days.

After the original influx of volunteers and as the threat of invasion receded, membership of the units tended to decline. In 1942 this trend was reversed when all men not involved in any form of civil defence were directed to the Home Guard. Sussex benefited from this by an increased membership of 11,000.

The idea of a local defence organization was not new. In 1804 a private army of eighty-one residents from Iping, near Midhurst, were prepared to defend their village against Napoleon. In the first war an underfunded Volunteer Training Corps struggled to survive, often subsidized by local initiatives. The 1940 programme was the first to establish a country-wide defence force. Each town had its own company and most villages could manage a platoon; certain potential soldiers faced a dilemma: to join their friends at home or enlist in the works unit? The Southdown bus company, the Southern Railway, the GPO and other large employers all formed companies with duties relevant to their trade.

Affiliated to the Home Guard, or using the title as a cover for their underground activities, were the blandly named Auxiliary Units. These small, localized patrols operated throughout the country and were, in effect, an embryonic British resistance. The first units were formed in March 1938 as an offshoot of the Special Intelligence Service. Only one of the early units operated in Sussex; this was based at the Star Brewery at Eastbourne. Four staff members were involved in the clandestine intelligence-gathering role,

which remained active until after the war. Following the fall of Dunkirk, plans were made to increase substantially the number of these secretive units. Sussex was allocated twenty-three, all but one, Staplefield, operating on or near the South Downs. Membership of each group was small, from six to eight being the usual number; each had its own bunker or hide-out, all coordinated from a manor house at Small Dole. Sixty years have passed since the formation of these groups and many of their members have died, taking with them their secrets of how and what was expected from them should the enemy arrive. This is one section of the Home Guard whose story will probably never be fully revealed.

There were other voluntary groups all combining to protect Sussex. Among them were the ARP (Air Raid Precautions) wardens, the Observer Corps, who were an essential link in the chain of defence against enemy bombing raids, the WVS (Women's Voluntary Service) and the Women's Institute, binding with each other to help the community. The Observer Corps was granted the 'Royal' title by King George VI, becoming the Royal Observer Corps in April 1941; shortly afterwards the WVS similarly became the WRVS.

The county's first contribution to the Continental war effort came in May 1940 when skippers and their little ships, from Chichester to Rye, answered the call to assist in the evacuation of the British forces from Dunkirk. Fighter aircraft from the Sussex airfields also took the opportunity to flex their muscles over the French beaches in preparation for the big battle. Two months later the fight at home began.

Air Activities over Sussex

There were five airfields in West Sussex operational at the time of the Battle of Britain and one in the east of the county. This sole representative, Friston, situated on the cliffs above Eastbourne, was designated an Emergency Landing Ground (ELG) and, as such, was never home to a permanent squadron. Tangmere was the single most important base in the county. Its aircraft were given the task of protecting the coast from Brighton to Bournemouth and it was supported by a satellite field at West Hampnett, now known as Goodwood. The three remaining stations, Ford, Shoreham and Thorney Island, were operational but concerned themselves mainly with maritime duties. During August German bombers targeted the Sussex fields, hoping to make them inoperable. On the 16th Tangmere was almost wiped out, two hangars and at least fifteen aircraft were destroyed. Two days later it was the turn of Ford and Thorney Island. Ford, apart from a few machine-guns, had no protection and paid the price, thirteen aircraft were lost together with most of the ground facilities. Replacement craft were found and, in spite of the destruction, the aircraft continued to fly. By the end of September the worst of the battle was over.

After the failure of the Luftwaffe to gain control of the skies above Britain, its attention switched to civilian targets. London was the first to suffer, shortly to be followed by Portsmouth and Southampton. Raids continued throughout the war, to be supplemented later by the pilotless V1 ('doodlebug') flying bomb and the V2 rocket and only petering out when the fields and launch sites were captured by the advancing Allied armies.

The coastal towns were the most at risk from the raids, Eastbourne claimed to have received more alerts than any other town in the southern counties, but it was Brighton that suffered the most damage; the most dramatic occurring in May 1943. Around noon twenty-five bombers blitzed the town, the most serious damage occurring in London Road where the brick railway viaduct was destroyed. Eerily, the railway tracks were left suspended over the road. Twenty-four residents lost their lives that day. But the worst incident in the county took place two months later. East Grinstead, being on one flight path to London, was accustomed to receiving German attention but on this July day a lone raider targeted the main shopping area, 108 people died and 253 were injured. The smaller towns also

suffered, typical was Petworth. At Michaelmas 1942 another lone bomber jettisoned his cargo over the town. A string of bombs fell across the boys' school, twenty-eight pupils and two masters perished.

Later in the war piloted raiders operated in tandem with the V1. The V1s were aimed for the metropolis but, with their primitive guidance system and susceptibility to air and ground attack, thousands never made it to their targets. As their trajectory should have been a straight line from launch pad to London, it follows that East Sussex, being under the main flight paths, was most at risk. As many as 775 hits were recorded; as expected, the heaviest concentration was near to the Kent border. Hitler's final terror weapon, the ballistic V2 rocket, hardly troubled Sussex or its people. There was no way of knowing of its imminent arrival: if you heard the explosion then you were safe.

The Land in Wartime

The greatest change that the Second World War brought to the face of Sussex was the desecration of the Downs. Now these hills were taken back 150 years to the period when Napoleon threatened. Again, out went pasture, in came arable. In the first conversion it was a gradual process spread over several years; twentieth-century government wanted instant results. In one season the sheep paths disappeared, to be replaced by a thin, hungry soil that needed an excessive input of artificial fertilizers in order to obtain a reasonable crop.

The transformation was accompanied by a strident campaign of propaganda ostensibly to steer the country towards self-sufficiency. Destroying our landscape, it was said, was but a small sacrifice, and anyway the land would soon recover. Recent surveys have exploded that argument, for it was found that land already in cultivation could have easily covered the country's needs. The Downs escaped in the first war; motive power was the horse and the ox, animals that proved difficult to manoeuvre on the steep slopes. By 1940 the tractor was king, the only sections of the Downs that escaped the plough were the scarp edges where there was a danger of the tractor's overturning. Much of this new land remains in cultivation today, so adding its harvests to the European food mountain.

The towns were not spared from the 'Dig for Victory' campaign; parks and gardens had open access for their railings had been despatched to the munition factories, flower beds now displayed prize vegetables not flowers. Individual residences had plots growing for the pot, not for table or window decoration.

Into this changing landscape came the Land Girls. The Women's Land Army was formed to fill the shoes of men called up for military service. They came from all walks of life into the unknown, soon to learn the skills of ploughing, stock-rearing, milking and the tending of various crops. Theirs was an all-weather occupation, but the only working uniform supplied to them was a set of dun-coloured bib and brace overalls. After hours, they changed into a smart outfit of green sweater, cord breeches with knee-length hose, topped by a wide brimmed hat, gear that was certain to attract the attention of the young Sussex blades.

In the immediate post-war years food rationing continued, along with the associated drive for home-produced food. Thus the need for this supplementary agricultural army remained and it was not until 1950 that the WLA was disbanded.

The Sussex countryside still contains a collection of Second World War artefacts, with many a truncated concrete obelisk lurking in a roadside hedgerow. These anti-tank deterrents were usually sited at strategic road junctions; they were certainly inconvenient for local movement but it is debatable whether they would have been effective against enemy tanks. Squat pillboxes still look out over river valleys; the design of these varied with their projected purpose, some were just anti-infantry machine-gun emplacements, while others were designed to house larger weapons. The largest concentration of the boxes was on the Ouse around Barcombe Mills, where there were at least ten covering all river crossings. A well-preserved example of anti-tank pillbox is in the grounds of Bodiam Castle, modern defences for an ancient building.

Before D-Day, more large expanses of open country, especially on the eastern Downs where the cultivation change was less marked, were purloined for troop training. In order for the men and equipment to reach these areas, ancient cart tracks and bridleways were given a new

THE DIEPPE RAID

Probably the greatest wartime disaster to affect the Sussex people was the badly planned raid on Dieppe in 1942. From the autumn of the previous year, the defence of the Sussex coast was entrusted to 1st Canadian Army, and the residents had grown accustomed to their speech. In August 2nd Canadian Infantry Division left its camps in West Sussex and set out for Newhaven, Shoreham and the Solent ports to embark on what was planned to be the largest raid to date on enemy-occupied Europe. The Germans were apparently warned of the raid, for the Canadians met with murderous small arms fire as they left their landing craft. Disaster followed disaster, culminating with an unspecified radio message that led to a premature ending to an attempt to rescue the survivors.

These unfortunates had no option but surrender. Out of a total raiding party of 6,000 fewer than 2,700 returned to England.

The official government line on this ill-fated foray pushed the invaluable lessons that had been learnt from the operation, these contributing to the eventual success of D-Day. Many feel that the lessons could have been learnt in a less expensive way.

The wartime connection between Canada and Sussex remains strong, sixty years on. Regular visits are still made by the veterans' association and each year a memorial service is held at Wisborough Green. The nearby Hawkhurst Court was home to one of the Canadian brigades, and it was there that the planning for the raid was made.

THE MULBERRY MIRACLE

The coastline of Normandy which was to receive the invasion had few harbours, those that did exist were tiny and would have been unable to accept the volume of traffic needed to sustain the invading army. Unloading direct on to the beaches would also have had its problems due to the large variation between high and low tide. The prognosis looked bleak until Winston Churchill recalled one of his First World War ideas: an artificial harbour that floated with the tide.

By early 1943 its structure had been formulated. The plan was to create an area of water, protected from the Channel swell by a series of breakwaters. In the calmer water would be jetties connected to the land. For the first time in history an invading army was to take with it its own harbour. Lt Cdr Robert Lochner RNVR was an Admiralty scientist who lived at Hammer, an isolated village in the north-west of the county. An electrical engineer in civilian life, he was given the task of solving the expected problems. His early experiments as to the feasibility of a floating boom were conducted, on a much reduced scale, in his bath using a flannel and then in his garden pond using a cut-down lilo! The project went ahead without too much difficulty; after numerous tests a decision was made in September to proceed with two such harbours, code-named 'Mulberry', delivery date: May 1944.

It was a massive undertaking to construct the individual sections of the harbours. The bulk of the work was concentrated in a small number of main depots, but one shipyard from Bosham also became involved. It was now the 'finest hour' for the waters of Pagham harbour, for they shared with Dungeness the honour of being the assembly points for the project.

From January onwards visitors were banned from Selsey; residents were issued with special passes and forbidden to approach the Pagham shoreline. The sea outside the harbour was closed to local fishermen, and, pointing skywards, were the barrels of numerous recently installed anti-aircraft guns. Daily the mysterious structures increased in size, the locals could only speculate on their purpose. Even when a practice assembly was disrupted by heavy seas, with parts breaking off the main unit and beaching, all remained top secret. The most plausible theory as to their purpose came with a leaked opinion from Bosham: they were the foundations for a proposed cross-channel bridge.

The giant caissons started their journey a couple of days after the combined force landed; but it was some time before the local people came to realize that they had witnessed the birth of the greatest Allied engineering feat of the Second World War.

concrete surface. South Hill, above the Cuckmere estuary, retains traces of these improved roads; some are succumbing to nature while the access road to the hilltop car park is kept in good order.

The Preparations for D-Day

Detailed planning for the invasion of Europe began in earnest early in 1943, over 1 million men were scheduled to be delivered into Normandy in the first three weeks of the campaign, plus, in the following three weeks, a further 2 million and 365,000 vehicles. The southern counties became the holding centre for this vast army, the size and numbers involved impos-

ing inconvenience and disruption to everyday life.

It was in early spring when Sussex began to notice an increase in military activity and visitor numbers. The Americans were coming over at 150,000 a month for a short training period, then a move further inland, their presence being replaced by British regiments. There was hardly a grand house in the county whose corridors did not echo to the sound of hobnailed boots. Hotels, village halls and any empty buildings that could supply lodging were quickly requisitioned. Those who missed the superior accommodation were forced to make do in tented camps. As the weather that spring was fine and warm, the 4,000 campers in Petworth Park were

The Community Shopping Centre, Tilgate.

New town housing at Crawley.

able to enjoy a final few weeks of sunbathing; these leisure activities being interrupted only when ˙they were visited by the Supreme Commander Gen Eisenhower and George VI. This army needed transportation, every patch of tree-covered road hid trucks and lorries, and, where suitable, complete sections of road were closed, to be turned into elongated lorry parks.

All the camps were sealed on 26 May, designated 'X' day. Military uniforms disappeared from the Sussex streets. Pubs, shops, cafés and cinemas were all out of bounds. The county realized that things were about to happen. This feeling was strengthened with the continuous movements of troops out of the county, all roads seemingly leading westward towards the mar-

Gatwick Airport.

shalling area centred on the Solent. England had enjoyed a good spring, with days of fine and settled weather, but, as feared, the weather broke at the beginning of June. After one postponement the campaign to free Europe from German oppression began on the 6th, D-Day.

In order to help provide air cover for the Allied ground forces in France, a series of auxiliary landing grounds (ALGs) were laid out. A total of twenty were sited in the south-east and along the Channel coast. Sussex, being the nearest county to the expected line of advance, had the lion's share, thirteen. It cannot be said that these ALGs were built for they consisted of a runway and little else. The temporary 'Semmerfeld' conversion from agricultural land to airstrip started in 1942 and was largely completed by the following summer. Many of the squadrons sent to the ALGs went with one purpose, that of gaining experience in operating from an airfield with minimum facilities, a situation they could expect to encounter on their transfer to France.

The operational life of these strips was expected to be short; in fact, Chailey and Coolham existed for only for two months. Three strips on the Manhood peninsula fared little better. Funtingdon, the largest of the western strips, survived for over a year; opening in September 1943, it was not until the following December that decommissioning took place. Deanland, the sole East Sussex field, was the largest and busiest. Opening in April 1944, one of its squadrons had the distinction of being the first to be airborne on D-Day, scrambling at 3 a.m. The V1 attacks on England began in June; as Deanland was close to the flight path zone of these weapons, it was designated, along with West Malling in Kent, an 'anti-diver' (that is, anti-V1) airfield. Entrusted to shoot down or tip over these pilotless aircraft, the crews using slower equipment achieved surprisingly good results. Because of the size of this strip, it often saw the arrival of a crippled bomber that was unable to reach its home base. These heavier aircraft were regarded as a nuisance, for their greater weight played havoc with the tracking and the day-to-day operations of the field.

The Final Fifty Years

Peace returned to Britain and Europe in 1945. Over the next fifty years the life of Sussex continued with an ever-increasing pace. Transport throughout the county was the first to feel the influence of the post-war Labour government when it started its policy of nationalization. The railways and road haulage became state-owned; Southdown continued as a public–private partnership until the late 1960s when the private sector relinquished its interests.

For the next decade the railways provided the only feasible transport for the medium- and long-distance traveller and, when the state took over, the four rail companies were in crisis since in the months on either side of D-Day the railways had carried loads far in excess of those for which they were designed and their infrastructure was in a poor state. The Sussex lines had served the county well, but, as the working classes found their freedom with the motor car, it was decided that it would be too expensive to bring many of the branch lines into good order and the closures began. The first to disappear was the East Grinstead to Lewes line, a section of which has been restored by volunteers and now operates as the nationally-famous Bluebell Line. The accountants' creed that money is paramount, now decided the fate of many of the county's secondary lines. The name of Beeching is now synonymous with rail closures, and when this East Grinstead chemist got to work it was goodbye to many of the local lines that had served the community for over a century; lines were axed with little apparent thought for the future.

Each individual closure may not have individually made a significant contribution, collectively they brought much more traffic on to roads already suffering from overuse. With the end of petrol rationing and the relative cheapness of the motor car, private ownership increased year on year. Compared with other 'poorer' neighbours, Sussex has fared badly in road improvements, only the London to Brighton A23 could be likened to a trunk road. The coastal A27 is a good example of the haphazard improvements inflicted on the county: stretches of dual carriageway occur, only to be bottlenecked in a residential area or, in the case of Arundel, terminate in a field.

As traffic in the towns increased, many called for a bypass, little realizing that, should their wish be granted, the economic life of the town would often suffer. The passing trade just passed, and the land between the new road and the town centre was an attractive proposition for the residential developer.

Successive governments have targeted Sussex with thousands of housing units, this spoliation of the countryside began in 1947 when it was decided that Crawley was to become one of the first new towns. On either side of Crawley, East Grinstead and Horsham have received their allocation of housing, and in the more recent years the emphasis on new dwellings has migrated southwards along the A23 corridor to Burgess Hill. In the last decade of the century villages within commuting distance of Gatwick have drawn the developers' eyes, and more green fields seem certain to be covered by bricks.

Industry returned to Sussex at the same time as the post-war increase in housing. The main complex concentrated on land between the new town of Crawley and the county boundary where it had easy access to the national motorway network. Other attempts to develop large-scale industrial units have met with little success; this is in part due to the weakness of the county's road and rail systems. Most of the larger towns have their own collection of factories; these are usually on out-of-town sites and coexist with the local retail park. Thankfully, Sussex has not had to endure the indignity of another period similar to that when the iron workings demolished vast areas of woodland. The county today can cope with its light industries, provided that their boundaries are kept under control.

Rural and Urban Difficulties

The county's towns and villages that are served by or have access to the railway lean towards becoming dormitory communities: vibrant at the weekend but lacking life in the week when the breadwinners are absent. Few Sussex workers, apart from those employed in agriculture, work in the areas adjacent to their homes. If the train is not used, then by necessity, the car makes its twice daily journey on the congested roads. The changing face of the high street also contributes to a ghost town feeling The local traders are ousted by the national and multinational names, which, in turn, if the catchment area is large enough and the profit potential is deemed acceptable, migrate to out-of-town complexes. The town councils do little to encourage local trade, imposing punitive parking fees on anyone who wishes to support the remaining traders. This imposition is not confined to Sussex, but outside the county, where free or cheap parking does still exist, then local trade remains buoyant. Individuality in the towns now hardly exists, thanks to the importation of the shopping precinct or mall, one retail area being a clone of another.

Over the years, local government funding appears to have been steered towards the urban communities. Two East Sussex towns, Hastings and Newhaven, believe that they have missed this largesse and consider themselves to be in danger of being labelled deprived areas. Not surprisingly, the two towns blame the poor transport links as a major factor in their decline. Rural Sussex has received many promises of assistance but delivery tends to be painfully slow.

The county's villages have seen a continual decline in both public and private services over the decades. In the years on either side of the 1939 war a regular bus service connected even the smallest village with the nearest town; now, for the non-car owner, a council-subsidized, infrequent and usually inconveniently timed service is on offer. Many of the local schools have closed, no longer thought cost-efficient, their pupils are transported daily several miles to an establishment that technically may offer an improved curriculum but which is unable to encompass the spirit of a local unit. The village

CRAWLEY NEW TOWN AND GATWICK AIRPORT

In October 1945 a government committee was set up to consider all matters relating to the establishment of a series of new towns. Six months later a New Towns Act was passed. Both Surrey and Sussex county councils realized the need for urbanization in the Ifield–Crawley–Three Bridges area, and, when the proposal came from London for a new town centred on Crawley, there was little official opposition. Generally, the long-established residents of the town were in favour, but there were a few pockets of spirited opposition which helped to delay the passing of the Act by over a year.

The plan was to divide the town into neighbourhoods, each with its own centre and amenities, to form a circle around the central retail and administrative area. As the majority of the first arrivals would be from London, an industrial area was to be sited to the north. Every encouragement was given to London-based companies to relocate, with their employees, from old, often war-damaged, factories into purpose-built premises in Sussex. Early in 1950 the then Princess Elizabeth opened the industrial estate, naming it Manor Royal; later in the year the first houses were ready for occupation.

When the new town was designated the population of the area was around 10,000; three decades later the figure had increased to 80,000 and is still rising. By 1970 the area intended for development was full and housing continued to expand into greenfield sites that were originally thought to be excluded from residential conversion. In fifty years Crawley, the New Town suffix abandoned years ago, has developed, after its expected early teething problems, into a major player in the Sussex team.

The link between Gatwick and Crawley was forged in the early 1950s when the government decided that Gatwick should become the second London airport. The county boundary was then moved northwards to bring the field under Sussex control. Today these two areas are so integrated and dependent on each other that it is difficult to envisage either operating as a separate entity.

Gatwick was a pre-war airfield operating from a site to the south of the present runway. The early years were not happy ones for the fledgling airport, crashes, the ever present risk of flooding, and the fact that it shared the ground with a racecourse did not find favour with potential passengers. It served as an RAF station during the war, derequisitioning from Air Ministry control was continually deferred, and in 1950, under governmental pressure, British European Airways began its love–hate relationship with the airport. Work on the new Gatwick started in 1953; the A23 Brighton road took a massive diversion, the old railway station closed and a new one was built with direct access to the airport terminal. For eighteen months the field was closed to all fixed-wing aircraft movements; then in June 1958 Elizabeth, now Queen, flew in to mark the official opening.

In its formative years Gatwick was seen as a bucket-and-spade holiday airport, an image not helped by the birth and subsequent death of many short-term charter operators. Slowly the major names in aviation began to appreciate the advantages that it could offer over the congested Heathrow. The throughput of passengers rose steadily, necessitating the opening of a second terminal in 1988. Today, Gatwick is the busiest single-runway international airport in the world, its future growth seemingly hindered only by a signed undertaking with West Sussex County Council that it would not seek a second runway before the year 2019.

---

policeman no longer looks after his patch, replaced by a motorized member of the force making fleeting visits from a centralized control. The numbers and types of shop decline, unable to exist on local support when many of the residents work away from the area. Often operating from the village shop is the Post Office, not strong enough to stand alone; if the retail business collapses then the public sector follows. The ultimate blow to the rural community would be the closure of the village pub; not all of the populace are customers, but it is the centre for socializing and discussion. Without it a village loses its soul.

The Resorts Before the Millennium

The resorts enjoyed the 1950s and the 1960s, holidays at home were still in vogue and it was only the rich and adventurous who travelled abroad. The cheap package brought an inrush of sun-hungry holidaymakers into the county, but this time their destination was Gatwick. The holiday camps and caravan parks kept their devotees, but the resorts had to diversify to remain solvent. No longer could they rely on the traditional one- or two-week holiday, their regular clients still kept in touch but only with a three- or four-day away break.

Brighton in particular developed a conference industry that today brings thousands of off-peak delegates, and their money, into the town. The foreign language schools fill much of the basic accommodation; London is, of course, the main attraction for this type of visitor, but unable to afford the capital's rates, the student turns to the south coast where the atmosphere is more amenable and the cost of living lower. When he has tired of the local entertainment, then London is only an hour away. The quieter towns were the target for many post-retirement émigrés, eager to enjoy what the coast offered for their golden years. This aged-related trend now appears to be in reverse as many young couples, driven from the London suburbs by soaring house prices, are finding their utopia on the Sussex coast.

Churchill Square Shopping Centre, Brighton.

Natural Effects on the Countryside

In the last fifty years nature has made repeated attempts to change again the face of the county. As the century drew to a close, she increased her attacks, by sea, wind and rain. Each winter the Channel continues with its aim to relocate the Selsey peninsula eastwards. Over the centuries this low-lying land has repeatedly changed its face and the land loss was accepted as inevitable. Now, with houses shadowing the shoreline, millions of pounds are spent annually in repairing

---

HILAIRE BELLOC

Belloc was born in France of Anglo-French parentage in 1870 and was only two when the family moved to England. Much of his childhod was spent at Slindon, where he started his love affair with Sussex. He was educated at Birmingham and Oxford; after graduating he left for France to complete his national service, then returned to England to become a naturalized British subject.

He moved to Shipley in 1906, buying Kings Land, a property that contained the village shop and a smock mill. From 1906 to 1910 he was Liberal MP for Stockport South but was not happy with politics and did not seek re-election. The mill at the foot of his garden was the youngest and tallest mill of its type to be built in Sussex. It started working in 1879 and ceased in 1926 when Belloc became irritated with the amount of traffic that was passing his study window. In spite of its enforced closure, he ensured that it was kept it in good order, and one of his first actions, when returning from his travels, was to doff his hat to 'Mrs Shipley'.

Belloc was a prodigious writer with over 100 books published. His first were children's stories, he then changed his interests to produce many historical works, interspersed with travel writings, mainly about Sussex and the surrounding counties. Over the years Belloc has been identified with Sussex, as Wordsworth was with the Lake District, this accolade was probably first earned by his semi-fictitious account of life in the county in the early years of the twentieth century. In *The Four Men*, the poet, the sailor, the old man and Belloc, wandered from Robertsbridge to the Hampshire border, swapping yarns, supping beer, meeting the locals and at all times keeping an observant eye on daily events.

Belloc spent many happy years at Kings Land, where he entertained many notables. G.K. Chesterton, who illustrated several of his books, was a regular visitor and Winston Churchill is known to have enjoyed a game of cards at his table. Belloc died in 1953 and is buried at the nearby Catholic church. Modest, to the end, he insisted that he wanted to be remembered as a farmer not a writer.

Mrs Shipley. Hillaire Belloc's smock mill.

the protective shingle banks. Thwarted in these seaborne attacks, nature has tried to gain revenge from the air.

Small tornadoes are not uncommon in Sussex, their short trail of destruction usually means no more than broken branches and uplifted house tiles. For a reason yet to be explained, Selsey has been the target for a series of more destructive whirlwinds. Houses in their paths have been decapitated and caravans in the camp sites destroyed. The great storm of October 1987 brought to Sussex a tangible reminder that natural forces are vastly greater than anything man can produce. The evening weather forecast was for a rough night, but not greatly different from the average blow. In the early hours the storm struck. The central core came ashore in the south-west and tracked in a north-easterly direction before taking its trail of destruction over the Kent–Surrey border and losing itself in the North Sea. Next morning Sussex and much of south-east England awoke to a state of chaos. The railways were at a standstill, innumerable roads were blocked and the electricity supply was cut over wide areas. The previous weeks had been wet, coupling this with the fact that the trees were still in full leaf, they were unable to withstand the near-hurricane-force winds. All parts of the county were affected, but it was the exposed hilltops where most trees were uprooted. Slowly the county returned to normal, power was restored, rail and roads were cleared of fallen trees and debris, and isolated communities brought back to life. The houses on Bedham Hill were among the hardest hit, here it was over two weeks before the last tree was cut up and their roads reopened.

Mention was made earlier of the flooding problems endured by the county towns and others. The rivers Ouse and Uck in the east, and the Lavant in the west, are the main culprits. Sussex itself must accept some blame for these tragedies The 'it may never happen' attitude prevailed throughout succeeding administrations. When it did, with dire consequences, then action was taken, albeit very slowly.

Whither Sussex?

The twentieth century saw Sussex and its people forced to accept greater changes to their lifestyles than in any previous period. In just a century the county has been transformed from a haven of easygoing tranquillity into frenetic activity. The cause of this can largely be blamed on technology. Much of the county has managed to distance itself from the the Silicon Valley-esque conglomerate imposed on the Thames Valley, but its tentacles have infiltrated all sections of the county structure. Transport, leisure, working practices and society itself have all undergone radical changes. Although many of the country's problems have bypassed Sussex, for a child born in 2002 life will be very different from that experienced by his or her parents and grandparents.

Hilaire Belloc had a vision when he wrote in *The County of Sussex*, published in 1935,

> its purpose is to make known Sussex to those who have not known it, through its physical character and its past. The moment is opportune for Sussex is in peril of dissolution, and anything that can help to preserve the memory at least of what Sussex was, is worthwhile.

This sentiment is equally applicable sixty-five years on.

Whither Sussex in the twenty-first century? No one knows but some signs are ominous. Central government looks set to continue its policy of forcing more people into the county. More people mean more houses, more cars and less of the land that the residents, both old and new, relate to as the real Sussex. One may hope that one of the county's greatest assets, the South Downs, will be afforded increased protection when its belated designation as a National Park takes effect. The coastal towns will still offer a day at the seaside, London will creep ever closer and the obstinate Sussex Hogs will continue the fight, 'not to be druv'.

INDEX